Japanese Museums

Laurance P. Roberts

The Connoisseur's Guide to

JAPANESE MUSEUMS

with a foreword by Laurence Sickman

PUBLISHED FOR THE JAPAN SOCIETY OF NEW YORK

by JOHN WEATHERHILL, INC., *Tokyo*

Distributed in Japan by
JOHN WEATHERHILL, INC., *Tokyo, Japan*
and in the rest of the world by
CHARLES E. TUTTLE CO., INC., *Rutland, Vermont*
with representation on the Continent by
BOXERBOOKS, INC., *Zurich*
in the British Isles by
PRENTICE-HALL INTERNATIONAL, INC., *London*
in Australasia by
PAUL FLESCH AND CO., PTY. LTD., *Melbourne*
and in Canada by
m. g. hurtig, ltd., *Edmonton*

Contents

Photographs of representative museums follow page 112

Foreword

Through the centuries the islands of Japan have been subjected to more than the normal share of disasters. Lightning, incendiary carelessness, and devastating civil wars have repeatedly laid waste by fire the wooden architecture of palaces and entire temple compounds with all they contained. Earthquakes and typhoons have taken a particular toll, heavier than most countries have had to bear. To this enumeration must be added the inevitable decay of such relatively fragile materials as silk and paper, wood and clay. Yet the creative energy and productivity of the Japanese people have been of such a nature and such a scale that, in spite of the forces of destruction, the quantity of ancient buildings and works of art surviving into the twentieth century is very near to overpowering.

Only in Japan, and not in the far older and vastly larger mainland of China, can one see examples of the classic wooden buildings from the eighth and ninth centuries, or trace the styles of Buddhist images in bronze, wood, and dried lacquer from their archaic beginnings through to their graceful decline.

Among the factors, such as the continuity of Buddhism, contributing to this phenomenon, one of the most basic is the Japanese cultural trait, developed to what may be a unique degree, of preserving by every possible means objects of beauty or historical significance. Traditionally this almost fanatical devotion to objects may have been influenced by the enormous value that must have been placed on the artifacts brought with so much labor from China in the early centuries of Japan's cultural growth. These works of art were not only of intrinsic merit in themselves but were also impressive material evidence of a civilization the Japanese were determined to make their own. The great mid-eighth-century treasury of Chinese and Chinese-inspired objects dedicated by the empress Komyo to the Great Buddha of Todai-ji, and still preserved in that temple's storehouse, the Shoso-in, is testimony enough of the cultural value these objects were thought to possess. Like Todai-ji, all temples of importance had their treasuries, and the hoarded contents have survived, in part at least, in surprising numbers to the present.

But not only the temples collected and preserved objects of merit. Together with their often remarked sensitivity to beauty, the Japanese also have a strongly developed acquisitive or collecting instinct. The laudable desire to own works of art most readily found expression among the families of the powerful feudal nobles and their more opulent retainers, and impressive collections were formed by this ruling class. Another Japanese trait, a distaste for ostentation, certainly contributed to that preservation so remarkable in the world history of collecting. Art objects were not scattered in profusion about the house but, rather, were wrapped in silk, placed in especially constructed boxes, and stored away in a fireproof treasure room to be enjoyed, as all works of art should be, on occasion. Again a precedent for such protective care can be found in the Nara-period treasures of the Shoso-in, where there are thirty-one cases for bronze mirrors, twenty-one of them still accompanied by the mirrors for which they were made. And so these precious things descend from generation to generation. Chronologically, one of the most recent examples of a great feudal collection is that of the Tokugawa family, assembled over a period of three hundred years.

With the emergence of Japan into the modern world, beginning in 1868, it was the great industrialists, members of the *zaibatsu* families, who with characteristic zeal took the place of the feudal nobles as collectors. Every aspect of Japanese art, especially the rarefied paraphernalia of the tea ceremony, was sought out and assembled in collections of unprecedented scale. It was this group of collectors that, with a widened interest in the arts of the Far East, acquired highly important Chinese objects of kinds not previously represented in Japan, such as archaic bronzes and ceramics of the T'ang and Sung dynasties. The Sumitomo collection of Chinese bronzes comes to mind as one of the most extensive in the world, while some of the most celebrated works of this kind are housed in the Nezu Museum.

But it was also in this same period of the Westernization of Japan that a new threat developed against the art treasures so miraculously preserved. This was the acquisitive enthusiasm of the burgeoning Occidental museums and collectors with their newly found world outlook on the arts. To meet this new danger the Japanese, beginning as early as the last quarter of the nineteenth century, initiated a series of laws for the protection of works of art, temples, and cultural property. These early laws, with later additions and emendations, are the most enlightened and practical of any nation of the world. It is through their consistent application that the tourist and scholar can enjoy today countless examples of Japanese art and architecture.

The ancient temples, their paintings and sculpture and the contents of their treasuries, the collections of feudal families and more recent industrialists, are now in large part available to the public, at one time or another, and often in varied ways. To the large national museums, like those of Tokyo and Kyoto, one must add a host of special museums of archaeology, drama, and the folk arts, in order to conceive the embarrassment of riches, occasionally mixed with a certain amount of dross, through which Laurance Roberts is our helpful, indeed indispensable, preceptor and guide.

With *The Connoisseur's Guide to Japanese Museums,* for the first time the museum visitor may be armed with a really comprehensive handbook to lead him through the bewildering variety of Japanese public and semi-public collections. Nor should the casual tourist be put off by the designation "connoisseur's guide" in the title. A good guidebook is not just informative; it is also an essential time saver. The hurried visitor can here select with ease exactly that museum or collection which will best gratify his particular interests and taste, he may learn how to get there, and, of special importance in Japan, know when it is open. Or, finding himself in a particular locality, he can quickly ascertain what museums in the vicinity are worth a visit for him. The scholarly specialist and those well familiar with Japan will be equally helped by the author's description of a museum's contents, its publications, percentage of material on display, and changing exhibitions.

In a word, this is a book of great value to anyone even superficially interested in the arts of Japan and China, and absolutely invaluable for scholars and students. And surely it is well named in that it provides an essential and hitherto lacking tool for connoisseurship in a fascinating field of art.

Laurance Roberts has personally visited every museum described, a feat of no mean proportions in itself. Moreover, he writes from a background of formal training in the Oriental-art field and with a keen sensitivity to beauty. His treatment of the museums and their contents is thorough, and his attention to detail always relevant. With the confusing proliferation of museums in Japan in the past two decades, a book of just such thoroughness and detail has become essential and, in fact, has been long overdue. Users of this guidebook are sure to feel a large debt of gratitude to the author.

LAURENCE SICKMAN, *Director*
William Rockhill Nelson Gallery of Art
Kansas City, Missouri

Author's Preface

New museums of art and archaeology and temple treasure houses have been built and opened in Japan at an astonishing rate since the Pacific War, and many of the older museums have done considerable remodeling and reinstallation. As a happy consequence, the vast holdings of both Chinese and Japanese art are far more easily seen and studied than before. It is not easy, however, for the Western visitor to find out the general nature and content of the museums, the quality of their collections, the amount normally on display, or even the times when the museums are open.

This guidebook to Japanese museums and treasure houses is designed to help the Westerner find his way among them. Not all the existing institutions or even all those mentioned in various publications are listed, but I believe that all those of any interest or importance to the connoisseur have been included.

Visitors to Japanese museums should remember that the best time of year for seeing the largest number of the finest objects is autumn—from about mid-October to the end of November. They should also remember that the collections, especially of paintings, are usually shown in rotation. In the large museums the display is apt to change at monthly or bimonthly intervals; smaller museums, such as those that are open only two or three times a year, change their display for each opening; temple treasure houses almost never change. Objects not on view can sometimes be seen upon the presentation of proper credentials and by giving advance notice, but this does not always apply to very rare or fragile objects. Since no polite warning can give any indication of the capriciousness of *all* Japanese museums as regards opening and closing dates or the availability of the collections, visitors would be well advised never to go to any museum before checking to make sure it is open and the collection on view.

The following brief notes will be of help to the reader as he makes use of this guide. The main text is arranged alphabetically by the English names of the museums, while the Indexes provide cross references by Japanese names, prefectures, and types of collections. Information concerning terms and proper names frequently used in the text will be found in the Glossary. All directions for reaching any museum read from the main railway station, except for Tokyo, Kyoto, and Osaka or unless otherwise noted. The address in Japanese, if shown to bus or taxi driver, should help in locating the building. Many of the local museum directors change every two years and are, in many cases, appointed by the local board of education. Hours of opening and closing, telephone numbers, and admission fees change frequently. Unless otherwise indicated in the text, all labels of objects are in Japanese only. All pre-Meiji names in the text are given in the traditional Japanese manner, with the family name first; post-Meiji names are given in the Western manner. Since many of the museums and practically all of the treasure houses are poorly lighted, it is advisable for the visitor to carry a flashlight.

The research for this guide was made possible by two very generous grants from the American Philosophical Society and another from the Bollingen Foundation. The Japan Society of New York has generously underwritten the costs of publication. And the Tokyo staff of John Weatherhill, Inc., has given much time and editorial help to the project. I am sure that anyone to whom the guide is of use will join me in my feeling of gratitude to these four organizations.

Many persons should also be mentioned by name. Without the help given me by Mr. Kikuji Yonezawa, Mr. Yasuo Inoue, and other members of the staff of the Kokusai Bunka Shinkokai, this work would never have been completed. I am also deeply grateful for the help and advice given me by Professor Yukio Yashiro and for the assistance received from Dr. Nagatake Asano, Director of the Tokyo National Museum, and Mr. Shigetaka Kaneko, staff member of the same museum. Professor J. Edward Kidder kindly located a number of archaeological museums for me. To all the museum officials who were everywhere endlessly kind and patient in answering my many questions, and to my interpreters, who were indefatigable in their willingness to help in every way, I offer my warmest appreciation. To Miss Misako Yamashita, friend and companion to my wife and me in so many of our Japanese wanderings, I am vastly indebted, particularly for her great talent in winkling out information and her skill in finding a means of having closed doors open. No thanks can repay my wife for bravely accompanying me to every museum, for coping with the clerical work, and for typing the manuscript.

Above all, I am grateful for the encouragement and help given me during this long project by Professor Rensselaer Lee, Professor Benjamin Rowland, and Dr. Laurence Sickman. The greatest spur to my own interest in the study of Japanese art came from the enthusiasm for all things Japanese and the taste and discrimination in them which the late Louis V. Ledoux shared with all those fortunate enough to have known him.

ART PERIODS OF JAPAN

The controversy over dating Oriental art periods seems endless. In the following three tables I have chosen to follow, in general, the chronology used in Sherman Lee's A History of Far Eastern Art.

Archaeological Age . . . . c. 4000 B.C. to A.D. 552
        Jomon . . . c. 4000 B.C. (?) to c. 200 B.C.
        Yayoi . . . . . c. 200 B.C. to c. A.D. 250
        Kofun . . . . c. 250 to 552
Asuka 552–645
Nara 645–794
        Hakuho (Early Nara) 645–710
        Tempyo (Late Nara) 710–794
Heian 794–1185
        Jogan (Early Heian) 794–897
        Fujiwara (Late Heian) 897–1185
Kamakura 1185–1336
Nambokucho (Northern and Southern Courts) 1336–1392
Muromachi (Ashikaga) 1392–1573
Momoyama 1573–1615
Edo (Tokugawa) 1615–1868
Meiji 1868–1912
Taisho 1912–1926
Showa 1926–

ART PERIODS OF KOREA

Three Kingdoms . . . . 57 B.C. to A.D. 668
        Koguryo dynasty . . . 37 B.C. to A.D. 668
        Paekche dynasty . . . 18 B.C. to A.D. 663
        Old Silla dynasty . . . 57 B.C. to A.D. 668
United Silla 668–935
Koryo period 918–1392
Yi dynasty 1392–1910
Period of Japanese rule 1910–1945
Republic 1945–

ART PERIODS OF CHINA

Shang or Yin dynasty . . . . c. 1500 B.C. to c. 1100 B.C.
Chou dynasty . . . . c. 1100 B.C. to 221 B.C.
      Period of the Warring States   481–221 B.C.
Ch'in dynasty . . . . 221–206 B.C.
Han dynasty . . . . 206 B.C. to A.D. 221
Six Dynasties 221–589
Sui dynasty 589–618
T'ang dynasty 618–906
Five Dynasties 906–960
Sung dynasty 960–1280
Yuan dynasty 1280–1368
Ming dynasty 1368–1644
Ch'ing dynasty 1644–1912
Republic 1912–

JAPANESE NATIONAL HOLIDAYS

January 1 . . . . New Year's Day
January 15 . . . . Adults' Day
February 11 . . . . National Foundation Day
March 21 or 22 . . . . Vernal Equinox Day
April 29 . . . . Emperor's Birthday
May 3 . . . . Constitution Day
May 5 . . . . Children's Day
September 15 . . . . Respect-for-the-Aged Day
September 23 or 24 . . . . Autumnal Equinox Day
October 10 . . . . Physical Education Day
November 3 . . . . Culture Day
November 23 . . . . Labor Thanksgiving Day

There is also the New Year's season, which lies anywhere between December 25 and January 7, depending on the individual institutions.

PUBLISHER'S NOTE: In their prefatory remarks both Mr. Sickman and Mr. Roberts have noted the great proliferation of museums and galleries in Japan since World War II. In fact, things change from day to day. As an example, still another important gallery has recently opened in Tokyo, after this book was already in page proof. This is the **Idemitsu Art Gallery** in the new International Building, which also houses Tokyo's new Imperial Theater. The collection, made by the well-known oil magnate Sazo Idemitsu, includes many paintings and calligraphy scrolls by the Zen monk Sengai, famous examples of old Karatsu ware, and fine ceramic works from China, Egypt, and Iran. Overlooking the Imperial Palace, the new gallery is beautifully located and its display is truly outstanding.

We hope this book will prove so useful that future editions will be needed. In them it will be possible to include such new galleries and the other changes that will undoubtedly have taken place in the meantime.

1. Abashiri Municipal Local Museum (Abashiri Shiritsu Kyodo Hakubutsukan), Katsuragaoka Koen-nai, Katsura-machi, Abashiri, Hokkaido. Tel. Abashiri 3039.

網走市立郷土博物館　網走市桂町　桂ケ岡公園内

Director: Kiyoe Yonemura. **Hours:** 9–4, closed Mon. and Dec. 28–Jan. 4. **Adm.:** ¥20. **Route:** The museum, an old-fashioned two-storied Western-style building, is in Katsuragaoka Park on a bluff overlooking the town. No bus runs directly to the museum, but the taxi ride is less than 5 min.

An interesting and quite extensive collection of local archaeology and material illustrating the life of the Ainu, Gilyak, and Oroko peoples, housed on the second floor of the building.

The archaeological section is noted for the finds from the nearby Moyoro shell mound, consisting largely of pottery vessels of varying sizes and stone and bone tools. In date, they correspond to the late Jomon and Yayoi periods on Honshu. There are also one quite large and many small pottery vessels from other sites of the Zoku-Jomon culture and several high-stemmed cups of the Satsumon period, as well as stone and bone objects of both periods.

The Ainu material covers a wide range. There are garments from both Hokkaido and Sakhalin (the latter showing Russian influence), many handsome necklaces, swords, and a great variety of libation wands. Plain wooden food vessels, lacquered cups and stands, and large circular lacquered boxes are almost as numerous. There is a display of a stuffed bear wearing all the ornaments for the bear ceremony as it was practiced on Sakhalin; and another shows the arrangement of mats, lacquer vessels, and other objects used in a religious ceremony in Hokkaido.

To illustrate the life of the Gilyak in Siberia and northern Sakhalin, the museum shows their fur and cloth garments (Chinese in style and cut), weapons, sleds, birchbark dippers, wooden spoons, and objects used by their shamans. Similar displays depict the traditions of the Oroko, another tribe from Sakhalin.

• COMMENTS • The quality is good, the display adequate. The ethnological material changes once a year, about half the collection being on view at any one time. Changes are made in the archaeological section twice a year. Excavations continue. There is a pamphlet in Japanese. The museum is worth seeing if one is in Hokkaido.

Note: There is a branch of the museum beside the site of the Moyoro shell mound, near the shore (2-chome, Higashi, Kita Ichijo; 9–5 in summer, 9–4 in winter; closed Mon. and national holidays; ¥20). Take the Shinaijunkan bus for Kawamukai Mawari and get off at Moyoro Taizuka Iriguchi. The dirt road to the right of the bus stop leads directly to the shell mound. A log building has been set up to house a cross section of the mound, showing pottery of various epochs and several burials. The installation is well done, the exhibition interesting. Illustrated pamphlet in Japanese.

2. Aichi Prefectural Cultural Center Art Museum
(Aichi-ken Bunka Kaikan Bijutsukan), 8, 8-chome Kuyacho, Higashi-ku, Nagoya, Aichi-ken. Tel. Nagoya 971-5511.

愛知県文化会館美術館　名古屋市東区久屋町８丁目８番地

Director: Vice-Mayor of Nagoya. **Hours:** 9–5; closed for New Year season. **Adm.:** depends on exhibition. **Route:** The cultural center, a large new building occupying almost an entire city block, is near the Sakae-machi stop on the Nagoya subway line that goes to Higashiyama Koen (3 min.), or the same stop on the city bus line (10 min.).

The art museum, a handsome series of exhibition rooms on the second floor of the cultural center, houses temporary loan shows, usually of contemporary Japanese or Western art. The center has no permanent collection.

3. Aikawa Archaeological Hall (Aikawa Kokokan),
Nishi-machi, Isezaki, Gumma-ken. Tel. Isezaki 82.

相川考古館　群馬県伊勢崎市西町

Director: Mr. Aikawa, owner. **Hours:** 1–4, Sat.; 9–4, Sun., on previous appointment made by telephone or in writing. **Adm.:** free. **Route:** Isezaki is most easily reached from Tokyo by the Tobu line. From Isezaki station, take bus for Honjo; get off at the Nishi-machi stop (10 min.) and walk ahead to the first gate in traditional Japanese style on the right side of street. This is the entrance to the owner's house, through which one reaches the museum.

A very fine collection of *haniwa,* plus some other Kofun material and a few Jomon-period objects, housed in a two-story building. The cream of the collection consists of three very large *haniwa* standing figures, kept in special boxes on the ground floor, and a smaller seated figure playing a musical instrument, which is on the upper floor. One of the tall figures is dressed in armor; the other two wear ordinary clothes; all three are remarkable for their size and the details of their dress. The figure holding the musical instrument is unique. There are also a large number of *haniwa* human heads and torsos, several horses' heads, some tall quivers, and a great many of the cylinders from which the upper part has been broken. A damaged figure of a man represented in the nude is very rare. The other Kofun material includes some Sue-ware jars, iron swords, excellent *magatama,* and tubular beads.

• COMMENTS • The quality of the *haniwa* is excellent. Little attempt is made at display, and the very scanty labels are in Japanese only. Sixty percent of the material is on view; no changes are made in the installation. No publication, but a few postcards are available.

4. Aikawa Local Museum (Aikawa Kyodo Hakubutsu-kan), Kitazawa, Aikawa-machi, Sado-gun, Niigata-ken. Tel. Aikawa 279.

相川郷土博物館　新潟県佐渡郡相川町北沢

Director: Zembei Nishino. **Hours:** 7–5. **Adm.:** ¥30. **Route:** Take Honsen (main line) bus for Aikawa from bus terminal near boat landing at Ryotsu. Get off at last stop in Aikawa; continue on foot along the main street and turn right after crossing a stream. The museum, a two-story wooden building, is at the top of the street. (The sightseeing bus from the boat landing makes a scheduled stop at the museum.)

A rather small collection of folk art, historical material, objects relating to the local gold-mining industry, and some natural history, housed on the ground floor of the museum.

The folk-art section includes costumes used by the Sado folk dancers and a charmingly painted wooden panel illustrating a folk dance peculiar to Aikawa. Among the historical material are portraits of Ogura Dainagon, an Edo courtier exiled to Sado, as well as his writing box, stirrups, and samples of his calligraphy. To illustrate the history of gold mining on Sado, there are scrolls of the Edo period depicting the whole process of mining and refining. There are also miners' lamps and ladders and a collection of coins.

· COMMENTS · The quality is fair, the display adequate. The gold-mining display never changes; alterations are made once or twice a year in the folk material. There is no pamphlet, but the museum is described in the illustrated guide to Niigata Prefecture put out by the Niigata Prefectural Museums Association. Visitors to Sado will find the mining exhibits of some interest.

5. Aizu Memorial Exhibition Room of Oriental Arts (Aizu Kyoju Kinen Toyo Bijutsu Chinretsushitsu), Waseda University, Totsuka-cho, Shinjuku-ku, Tokyo. Tel. Tokyo 203-4141, ext. 384.

会津教授記念東洋美術陳列室　東京都新宿区戸塚町
早稲田大学

Director: Professor Kosei Ando. **Hours:** 12–3, Tues., Thurs., Sat.; closed Jul.–Aug. and Dec. 20–Feb. 1. (It can, however, be opened on advance request made by telephone.) **Adm.:** free. **Route:** Take Yamate line to Takatanobaba, then bus to Waseda Seimon-mae, the stop directly in front of the university's main gate. The museum is in a rather small brick building to the left of and across the street from this gate, with its entrance on the far side of the building, down a short path past the quarters of the Student Center. The entrance to the exhibition room is on the right on the ground floor. (The university may also be reached from the Waseda stop on the new Tozai subway line.)

A rather small but interesting collection of Chinese objects from the prehistoric period through the T'ang dynasty. The earliest pieces are two prehistoric painted jars, unusual for their small size, from northwest China. Next come some fragments of inscribed oracle bones and a few small jades of the Yin dynasty, some small Chou bronze vessels, a few bronze chariot fittings and belt hooks of the Warring States and the Han dynasty, and two curious figures in wood from the same period. There is also a small selection of bronze mirrors ranging from the Warring States period through the T'ang dynasty, a number of gilt-bronze T'ang Buddhist figures, and a small T'ang white marble one.

The bulk of the collection, however, consists of ceramics from the Han through the T'ang dynasty. There are large Han painted pottery vases and pottery models of stoves, wellheads, and farm buildings for use in graves, as well as many tomb tiles. There is a good selection of figurines, including two rare tall thin ones with detached arms. The Six Dynasties and the T'ang dynasty are equally well represented by large and small figurines and a variety of glazed pottery vessels.

The collection also contains a few Korean ceramic bottles of the Koryo dynasty, a Gandhara stone head, and several small Indian bronze figures of Hindu deities.

• COMMENTS • The quality is generally good, but little attempt is made at display. About seventy percent of the collection is on view; the remainder is stored in boxes beside the cases and along the walls of the room. The exhibits seldom change. Anyone interested in this particular aspect of Chinese art will find this collection well worth visiting.

6. Akita City Art Museum (Akita-shi Bijutsukan), 6 Uenaka-jo, Senshu Koen, Akita, Akita-ken. Tel. Akita 2-7575.

秋田市美術館　秋田市上中城6番地　千秋公園内

Director: Shin'ichi Kitajima. **Hours:** 9–5, Apr.–Sept.; 9:30–4:30, Oct.–Mar.; closed Mon., Dec. 28–Jan. 11, and when exhibitions are being changed. **Adm.:** ¥20 (¥50 for special exhibitions). **Route:** Walk down the right-hand side of the street leading away from the station, turn right on the road that bisects a lotus pond, and proceed a short distance uphill through the woods of the park (about 15 min.). The museum is a small new one-story building in the International style, to the right of the road.

This museum, the display section of which consists of the entrance and a single case-lined room, is to all intents and purposes only an exhibiting gallery. Its permanent collection is limited to a few paintings, in a style part Oriental, part Western known as *yoga* (foreign painting) or *ranga* (Dutch painting), by Odano Naotaki, a local 18th-century painter, and by Shiozan, the local daimyo.

The museum puts on some 15 loan exhibitions a year. In 1965 its schedule included shows of swords and armor, local history, art of the Muromachi period, and a group of paintings by Tessai.

• COMMENTS • The displays are well arranged, and there

is an illustrated folder in Japanese. The museum's own paintings are not generally on view but may be seen on request. The museum is worth visiting if one is in the district.

7. Arita Ceramic Museum (Arita Toji Bijutsukan), 3-ku, Arita, Matsuura-gun, Saga-ken. Tel. Arita 672.

有田陶磁美術館　佐賀県松浦郡有田市３区

Director: Superintendent of Arita Board of Education. **Hours:** 9–5; closed Mon., national holidays, and New Year season. **Adm.:** ¥20. **Route:** Turn left on the main street, which is about 200 yards from the station square, and walk for about 20 min. The museum is on the left side of the street and is the right-hand one of three buildings set around a small open space. (The other buildings are offices of the Arita Chamber of Commerce.)

A rather small but extremely interesting collection of the ceramics of the region and documents pertaining to their history, charmingly shown in an old ceramic godown. On the ground floor are good examples of Imari, Karatsu, Kakiemon, and Nabeshima wares, as well as pieces recovered from the kiln sites. Especially interesting items are a small jar decorated in underglaze blue, dated 1636 and signed Kujiro, and several shell-shaped moulds.

Examples of blue-and-white Korean wares of the Yi dynasty, excavated in the neighborhood, are shown on the upper floor along with documents relating to the history of the kilns in this ceramic center. Among the latter is a pass of the Edo period permitting the bearer to enter the district.

· COMMENTS · The quality is excellent, the display good. Changes are made in the exhibition about three times a year; about fifty percent of the collection is generally on view. An illustrated booklet in Japanese, issued by the museum, describes the history of the local wares, contains a map of the kiln sites, and lists at the back the contents of the museum. By the very nature of its collection, this museum is of importance chiefly to specialists in ceramics, but its interest to them, particularly in view of the excavated objects, is great. Others will find that the quality of the exhibits and the pleasant atmosphere of the museum make a visit worth while.

8. Asahikawa Local Museum (Asahikawa Shiritsu Kyodo Hakubutsukan), 2-chome, Hanasaki-cho, Asahikawa, Hokkaido. Tel. Asahikawa 5-3017.

旭川市立郷土博物館　旭川市花咲町2丁目

Director: Hiromitsu Mukaiyama. **Hours:** 9:30–4:30; closed Mon., national holidays, and Dec. 28–Jan. 3. **Adm.:** ¥40. **Route:** Take bus No. 6 to Gokoku-jinja-mae and enter the grounds of the shrine. The museum, a ferroconcrete building with a Japanese-style roof, is to the right of the shrine buildings.

A small collection of Ainu material and an even smaller one of Japanese archaeology, exhibited in the entrance hall and the left wing of the building. An Ainu house, storehouse, and bear cage are set up in the entrance. Ainu garments, necklaces, lacquer vessels (made by the Japanese for Ainu use), swords, bows and arrows, and mats that serve as curtains in both religious ceremonies and houses are shown in center cases in the gallery to the left, while dioramas illustrating Ainu life line one wall. In the same room are a number of pottery vessels and stone and bone implements, mostly of the Satsumon period.

• COMMENTS • The Ainu material is good; but the display is hardly adequate, and a general air of disintegration hangs over the museum. Only an enthusiast of Ainu culture would be interested.

9. Atami Art Museum (Atami Bijutsukan), Momoyama, Atami, Shizuoka-ken. Tel. Atami 81-6247.

熱海美術館　静岡県熱海市桃山

Director: Yoji Yoshioka. **Hours:** 9–4; closed Thurs., Dec. 24–31, Jul.–Aug., and when exhibition is being changed. **Adm.:** ¥100. **Route:** The museum is on the upper floor of the Hall of Messianity, which stands in the grounds of the Church of World Messianity on a bluff overlooking Atami and the coast of the Izu Peninsula, surrounded by a large garden. As no bus runs directly to the museum, and as the climb to it is long and steep, it is advisable to take a taxi (5 min.).

A very fine collection formed by the late Mr. Mokichi Okada and now belonging to the Church of World Messianity. It contains Chinese and Japanese painting, calligraphy, and sculpture; Chinese bronzes; and Japanese pottery, lacquer, metalwork, and prints. There is also a Gandhara stone Bodhisattva.

Of special note among the Chinese paintings is one of the T'ang dynasty from the Turfan region of Central Asia, done in strong colors on paper and showing a lady and her attendants standing under a tree. From the Sung dynasty are two *kakemono* of landscapes attributed to Ma Yuan, an album painting of a bird and flowers attributed to the emperor Hui Tsung, and two *kakemono* of birds attributed to Mu Ch'i. Other paintings include a winter scene attributed to Ma Lin and one of birds and another of Han Shan and Shih Te attributed to Liang K'ai. Buddhist figure pieces and a charming album sheet of fish are credited to Yuan artists, while a good bird-and-flower painting is placed in the Ming dynasty.

The earliest Japanese painting is a section of the *Inga-kyo* of the Nara period. A copy of the *Hokke-kyo* has delightful Heian painting on its end paper. The Buddhist figure paintings are mainly of the Kamakura period, with one dated 1327; and from the same period are small paintings of several of the Thirty-six Poets, accompanied by their verses, a large portrait of Minamoto Yorimasa, and another of the priest Saigyo. There are a Muromachi portrait of Ikkyu and a self-portrait of Matabei. Large screens with landscape designs show Yusho at his best. Other Momoyama screens depict a hunt, a picnic, cherry-blossom viewing, and scenes along the Inland Sea. Of two pairs of *namban* screens one shows Western traders in Japan and the other, obviously copied from European prints, Westerners playing musical instruments. A celebrated pair of twofold screens of plum blossoms on a gold ground is by Korin. Koetsu is represented by a fragment of his famous scroll of poems written against a background of deer and by another written on a ground of trees and flowers. There is a very large section of paintings by such *ukiyo-e* artists as Choshun, Hiroshige, Hokusai, Kaigetsudo Ando, Kiyonobu, Shunsho, and Utamaro. (There are also prints by many of these artists as well as by others.) The more recent development of Japanese painting is shown in the works of Taikan Yokoyama and Seison Maeda.

Chinese calligraphy is represented by two large characters written by the Sung priest Wu Chun and by verses and inscriptions written by various Yuan masters. The extensive section of Japanese calligraphy includes a large album with specimens of writing from the 7th to the 14th century, *shikishi* of the late Heian period, and a letter by Fujiwara Toshinari (1114–1204), to name but a few items. There are also samples of the writing of the Kamakura priests Daito Kokushi and Muso Soseki and, from the Edo period, poems written by the priest Ryokan and samples of the writing of such tea masters as Kobori Enshu.

Chinese sculpture includes a medium-sized Northern Ch'i stone stele of a Buddha and two attendants and two fine gilt-bronze figures of Bodhisattvas, one Sui and the other T'ang. In Japanese sculpture, there are small bronze Buddhist figures of the Asuka and Nara periods and several wooden figures of the Heian and Kamakura periods; the finest pieces among the last are a large seated Amida Nyorai with two smaller attendants.

Among the Chinese bronzes are two fine *yu* and a *chia* from the Yin dynasty, a middle-Chou *kuei,* and a Warring States *ting.* There are also Han and T'ang mirrors.

In the section of Japanese pottery are five Momoyama Oribe dishes, a tea bowl made by Koetsu for the tea master Kobori Enshu, a bowl made by Dohachi, and a large jar with a lovely design of wisteria by Ninsei. Japanese lacquer includes good Muromachi *tebako,* an Edo picnic box, and a fascinating writing box with a figure design in mother-of-pearl and lead, attributed to Koetsu. Metal objects used in the Buddhist ritual are of the Heian and Kamakura periods.

• COMMENTS • The quality is excellent, the display good. There are labels in English, save for the calligraphy, which, as usual, has Japanese labels only. About fifteen percent of the collection is normally on view, but this figure varies according to the exhibition, which changes about once a month. Objects not on view may be seen on request made in writing one week in advance. *Ukiyo-e* paintings are usually shown in January, tea-ceremony objects in March, the best pieces from the collection in February and November, the less rare pieces in the spring and autumn. In December there is an exhibition made up of items from previous shows. Some of the sculpture is always on view. There is an illustrated catalogue of selected objects from the Atami and Hakone museums as well as an illustrated folder on these museums; both publications are in Japanese and English.

Note: This museum is under the same direction as the Hakone Art Museum (No. 32), and objects from Hakone are sometimes shown here.

10. Beppu University Ancient Culture Museum
(Beppu Daigaku Jodai Bunka Hakubutsukan), Kamegawa, Rikushoen, Beppu, Oita-ken. Tel. Beppu 6-0101.

別府大学上代文化博物館　大分県別府市亀川六勝園

Director: Professor Mitsuo Kakogawa, Dean of Department of Literature. **Hours:** 9–5, when the university is open. Otherwise, inquire at university office. **Adm.:** free. **Route:** The university lies to the north of Beppu, on the left of the coast road. A bus runs occasionally from the station to the gate of the university, taking about 40 min. By taxi, the trip takes 15 min.

A very interesting collection of Japanese archaeology, of which about one-third is housed (autumn of 1965) in a classroom in one of the new university buildings.

The collection consists of about 100 complete pottery vessels and a large group of fragments from all stages of the Jomon period, Jomon stone implements, much Yayoi material, and some Kofun material. (Northern Kyushu is particularly rich in Yayoi finds, and many pieces come from the Kunisaki Peninsula and from Asajimachi.) The early- and middle-Jomon vessels are very good; to be especially noted are the early pointed Jomon vessels, an unusual late-Jomon high-footed dish, and a striking middle-Jomon *kaen-toki* vase.

· COMMENTS · The quality of the material is excellent. There is no folder or catalogue of the collection, but there is a catalogue of a loan exhibition of Jomon culture held in 1954 which lists many and illustrates a few of the museum's pieces. The specialist will find the museum well worth visiting.

Note: It is planned to build a museum for the collection on the university campus.

11. Bridgestone Art Museum (Bridgestone Bijutsukan), 1, 1-chome, Kyobashi, Chuo-ku, Tokyo. Tel. 561-6317.

ブリヂストン美術館　東京都中央区京橋1丁目1番地

Director: Shojiro Ishibashi. **Hours:** 10–5:30; closed Mon. and Dec. 28–Jan. 4. **Adm.:** ¥50. **Route:** The museum is located on the second floor of the Bridgestone Building in downtown Tokyo, midway between the Kyobashi and Nihombashi stations on the Ginza subway line.

The collection consists of Western paintings, prints, sculptures, pottery, and metalwork, and of paintings by Japanese artists working in the Western manner. Except for a few Flemish and Dutch paintings of the 17th century, three Guardis, and a Gainsborough, the Western paintings (about 125) are by all the well-known French artists of the 19th century, the artists of the School of Paris, and the Italians de Chirico and Marini.

The Japanese painting section (about 170 items) is made up exclusively of works in the Western manner. A few date from the early 19th century, the majority from the last half of the 19th and first half of the 20th century. Paintings by Takeji Fujishima, Shigeru Aoki, Sotaro Yasui, and Tsuguji Fujita are the most numerous.

The sculpture includes objects ranging from ancient Egypt and classical Greece and Rome through medieval France to works by such modern artists as Degas, Rodin, Bourdelle, Maillol, and Despiau. Works by Zadkine and Emilio Greco are the latest acquisitions. Among the more than 80 prints are works by Rembrandt, Manet, Whistler, Toulouse-Lautrec, and Picasso.

There are 11 pieces of Roman metalwork and about 200 pottery vessels from pre-Columbian Peru, the classical world of the Mediterranean, medieval Persia, Mesopotamia, Syria, and 16th-century Spain.

• COMMENTS • The quality is uneven. The display is good, though to Western eyes it is rather surprising to find framed Western paintings hung in the deep vitrines generally reserved for the showing of Japanese paintings. The labels are adequate in both Japanese and English, and there are illustrated catalogues in both languages.

Note: Above half the collection is on view at the Ishibashi Art Museum (No. 53) in Kurume, a sister museum under the same management. Items in the exhibitions change from time to time, but there is no regular schedule; between the two museums, the bulk of the collection is on view at all times.

12. Chido Museum (Chido Hakubutsukan), 1 Yanaka Shin-machi, Tsuruoka, Yamagata-ken. Tel. Tsuruoka 1199.

致道博物館　山形県鶴岡市家中新町 1 番地

Director: Matataro Inuzuka. **Hours:** 9–5; closed about Nov. 20–Apr. 1 and when exhibition is being changed. **Adm.:** ￥50. **Route:** Walk straight ahead from the station, cross the Uchi River, and turn right on the large street that leads to Oyama. The museum is on the right, shortly after a second crossing of the Uchi River, set back from the street, behind a white-painted late-Victorian-style frame house, on the west side of Tsuruoka Park (20 min.). The bus from the station, going towards Yunohama, stops near the museum (10 min.).

A good collection of local folk art and archaeology and some of the possessions of the Sakai family, the former daimyo of the region. The museum was founded in 1950 by the head of the Sakai family. The folk art is partially housed in the Japanese-style building which was originally the official residence of the daimyo; adjoining this early building is a handsome new one, built in 1961 to house the archaeology, the remaining folk arts, the other exhibits, and the offices.

The extensive folk-art collection (some 2,000 pieces) contains peasant cotton garments; straw raincoats, hats, and sandals; wooden farm and household utensils; tables; wooden storage chests and sakè containers; lanterns, lacquer smoking sets, straw toys, and pottery dolls; and a loom and a spinning wheel. The elaborately decorated *bandori* (cushions that are placed on the back and held in place by straps over the shoulders and under the arms to aid the bearer in carrying heavy loads of rice or charcoal) are a special feature. One room is set up as a typical farm living room. The accounting equipment for an old-fashioned shop is also on view.

The equally large archaeological collection contains Jomon pottery vessels and figurines, stone implements, jewels, *haniwa,* Sue and Haji vessels, all excavated locally in the Shonai region.

Among the possessions of the Sakai family are swords

(three are signed Nobufusa, Sanemitsu, and Yoshimitsu, respectively, and are dated in the Kamakura period), armor of the Muromachi and Edo periods, calligraphy (chiefly by members of the family, but also a fine three-character inscription by the Chinese priest Wu Chun of the Sung dynasty), paintings by members of the family and the Kano artists Tan'yu and Naonobu, and regional documents.

There is a tea-ceremony house in the Japanese-style part of the museum, and on the upper floor of the new building is a gallery set aside for temporary exhibitions.

• COMMENTS • The folk-art collection is excellent and alone makes a visit to the museum worthwhile. The archaeology will attract the specialist, for the museum carries on a very active archaeological campaign, and the display generally consists of the most recent finds. The installation is excellent. Five to ten percent of the folk art is generally on view, one percent of the archaeological material, and some of the Sakai family possessions. The folk-art exhibitions are changed a little every two or three months. The museum mounts about 18 temporary loan shows a year with the emphasis on local arts and crafts. There is an illustrated pamphlet in English, another in Japanese, and an illustrated booklet describing the folk-art collections, also in Japanese. A catalogue, briefly illustrated and in Japanese only, of an exhibition of the Sakai family possessions gives some idea of their extent. The museum looks out over a large and lovely garden.

13. Chikubushima Treasure House (Chikubushima Homotsukan), Chikubushima, Biwa-ko, Shiga-ken. Tel. none.

竹生島宝物館　滋賀県琵琶湖竹生島

Director: Chief Priest. **Hours:** 10–4, Mar. 15–Nov. 15. **Adm.:** ¥50. **Route:** Chikubushima, a small island at the northern end of Lake Biwa, may be reached by excursion steamer from either Hamaotsu or Hikone. The treasure house, a small one-room building in very bad repair, is to the right of and above the main building of the Hogan-ji, which is approached by a steep flight of stone steps leading up from the boat landing.

A collection of some of the objects belonging to the Hogan-ji. Among the pieces on display are statues of Dainichi

Nyorai and a Sho Kannon (assigned to the Kamakura period), the emperor Komyo's copy of the *Daihannya-kyo,* a Benzaiten *mandara,* a bell used by Kobo Daishi, a *shakujo* of the Kamakura period, a copy of the *Gosen Wakashu* written by a pupil of the priest Honen Shonin, a Buddhist painting said to be by Chodensu, and Noh masks and musical instruments.

• COMMENTS • The quality is fair, but the paintings, sutras, and documents for which this treasure house was noted are now divided between the national museums in Nara and Tokyo. The display is adequate. A booklet describes the temple buildings and lists the possessions of the treasure house. As it now stands, the treasure house is hardly worth visiting, though the lake trip can be very pleasant and the site of the temple is picturesque.

14. Chofu Museum (Chofu Hakubutsukan), 2162 Toyo-ura-mura, Shimonoseki, Yamaguchi-ken. Tel. Shimonoseki 45-0555.

長府博物館　山口県下関市豊浦村 2162 番地

Director: Soichi Tsubaki. **Hours:** 9–5; closed Mon., day after a national holiday, Dec. 29–Jan. 1, and when exhibitions are being changed (usually twice a year). **Adm.:** ¥30. **Route:** The museum is at Chofu, 9 miles from the center of Shimonoseki. Take bus to Chofu and get off at the Kosan-ji, which is on the slope of a hill, to the left of the main road, and approached by several flights of steps. The museum, a Western-style ferroconcrete building, is beside the temple.

A small museum with a mixed collection of local archaeological finds, sculpture, paintings of the 19th century, examples of local painting and calligraphy, and ceramics. There is also a group of mementos of General Nogi (commander of the Japanese army in the Russo-Japanese War and victor at Port Arthur) which includes a full-length statue of the general and many of his personal possessions.

The archaeological section contains some stone implements of the prehistoric period, Jomon and Yayoi pottery, Yayoi metalwork, *haniwa* figures and ornaments of the Kofun period, and roof tiles of the Nara period. Among the 19th-century paintings are works by Hogai and Kaisen. The local ceramics include such wares as Hoshisato, Takaha, and Wado.

To the left of the first flight of steps leading to the museum is a small open plot of ground with a number of early tombs.

• COMMENTS • The quality of the collection is uneven, the display adequate. Less than fifty percent of the items are normally on view, and sometimes even less, as the museum is host several times a year to temporary exhibitions of local arts and crafts. There is a small pamphlet in Japanese illustrating the collections and describing the museum's activities.

15. Chuson-ji Treasure House (Chuson-ji Sankozo), Chuson-ji, Hiraizumi-machi, Nishi Iwai-gun, Iwate-ken. Tel. Hiraizumi 200.

中尊寺讃衡蔵　岩手県西磐井郡平泉町　中尊寺内

Director: Chief Priest. **Hours:** 8–5, Apr.–Oct.; 8:30–4:30, Nov.–Mar. **Adm.:** ¥150. **Route:** The temple precincts are on a hill about 1 mile northwest of Hiraizumi station. Buses run to the foot of the hill; it is then about 30 min. on foot up a walk lined with cryptomerias. The treasure house, an L-shaped two-story building in ferroconcrete, is near the level open space at the far end of the temple precincts, opposite the new site for the Konjikido. (By taxi, it is possible to use a back road and to arrive within a few yards of the building.)

A superb collection of the art of the late Heian period, when a branch of the Fujiwara family controlled the north of Honshu.

The sculptures include a Dainichi Nyorai, a Senju Kannon, a large seated Amida, and two Yakushi. A temporary but most important feature of the display is a group of gilt-wood Buddhist figures from the daises in the Konjikido. The famous Ichiji Kinrin, a seated figure with the original coloring well preserved, is kept in a locked room on the upper floor and can be seen by applying at the entrance and paying ¥200 more.

Among the most remarkable objects in the collection are the three gilt-wood coffins of Kiyohira, Motohira, and Hidehira, leaders of the Fujiwara family. Also on view are the fragments of swords, two wooden halos, the reliquaries, rosaries, pillows, and pieces of the shrouds and priests' robes that were found in the coffins.

15

The sets of the *Issai-kyo,* formerly kept in the Kyozo, are now stored in the treasure house along with their lacquer boxes. Three sections, in gold and silver on dark-blue paper, are shown, as are three paintings of the Jukkai Hoto *mandara.*

Among the pieces of metalwork are a well-known and very beautiful gilt-bronze *keman* from the Konjikido and a *kei* with a design of peacocks. The furniture includes a sutra table, a *kagen-kei,* and other altar fittings.

· COMMENTS · The quality is superb, the display well arranged. The exhibition does not change. There are an illustrated pamphlet and an illustrated booklet on the temple and the treasure house, both in Japanese only.

Note: The Konjikido, built in 1124 by Fujiwara Kiyohira and elaborately decorated on the interior in lacquer and mother-of-pearl, was enclosed in the Kamakura period by an outer building for protection; this now stands empty, as a new protective building is being erected opposite the treasure house and the Konjikido is in Tokyo for restoration, which should be finished in 1968.

16. Daigo-ji Treasure Hall (Daigo-ji Reihokan Hoshu-in), Daigo-ji, Daigo Higashioji-machi, Fushimi-ku, Kyoto. Tel. Daigo 2.

醍醐寺霊宝館宝聚院　京都府伏見区醍醐東大路町　醍醐寺内

Director: Ryuken Sawa. **Hours:** 8–4, Apr. 1–May 15 and Oct. 15–Nov. 20. (Check before going.) **Adm.:** ¥50. **Route:** Bus No. 39 from Keihan Sanjo passes the Daigo-ji, which is about 2 miles north of the Kobata station of the Japanese National Railways. Enter the main gate of the temple and take the small road to the right; the second entrance on the left leads to the treasure hall.

A superb collection of painting, calligraphy, sculpture, lacquer, metalwork, and temple documents of great importance for the study of Japanese art of the Heian and Kamakura periods and of the early 17th century.

The oldest painting is of the Nara period: a section of the *Kakogenzai Inga-kyo.* One of the best-known items is a sketch in ink on paper of Fudo Myo-o standing on a rock, by Shinkai and dated 1283. Also by Shinkai are a Bishamonten of 1278 and a Kongo Doji of 1280. Other sketches of a similar type (they are perhaps preliminary studies for a painting

16

to be done in color or models in a copybook) show a standing Fudo, a head of Fudo, and two disciples.

Among the large Buddhist paintings are a Monju crossing the sea (Kamakura period), a three-faced, eight-armed Gozanze Myo-o of the late Heian or early Kamakura period, and a Kishimojin called Chinese of the late T'ang or early Sung dynasty. There are also a Gundari Myo-o of the Heian period and an Amida triad, a Jizo, and a Kokuzo, as well as many portraits of priests—all of the Kamakura period.

The sutras include a copy of the beginning of the *Dainichi-kyo* in Kobo Daishi's handwriting and a sutra copied by the emperor Goyozei in 1593. There are also paintings of the Ryokai and the *Ninno-kyo mandara*.

The treasure hall is famous for its calligraphy, with writings of the emperors Godaigo and Gouda, a letter written by the monk Rigen in 907, and poems written on the occasion of a flower-viewing festival in 1598, to name but a few. It is equally noted for the screen of Bugaku dancers and the pair of twofold screens with fan-shaped designs on gold paper by Sotatsu. There are also three pairs of six-fold screens: one showing the training of horses and another with a design of painted curtains are of the Momoyama period; the third, of red maples, is by Sekkei.

The collection is almost as rich in sculpture. To be especially noted are a Kongo Yasha Myo-o dated 940, a charming Sho Kannon of the early Heian period, two Nyoirin Kannon, a seated Amida Nyorai, and a Kichijoten, all assigned to the middle or late years of the Heian period. From the Kamakura period are a Fudo by Kaikei and a Jizo.

There are also such items as sutra boxes and metal objects used in the temple ceremonies (including a scepter, a bell, and a *vajra* of the Heian period), *kesa,* a bowl said to have been used by Rigen, bamboo flower baskets and small mirrors of the Heian period, and an incense burner by Ninsei.

• COMMENTS • The quality is excellent, the installation handsome. The exhibition, save for the larger sculptures, changes each time the treasure hall is open. About 60 objects are shown at any one time, and each exhibition has a check list in Japanese. There is also a handbook describing

17

the temple and, very briefly, the collection, and a larger handbook illustrating and describing the temple buildings and a few of the items in the treasure hall; both of these are in Japanese. The treasure hall should not be missed if it is open when one is in Kyoto.

17. Dazaifu Temman-gu Treasure House (Dazaifu Temman-gu Homotsuden), Dazaifu Temman-gu, Dazaifu-machi, Tsukushi-gun, Fukuoka-ken. Tel. Dazaifu 25.

太宰府天満宮宝物殿　福岡県筑紫郡太宰府町

Director: Nobusada Nishitakatsuji. **Hours:** 8–5, Apr.–Oct.; 8:30–5, Nov.–Mar. **Adm.:** ¥50. **Route:** Dazaifu can be reached in about 35 min. on the Nishi Nippon Electric Railway from Fukuoka. (Some trains run directly to Dazaifu; on others, change at Futsukaichi.) On leaving the Dazaifu station, turn right onto the main shopping street, at the end of which is the entrance to the grounds of the shrine. Cross the three arched bridges which lead to the main building; then bear right to the museum, which is housed in two adjoining ferroconcrete buildings.

A good collection of paintings, calligraphy, documents, sculpture, arms and armor, porcelain, lacquer, masks, writing materials, metalwork, and archaeological objects. The shrine is dedicated to Sugawara Michizane (845–903), the celebrated man of letters and adviser to the Kyoto court who, banished to Kyushu, was posthumously deified and is worshiped as the god of learning and calligraphy. A large part of the collection centers around him. Of particular interest in this connection are two samples of his calligraphy and his copy of the *Hokke-kyo* in eight scrolls. In addition, there is a copy in three scrolls, which was made in 1615, of the *Temman-gu Engi* (which relates the story of Michizane's life) and a late-17th-century set of *kakemono* on the same subject, as well as many portraits of Michizane. A large number of the last are fairly recent, and a most amusing one is by the priest Sengai. There is also a sword that belonged to Michizane.

Probably the most important document is a Kamakura-period history of the shrine. There is also a memorandum of a gift from Hideyoshi, a manuscript (the *Kan'en*) of the early Heian period, and some delightful scrolls of poetry dated 1317. The shrine's autumn festival is charmingly recorded in a long Edo-period scroll. There are a number of metal and pottery Heian sutra boxes, a mirror dated 1593, and some huge writing brushes and inkstones.

Among the Chinese items are a large Ming painting of a plum branch, small dishes of "northern celadon" of the Sung period, and Ming celadon plates. An anchor from a Mongol warship recalls the unsuccessful attempt made by the Mongols to invade Kyushu in 1274 and again in 1281.

In the archaeological field are pieces of Yayoi pottery and, from the Kofun period, a group of Sue-ware vessels, some *magatama,* and tubular beads.

• COMMENTS • The quality and the installation are good, and there are some English labels. About seventy percent of the collection is normally on view. There is a small leaflet in Japanese listing the objects that are usually on display.

18. Ehime Cultural Hall (Ehime Bunkakan), Fukiage Koen, Yamazato-dori, Imabari, Ehime-ken. Tel. Imabari 2-0534.

愛媛文華館　愛媛県今治市山里通　吹上公園堀端

Director: Kaneichi Ninomiya, owner. **Hours:** 10–4; closed Mon. and day after a national holiday. (It can, however, be opened at any time on previous request.) **Adm.:** ¥20; free for special exhibitions. **Route:** Take bus for Imabari Sambashi, get off at Fukiage Koen-mae (the stop at the castle grounds) and walk south along the moat on the west side of the castle. The museum, a small Japanese building, is behind a cement wall, opposite the southwest corner of the castle precincts. (From the boat landing, walk east for 10 min. to the corner of the park, then as above.)

An interesting collection of Chinese, Japanese, and Korean ceramics, Japanese lacquer, a few Japanese swords, and fragments of Japanese poems.

In the early Chinese group are Han and T'ang grave figurines, a Han green-glazed jar, a T'ang dragon-handled vase, and a T'ang three-color pitcher with a bird's-head spout. The Sung dynasty is represented by celadons, Tz'u-chou bowls, and a Ju dish, among other pieces. From the Ming dynasty are marked pieces of the Hsuan-te, Wan-li, Chia-ching, and T'ien-ch'i periods. There are also a few objects from the Ch'ien-lung period, such as a yellow-and-blue glazed plate and a red-glazed vase.

The Japanese ceramic pieces are largely Old Karatsu dishes, vases, and tea bowls. Among the lacquer items from the Edo period are a clothes box, a writing box, a bookcase, and many *inro*. The Korean ceramics include a celadon bowl of the Koryo dynasty and several jars of the Yi dynasty.

A sword, assigned to the Kamakura period, is inscribed Ichimonji, and another, of the Momoyama period, is inscribed Kuniyasu.

• COMMENTS • The quality is good and the installation pleasantly arranged. About ten percent of the some 500 pieces in the collection is usually on view; the exhibition changes four times a year. The museum is worth visiting.

19. Ehime Prefectural Local Art Museum (Ehime Kenritsu Kyodo Geijutsukan), 19 Ichiban-cho, Matsuyama, Ehime-ken. Tel. Matsuyama 2-3711.

愛媛県立郷土芸術館　愛媛県松山市一番町 19 番地

Director: Under the prefectural office. **Hours:** 9–4:30; closed for New Year season and when exhibition is being changed. **Adm.:** ¥30. **Route:** Take tram for Dogo and get off at Ichiban-mae (15 min.); walk back about 100 yards to the first street on the right. This turns into a winding driveway at the top of which is the museum, a large house built in the Western style at the turn of the century.

A small collection (with many of the items on loan from a nearby shrine) of Japanese archaeology, swords, armor, local ceramics and paintings, housed on the second floor of the museum building. There are also displays of sword and pottery making. This material, however, is apt to be put aside in favor of a number of temporary loan shows of considerable quality, such as that of local archaeology held in the autumn of 1965.

• COMMENTS • The display is adequate. The temporary exhibitions rather than the permanent collection would justify a visit.

Note: The tower of the castle which crowns the hill behind the museum building, and which in itself is worth visiting, shows a collection of arms and armor. There is a ropeway to the top of the hill.

20. Fujii Museum (Fujii Saiseikai Yurinkan), 44 En-shoji-machi, Okazaki, Sakyo-ku, Kyoto. Tel. Kyoto 77-0005.

藤井斉成会有隣館　京都市左京区岡崎円勝寺町 44 番地

Director: Shizu Fujii. **Hours:** 12–3, 1st and 3rd Sun. each month except Jan. and Aug. **Adm.:** free. **Route:** Take tram No. 6 from station and get off at Higashiyama Niomon; walk right (east) for about 200 yards towards the entrance to Okazaki Park. The museum, a large Western-style building with a yellow tiled roof, is on the right side of the street.

A large collection of Chinese painting, sculpture, jades, bronzes, pottery, porcelain, lacquer, costumes, and furniture. There are also a few Gandhara sculptures, Indian bronzes, and Japanese mirrors.

The sculpture, shown on the ground floor, is somewhat uneven in quality. Among the better Buddhist pieces are a stele dated 535, a tall Bodhisattva of the Sui dynasty, and a standing T'ang Buddha. There are also a smaller seated Buddha, dated 639, and two large guardians from the caves of T'ien-lung-shan. Several wooden figures are labeled Sung. On the same floor are good Han pottery tomb slabs and roof tiles, inscribed stone slabs from T'ang tombs, and a fragment of a stele with an unusual inscription of a classical text with each character written in three different forms. There is also a case containing the Gandhara stone figures and reliefs.

An excellent group of early bronzes occupies the second floor. There are fine vessels of the Yin and early Chou dynasties, notably two *ting,* a *ku,* and a *kuei.* A *hu* of the Warring States period has an inlaid design, and a small box of the same period is topped with human figures. There are many Han bronze vessels, large drums, and a series of unusual weights, as well as a few pieces of lacquer from Lo-lang. Mirrors date from the Han to the T'ang dynasty and ritual jades from the Chou and Han dynasties. One case contains metal coins and cowrie shells, another the molds for coins. A medium-sized 5th-century gilt-bronze Buddha is unusual in that it resembles a figure from Gandhara.

There are some 500 paintings in the collection, the majority representing the Ming and Ch'ing dynasties, although a few have earlier attributions. These are exhibited on the third floor. A good landscape is ascribed to the Sung artist Hsu Tao-ning. Other paintings are by the Sung artists Ma Ho-chih, Emperor Hui Tsung, and Hsu Ch'ung-ssu, while a scroll, *Secluded Bamboo and Withered Tree,* is ascribed to the Yuan artist Wang T'ing-yun. There are a scroll of the Sixteen Lohan by Ch'ou Shih-chou of the Ming dynasty and paintings by Shih T'ao and Lang Shih-ning (Castiglione) of the Ch'ing dynasty. Brushes, seals, ink sticks, and inkstones complement the painting display.

Among the documents are a copy (said to be of the T'ang dynasty) of the *Spring and Autumn Annals,* a scroll attributed to Su Tung-p'o, a document of the Ming emperor Hsuante, and calligraphy of the Ming painter Tung Ch'i-ch'ang.

Good Han and T'ang pottery grave figurines and large porcelains of the Ming and Ch'ing dynasties are also exhibited on the third floor. Among the Han pieces are a tall tower and a house, the latter painted with two rows of figures on balconies.

Pieces of elaborately decorated furniture are scattered throughout the galleries, and in a separate case is a robe said to have been worn by the emperor Ch'ien-lung.

• COMMENTS • The quality is good to excellent. The display is crowded, but the objects can be adequately seen and there are some labels in English. Most of the collection is normally on view, save for the paintings and documents, of which ten or twelve different ones are shown each time the museum is open. There is an illustrated folder in Japanese which lists some of the more important items. The collection is of very great interest to any student of Chinese art and should by all means be visited. The museum may be specially opened, and the paintings not on view may be seen, if application is made in writing a week in advance and provided the weather is good.

21. Fujita Art Museum (Fujita Bijutsukan), 40 Amijima-cho, Miyakojima-ku, Osaka. Tel. Osaka 351-0582.

藤田美術館　大阪市都島区網島町 40 番地

Director: Tomiko Fujita. **Hours:** 10–4, Apr., May, Oct., and Nov.;

closed Mon. (Check before going. Students may be allowed to see the collection at other times on previous application.) **Adm.:** ¥100. **Route:** The museum, which is about 2 miles east of the Osaka main station and to the north of Osaka Castle, is not far from the Higashi Noda stop on the Keihin Electric Railway to Kyoto, or same stop on municipal tramline. It stands in ample grounds, enclosed by a high wall, on the site of the former residence of Baron Fujita.

A superb collection, assembled by the late Baron Fujita and his sons, of Chinese and Japanese painting, calligraphy, sculpture, ceramics, lacquer, textiles, and metalwork, and Japanese tea-ceremony objects. It is stored in two concrete godowns and exhibited in a third.

Among the early Japanese paintings are one scroll of the *Kegon Gojugosho Emaki* and one scroll of the *Murasaki Shikibu Nikki Emaki,* both Kamakura, 13th century; a segment of the *Shungyu Ekotoba,* Kamakura, late 13th or early 14th century; twelve scrolls of the *Hossoshu Hiji Ekotoba* attributed to Takashina Takakane, Kamakura, 14th century; and, also from the Kamakura period, a portrait of one of the Thirty-six Poets, a hanging scroll of a Rakan, and a painting of the Paradise of Amida. From the 15th century are two landscapes attributed to Dasoku, a figure painting by Reisai, and another attributed to Sotan. A painting of Fugen and a river scene are assigned to the Muromachi period, and there are twofold and sixfold screens of the Kano school from the Momoyama and Edo periods.

Paintings by Masanobu, Moronobu, and Choshun represent the *ukiyo-e* school, and there is a scroll by the 19th-century painter Tamechika illustrating the *Heiji Monogatari.*

Among the Chinese paintings assigned to the Sung dynasty are a triptych of Sakyamuni, Manjusri, and Samantabhadra; a fan-shaped painting, *Li Po Looking at a Waterfall,* attributed to Ma Yuan; two *kakemono,* Han Shan and Shih Te and a bird on a pine branch, attributed to Liang K'ai; and another of Pu Tai, attributed to Li Lung-mien. A pair of landscapes attributed to Kao Jan-hui and an album painting attributed to Yu Chien are designated Yuan. There are examples of Chinese calligraphy of the Sung dynasty and of Japanese calligraphy of the Kamakura and later periods.

23

The sculpture section includes two small Chinese stone steles of the Northern Wei and T'ang dynasties respectively, an eight-sided pillar of the 6th century, and a unique gilt-bronze figure of Maitreya seated cross-legged on a bird. There is also a Japanese painted clay statue of a Rakan of the Nara period.

Japanese ceramics, largely tea-ceremony objects, abound, and they date from the Muromachi to the Edo period. To name a few: a Raku-ware bowl by Chojiro, a tea bowl by Ninsei, and examples of Hagi, Seto, Karatsu, Takatori, and Shigaraki wares. The collection also contains Chinese Sung-dynasty *temmoku* tea bowls with oil-spot, hare's-fur, and leaf decoration, and a yellow *temmoku* bowl. In addition there are many porcelain incense boxes of the Ming dynasty and several pieces of Dutch Delft ware.

There are a great number of other tea-ceremony objects in the collection, such as bamboo spoons and whisks, Old Ashiya teakettles, tea caddies, stands for the kettles, and fans.

Among the Japanese lacquer items are a Heian sutra box and Kamakura and Muromachi incense boxes. There are also a lacquered wooden *oi* of the Kamakura period and a bamboo sutra cover of the Fujiwara period. The Chinese lacquer is all of the Ming dynasty.

In the textile field are a Chinese Ming embroidery portraying Pu Tai, Han Shan, and Shih Te and a fragment of a fine tie-dyed material of the Momoyama period. The collection also contains a notable number of Chinese and Japanese ink sticks and seals.

· COMMENTS · The quality is excellent, and the display, especially the lighting, is good. One to five percent of the collection is normally visible, though the Chinese sculpture is always on view. A large part of each exhibition is generally devoted to tea-ceremony objects, and each show is accompanied by an illustrated catalogue. There is a brief illustrated catalogue of objects associated with the tea ceremony. All the publications are in Japanese only, except for the catalogue of the autumn of 1964. Behind the buildings is a charming garden with a teahouse.

22. Fukui Municipal History Hall (Fukui Shiritsu Rekishikan), 121 Asuwayama-machi, Fukui, Fukui-ken. Tel. Fukui 2-5517.

福井市立歴史館　福井市足羽山町 121 番地　足羽山公園内

Director: Hatsui Taniguchi. **Hours:** 8:30–5, Mar.–Oct.; 9–4, Nov.–Feb.; closed Mon., day after a national holiday, and Dec. 29–Jan. 3. **Adm.:** ¥20. **Route:** The museum, a small, well-designed modern building, is pleasantly situated in Asuwayama Koen, overlooking the town. The bus for Sekijuji stops at Asuwayama Koen Noboriguchi, which is at the bottom of the hill, with a long, steep flight of steps leading up to the museum. By taxi, the museum is about 5 min. from the station.

A collection of local archaeology, mementos of local notables, documents relating to local history, and dioramas of early industrial scenes.

The portraits, possessions, and calligraphy of the region's notable men and a large painting of the middle Heian period of Amida and attendants are shown on the ground floor. On the upper floor are Sue-ware vessels, Kofun swords, a quiver, and jewelry from local excavations; a screen depicting Asuwayama in the Edo period; photographs of Fukui in the late 19th century; and the above-mentioned dioramas.

• COMMENTS • The quality is good of its kind, and the display is well done. One-third of the collection is normally on view, and changes are made in the exhibition five or six times a year. A special loan exhibition is generally held once a year. There is a small illustrated pamphlet in Japanese. The museum is of interest chiefly to the specialist in local history or archaeology.

23. Fukui Prefectural Okajima Art Memorial Hall (Fukui Kenritsu Okajima Bijutsu Kinenkan), 1 Hoei Naka-machi, Fukui, Fukui-ken. Tel. Fukui 3-4347.

福井県立岡島美術記念館　福井市宝永中町 1 番地

Director: Hajime Kuga. **Hours:** 9–4:30, Apr.–Sept.; 9:30–4, Oct.–Mar.; closed Mon., last day of each month, national holidays, and Dec. 28–Jan. 5. **Adm.:** ¥20. **Route:** The museum is a two-story modern building. It can be reached in 5 min. by taxi; there is no convenient bus.

A small collection of Chinese, Tibetan, and Japanese metalwork, costume jewelry, and coins; Japanese lacquer, tobacco pouches, and pipes; and other items collected in the United States—all donated, together with the building, by Mr. Okajima to the city of Fukui.

Among the bronzes are small Chinese Buddhist figures of the Sui and T'ang dynasties and Tibetan Lamaist deities. There is a great deal of Japanese sword furniture (largely of the Edo period and of good quality), such as a *mitokoromono* (set) by the Goto school, and a small knife or *kozuka* by Yokoya Somin. The interesting group of tobacco pipes, cases, and pouches and some good lacquer writing boxes and tables are also of the Edo period. In addition, the collection has some Chinese jewelry and miniature pewter vessels and Japanese metal vases, lamps, sutra boxes, incense burners, and a set of toy tea-ceremony vessels.

The coins include a good representation of the gold coins of the Edo period (*oban* and *koban*) and a number of foreign commemorative ones.

• COMMENTS • The collections, chosen with care and taste, are pleasantly arranged in a building well adapted to its purpose. There is a small handbook in Japanese. The exhibition is changed four times a year, with borrowed objects supplementing the regular collections, half of which are normally on view. Special loan shows are arranged for May and November. The museum is worth a visit.

24. Fukuoka Art Museum (Fukuoka Bijutsukan), Fukuoka-ken Bunka Kaikan, 1-go, 2, 5-chome, Tenjin, Fukuoka, Fukuoka-ken. Tel. Fukuoka 74–8591/5.

福岡美術館　福岡市天神5丁目2番地1号　福岡県文化会館内

Director: Sanji Mizoe, Director of the Bunka Kaikan. **Hours:** 10–6; closed Mon. **Adm.:** free. **Route:** Take tram No. 8, 15, or 16, and get off at Shimin Kaikan-mae (about 20 min.). The museum is in the Bunka Kaikan (Cultural Hall), a large new building with a tall tower and faced with red brick, set back from the street on the left.

This museum, which opened in October 1964, occupies a large gallery on the second floor of the city's new Cultural Hall. It is now run as an exhibition hall, as it has no collection of its own, though it is planning to create a collection of the contemporary art of Kyushu. It organizes one loan show a year, in the autumn; at other times it lends its space to private groups.

The museum's loan exhibitions have, as of November 1965, included one of Momoyama painting and one of the art of the Meiji and Taisho periods.

• COMMENTS • The shows are well arranged in the handsome gallery. The museum's own exhibitions are accompanied by illustrated catalogues, and there is an illustrated pamphlet and a booklet on the Bunka Kaikan. The museum is worth visiting for its own exhibitions and for the architecture of the building.

25. Gakuen-ji Treasure House (Gakuen-ji Homotsu-den), Bessho-machi, Hirata, Shimane-ken. Tel. Kawashimo 608.

鰐淵寺宝物殿　島根県平田市別所町

Director: Chief Priest. **Hours:** 9–5, Jul. 28 and 29, if not raining, or on any fine day if written application has been made well in advance. **Adm.:** ¥50. **Route:** The temple is in a narrow wooded valley, rather far from Hirata (which can be reached from either Matsue or Taisha by the Hohoku private electric railway) and near the coast of the Japan Sea. Take bus from Hirata for Kawashimo; get off at Shogaku-mae (40 min.) and walk ahead, crossing the bridge on the left. Continue uphill along a dirt road, following a stream (about 1 hr.). The temple precincts are at the end of the road, with the treasure house, a small godown-type building, to the right and halfway up the long flight of steps leading to the Kondo.

An important collection of Japanese painting, calligraphy, sculpture, and metalwork, belonging to the temple.

Among the *mandara* are an Ichiji Kinrin (late Heian to early Kamakura) and a Sanohonchibutsu (Kamakura period). The portraits include a likeness of Mori Motonari (the daimyo of what is now Hiroshima Prefecture) of the Muromachi period and one of the priest Eigen Honin of the Momoyama period.

The documents are very interesting. Among them are an order of the emperor Gomurakami for the raising of troops to fight for the Southern Court during the Nambokucho period, a copy of a law promulgated in 1355, an order of the emperor Gonara, and a letter written by one of the ladies of his court. A letter from one priest to another is dated 1215.

The earliest piece of sculpture is a gilt-bronze standing Kannon dated 692. A variety of figures, in wood and metal, are assigned to the Heian and Kamakura periods.

There are also a stone sutra box dated 1151, many Heian and Kamakura mirrors, good *kakebotoke* of the Heian period, and a lovely *kei* of the same date.

· COMMENTS · The quality is excellent, the display adequate. The importance of the collection and the beauty of the setting of the temple repay the visitor for the difficulty of the trip.

26. Gallery of Horyu-ji Treasures, Tokyo National Museum (Horyu-ji Homotsuden, Tokyo Kokuritsu Hakubutsukan), Ueno Koen, Taito-ku, Tokyo. Tel. Tokyo 822-1111.

法隆寺宝物殿　東京国立博物館　東京都台東区上野公園

Director: Nagatake Asano. **Hours:** Open on Thurs. only, if not raining; also, if humidity within building rises above 70%, museum will be closed. **Adm.:** ¥50. **Route:** The gallery, a small ferroconcrete building in Japanese style, is within the grounds of the Tokyo National Museum (No. 184), to the left of the main gate. It is about a 5-min. walk from the Ueno stop (near which there is a map of the park) on either the Hibiya or the Ginza subway line.

A collection of rare and beautiful objects, many from the Asuka and Hakuho periods, which were presented by the authorities of the Horyu-ji at Nara to the Imperial Household in 1876 and are now on loan to the Tokyo National Museum. Just over 300 items in all, they are housed in a very handsome new building, opened in 1962.

As is natural in temple collections, many of the objects are connected with Buddhism. In the rich sculpture section are a large group of gilt-bronze figures of Buddhas and Bodhisattvas of the Asuka and early Nara periods, including a Bodhisattva with a date of 651, which are indispensable for the study of early Buddhist sculpture. Many of the bronze halos that accompanied such figures are on view. There are also ten bronze repoussé plaques with Buddhist figures of the Nara period and, from the Asuka period, a charming and very rare group portraying Queen Maya, surrounded by her attendants, giving birth to the Buddha.

The masks are equally fine, with 31 Gigaku masks of the Asuka and Nara periods, a Bugaku mask of the Nara period, and a demon mask made in 1294. Nowhere else can these early masks be seen to better advantage.

The paintings are a small group, but they include screens illustrating the life of Shotoku Taishi (painted in 1069), four Kamakura *kakemono* on the same subject, and Buddhist paintings and sutras of the Heian period mounted on screens.

The somewhat larger document section contains such extraordinary pieces as the record of an imperial donation to the Horyu-ji in 756, a Chinese copy of the *Hokke-kyo* dated 694, sutras in Sanskrit characters of the T'ang dynasty, and a fragment of the *Kengyu-kyo* of the Nara period. There are also Heian-period copies of the *Hokke-kyo*, the *Butsumyo-kyo,* and the *Shoman-gyo;* a catalogue of the *Kokinshu* written in the Kamakura period by Kenshin; and sutra covers of the same period, as well as daily records of the Horyu-ji.

Among the textiles are a few patterned and embroidered silks of the Asuka period and many more of the Nara period. There are also some felt rugs of the Nara period.

The many fine pieces of metalwork include a canopy, with pendant banners, for a Buddhist image (Asuka period); a variety of objects used in the Buddhist ritual (Nara to Kamakura periods); superb T'ang mirrors; long-handled incense burners of the Asuka period; and a great variety of Nara bottles, bowls, and spoons.

The collection also contains a *koto* of the T'ang dynasty with a date corresponding to 724, stirrups of the Asuka period, and Nara-period inkstones, miniature wooden pagodas, a sutra box, lacquered leather boxes, needle cases, rosaries, wood for incense, a bamboo cabinet, a foot rule, a bow and arrows, and wooden drums. A chest on legs, with mother-of-pearl inlay, dates from the Heian period, and a lacquer and mother-of-pearl lampstand is from the Kamakura period.

• COMMENTS • The quality is superb, the objects rivaling those in the Shoso-in. The display is excellent, and the labels are in Japanese and English. Almost all the objects are on view. There is a very good completely illustrated catalogue in Japanese with an English summary.

27. Gifu University Local Museum (Gifu Daigaku Gakugeigakubu Kyodo Hakubutsukan), Gifu Daigaku, Nagara, Gifu, Gifu-ken. Tel. Gifu 2-4161, ext. 48.

岐阜大学学芸学部郷土博物館　岐阜市長良
岐阜大学学芸学部内

Director: Yasaburo Hiyoki. **Hours:** 9–5; closed Sun., half a day Sat., and national holidays. **Adm.:** free. **Route:** Take bus for Obusa and get off at Daigaku-mae (20 min.). The museum is in a small new building at the rear of the university campus.

A medium-sized collection of Japanese archaeology, a few pieces of armor, and a very large collection of documents referring to local history, housed in part of the building.

There are some 700 Jomon stone implements and fragments of pottery, and a slightly larger number of fragments of Yayoi pottery. From the Kofun period there are nearly 200 objects, including high-stemmed cups, jars, and other items, and from later periods a few pieces of armor and some swords. In addition, there are rubbings of ancient tiles and some mirrors.

The museum is best known for its collection of more than 25,000 documents pertaining to local history, of which a very few (such as an early-17th-century wooden signboard with an edict against Christianity) are normally on view.

• COMMENTS • The quality of the objects is fair, the display poor. All but a very few of the objects and documents are usually kept in an open storeroom on the ground floor.

28. Goto Art Museum (Goto Bijutsukan), 111 Tamagawa Kaminoge-cho, Setagaya-ku, Tokyo. Tel. Tokyo 701-5932.

五島美術館　東京都世田谷区玉川上野毛町 111 番地

Director: Hideto Ito (Kiyoshi Nishimura, Vice-Director). **Hours:**

9:30–4:30; closed Mon., Dec. 27–Jan. 4, and sometimes when exhibition is being changed. **Adm.:** ¥50. **Route:** The museum is in the southwest section of the city. Take Keihin line from Tokyo Central Station to Oimachi, change to Tokyu Oimachi line, and get off at Kaminoge. On leaving the station, walk straight ahead, cross the main highway, and take the second street on the right. The museum, a large new building, is on the left, about 100 yards from the corner and set back from the street.

The private collection of the late Mr. Keita Goto forms the nucleus of this superb group of Chinese and Japanese paintings, calligraphy, sutras, and ceramics; Chinese mirrors and early jades; Japanese tea-ceremony, lacquer, and archaeological objects; and a few Korean ceramics. The museum, a very handsome one-story building, was designed by Isoya Yoshida and opened in 1960.

The collection is perhaps best known for its sections of the *Genji Monogatari* scroll, a masterpiece of Heian painting. *Emakimono* of the Kamakura period include six segments of the *Murasaki Shikibu Nikki Emaki,* a segment of the *Jigoku Zoshi,* another of the *Zen Kunen Kassen Emaki,* and three segments of the *Kitano Tenjin Engi.* There are also portraits of poets, a painting of a famous carriage bull (one of the "Ten Fast Bulls"), and a charming scroll showing pairs of poets beside their poems (*Jidai Fudo Uta-awase*). Among the religious paintings are Heian portraits of priests drawn in ink; the Shi Tenno, similarly drawn but of the Kamakura period; and the *Manifestation of Manjusri,* the frontispiece of a Kamakura sutra. A fine painting of Kanzan is by Reisai, while Kenzan is represented by a charming circular painting of a pine tree under snow and screens of the flowers of the four seasons, Korin by an equally delightful painting illustrating the *Ise Monogatari,* and Koetsu by part of his famous deer scroll.

There is a fascinating group of sutras. Several date from the Nara period, such as a section of the *Inga-kyo,* a portion of the *Kegon-kyo,* and a portion of the *Hokke-kyo.* A section of the *Kongo Hannya-kyo* is in Kobo Daishi's handwriting, and other Heian sutras include a copy of the *Hokke-kyo* attributed to Tofu, an *Amida-kyo,* a section of the *Hokke-kyo* with each character inscribed in a stupa, and another section of the same sutra on a ground of birds, butterflies, and flowers. A *Kanfugen-kyo* is bound in booklet form. A second copy of the *Inga-kyo* is of the Kamakura period, as is a sutra written in Sanskrit over elaborate drawings and another called *Menashi-kyo* (literally, "Eyeless Sutra") because the figures in the background of the text are faceless.

The collection is almost as well known for its Japanese calligraphy. There are many sections of such anthologies as the *Kokinshu,* the *Man'yoshu,* and the *Wakan Roeishu,* as well as *shikishi,* all of the Heian period, with attributions in some cases to Gyosei, Kinto, Sari, Tofu, or Tsurayuki. Two poems are in the handwriting of the emperor Gotoba. There are also examples of the calligraphy of Daito Kokushi, Muso Kokushi, and Ikkyu, of the Kamakura, Nambokucho, and Muromachi periods respectively, and a *shikishi* by Koetsu.

The Chinese paintings of the Sung dynasty include a bird attributed to Mu Ch'i, a duck attributed to the emperor Hui Tsung, and a painting of the sixth patriarch of the Zen sect. Sung and Yuan calligraphy is liberally represented. There are a number of Han and T'ang Chinese mirrors, of which four have inscriptions containing dates of the second half of the Han dynasty and a fifth is dated 650.

The collection is especially strong in Japanese tea bowls and tea caddies (many of which are named), water jars, and flower vases. Old Iga, Old Bizen, Shino, Seto, Oribe, and Yellow Seto wares are all represented, and there are named Raku tea bowls by Chojiro, Donyu, and Koetsu. Other tea-ceremony objects include spoons used by famous tea masters and Old Ashiya iron teakettles.

Among the Chinese Sung porcelains are Tz'u-chou vases with peony designs in black on white, *temmoku* tea bowls, and celadon vases and bottles. From the early Ming dynasty are bowls and bottles in underglaze blue and colored overglaze enamels. The Korean ceramics are mainly tea bowls with monochrome glazes.

Japanese archaeology is brilliantly represented by a group of gilt-bronze harness trappings of the Kofun period, excavated at the Saitobaru tomb site in Miyazaki Prefecture.

· COMMENTS · The quality is superb, the installation handsome. About ten percent of the collection is normally on view. The exhibition changes about six or seven times a year, and in the spring and autumn there are special shows with objects borrowed for the occasion and accompanying catalogues, in Japanese only. There is an illustrated leaflet in English describing the collection. A large book with illustrations of the most important items in the collection has a list of the illustrations in English.

29. Gumma Prefectural Museum (Gumma Kenritsu Hakubutsukan), 1353 Ichinomiya, Tomioka, Gumma-ken. Tel. Ichinomiya 42.

群馬県立博物館　群馬県富岡市一の宮 1353 番地

Director: Kiyomatsu Hayashi. **Hours:** 9–4:30; closed Mon., national holidays, and Dec. 28–Jan. 5. **Adm.:** ¥20. **Route:** Ichinomiya (known also as Joshu Ichinomiya: Joshu is an old name for Gumma Prefecture) is on the Joshu Dentetsu line from Takasaki to Shimonita, the third stop beyond Tomioka. From the station, walk straight ahead to the main road, turn left, and then right at the *torii* (about 10 min.). The museum, a yellow-plaster Western-style two-story building, is on the right, halfway up the road leading to the shrine.

A rather small collection of local archaeology and ethnology.

The archaeological section contains arrowheads and stone implements of the early Jomon period, some late-Jomon pottery jars, and Kofun-period iron swords, Sue-ware vessels, a very large stone *magatama,* and a group of *haniwa* which includes two large horses, a quiver, several small animals, and some human heads.

In the ethnological section are farm tools, straw raincoats, lanterns, tobacco pipes, stencils for dyeing cloth, and a collection of puppet heads. There are also a few swords and suits of armor of the Edo period.

• COMMENTS • The quality is fair to good, the display adequate. About thirty percent of the collection, including the more complete archaeological pieces, is usually on view, and changes are made in the exhibits three times a year. Much of the material, other than the archaeological, is on loan. There is no general pamphlet, but reports on the local excavations are available. The museum is of interest only to the specialist in archaeology.

33

30. Gyokudo Art Museum (Gyokudo Bijutsukan), 75 Mitake, Ome-shi, Tokyo. Tel. Ome 7-8335.

玉堂美術館　東京都青梅市御岳75番地

Director: Yusai Suzuki. **Hours:** 9–5; closed Mon. and Dec. 25–Jan. 4. **Adm.:** ¥50 (¥150 for special exhibitions). **Route:** The museum is at Mitake, on the Tama River, west of Tokyo. Take Chuo line from either Tokyo station or Shinjuku to Tachikawa; change to the Ome line and get off at Mitake (about 1½ hrs. from Shinjuku). Walk downhill from the station, cross the bridge over the river, turn left, and left again into the first paved driveway, at the end of which lies the museum.

A small collection of the paintings and sketches of Gyokudo Kawai (1873–1957), shown in a gallery in a charming Japanese-style building designed by Isoya Yoshida and opened in 1961.

The rather scant holdings of the museum are supplemented each spring and autumn by major paintings of Gyokudo borrowed for the occasion. Other loans fill out the exhibition during the summer and winter. About 20 paintings are on view each time, and some of Gyokudo's brushes, ink sticks, and inkstones are also on exhibit, as well as photographs of the artist. A room connected by an open passageway with the main building is set up as a reproduction of his studio and contains his painting equipment and some of his furniture.

• COMMENTS • The museum is worth visiting not only for the gentle and charming paintings in the Japanese style for which Gyokudo is so well known but also for its building, its garden, and its view. It was built at Mitake because Gyokudo lived there for many years and loved the countryside. The beautiful sand-and-rock garden was designed by Isoya Yoshida and Ken Nakajima and has a striking view over the river.

31. Hakodate Municipal Museum (Shiritsu Hakodate Hakubutsukan), 1-go, 17 Aoyagi-cho, Hakodate, Hokkaido. Tel. Hakodate 23–5480.

市立函館博物館　函館市青柳町17番1号

Director: Shigeo Kitakaze. **Hours:** 9–4:30, Apr.–Oct.; 9–4, Nov.–Mar.; closed Mon., national holidays, and New Year season. **Adm.:** ¥10 (¥100 for special exhibitions). **Route:** The museum, a large new ferroconcrete building, is in the park grounds, back from and somewhat to the left of the entrance. Take tram for Yachigashira and get off at Aoyagi-cho (15 min.). Turn right and walk uphill to the park entrance.

An interesting collection of local archaeology; of material illustrating the life of the Ainu, the Gilyak, and the Koryak; and of the (largely local) arts and handicrafts of the late Edo and Meiji periods.

The Jomon material, of all periods, comes from a variety of local sites; there are also finds from the Esan shell mound dating from the Zoku-Jomon period. Excavations by the museum staff continue.

The special features of the Ainu collection are screens depicting Ainu activities in each month of the year, scrolls with scenes of Ainu life painted by Tessai, and Japanese illustrated books on the same subject. The actual Ainu items were all collected early in the Meiji era.

The painting section is enlivened by works of Matsumae Hakkyo, a local artist of the late Edo and Meiji periods, and a view of Hakodate by Tessai. The local Hakodate ware, a quite charming blue-and-white, is well represented, along with more recent Kutani ware and Chinese porcelains from Swatow. Handsome wooden chests, lamps, inkstones, and sword guards may also be on display. Pottery by Kawai and a painting by Munakata bring the collection up to date. Many of these items were recently given to the museum by Mr. Hanamitsu.

• COMMENTS • The quality is good. The museum opened in April 1966, with the inaugural loan exhibition taking up most of the space and making it difficult to comment on any permanent installation. However, the well-lighted, ample galleries are excellently designed for their purpose and should provide a pleasant background for the collection. Anyone traveling in Hokkaido will find this museum worth visiting.

32. Hakone Art Museum (Hakone Bijutsukan), Gora, Hakone-machi, Kanagawa-ken. Tel. Hakone 2-2623.

箱根美術館　神奈川県箱根町強羅

Director: Yoji Yoshioka. **Hours:** 9–5, Apr.–Sept.; 9–4, Oct.–Nov.; closed Thurs. and Dec. 1–Mar. 31. **Adm.:** ¥100. **Route:** Take Hakone

Tozan Railway from Odawara to Gora; then, from same station, cable
car running between Gora and Sounzan, getting off at the second stop
(Koen-ue), which is beside the entrance to the museum grounds.

An excellent collection of pottery and porcelain from
China, Japan, Korea, and the Near East, housed in two
buildings. The first and smaller one, to the right of the
entrance, has an exhibition of Chinese and Japanese
ceramic techniques with tools, samples of clay, shards
from kiln sites, and photographs of potters at work and
of various kilns. It is very well arranged, with the objects
displayed in vitrines and in shallow drawers under the
vitrines and with enlarged photographs on the walls.

The main building, a little farther up the hill from the
entrance, houses the display collections in which Chinese
and Japanese ceramics predominate. Among the Chinese
pieces are a neolithic jar from Kansu; a Han watchtower,
hill jar, and oxcart; and a good selection of 3rd-century
Yueh ware. There are also a number of T'ang jars, dishes,
and pitchers and Yueh-ware vessels dating from the end
of the T'ang dynasty to early Sung. The Sung dynasty is
also represented by good Tz'u-chou jars, a fine Ting bowl,
pieces of Chun and Ju ware, and Lung-ch'uan celadons.
A blue-and-white bowl is assigned to the Yuan dynasty,
and there is a great variety of Ming pieces decorated in
colored enamels and in underglaze blue. A few pieces
from the Ch'ing dynasty have K'ang-hsi, Yung-cheng,
and Ch'ien-lung marks.

Japanese archaeology is represented by a Jomon urn,
Yayoi jars, a very good *haniwa* warrior, and Sue-ware
vessels from the Kofun period, as well as Nara-period tiles.
Most of the pieces come from known sites.

From the Momoyama period are Shino bowls, Yellow
Seto bowls and an incense burner, an Oribe pitcher, and
Old Bizen, Old Imari, Old Kutani, and Kakiemon pieces.
More Kutani and Imari vessels date from the Edo period,
as does an excellent series of Nabeshima plates. There is
also a fine piece by Ninsei and one by Dohachi.

In the section devoted to tea-ceremony objects are Seto
tea caddies and tea bowls of the Momoyama period and
Ido and Hori Mishima tea bowls of the Korean Yi dynasty.
Many of these are named pieces. There are also good
examples of Korean inlaid celadons of the Koryo period.

The Near Eastern group has some Iranian pieces dating from the 12th to the 14th century.

A charming garden of bamboo, maple, and moss, with a small teahouse, lies between the two buildings.

• COMMENTS • The quality is excellent, and the display is good. Some labels are in English. The exhibition is seldom changed, and, of the total collection of about 300 pieces, 200 are usually on show. There is a pamphlet in Japanese and English and a check list in Japanese.

Note: The museum belongs to the Church of World Messianity, and the collection was formed by the late founder of this church, Mr. Mokichi Okada. It is under the same director as its sister museum at Atami, and some of the objects are apt to be on loan at the Atami Museum (No. 9).

33. Hakone Shrine Treasure House (Hakone-jinja Homotsuden), 86 Oshiba, Motohakone, Hakone-machi, Kanagawa-ken. Tel. Motohakone 3-6031.

箱根神社宝物殿　神奈川県箱根町元箱根大芝86番地

Director: Yoshitaka Wakiyama, Chief Priest. **Hours:** 8–5. (If closed, inquire at the shrine office). **Adm.:** ¥20. **Route:** The shrine is on the eastern shore of Lake Ashi (known to foreigners as Lake Hakone), about 400 yards from the Motohakone stop on bus line running from Odawara station via Miyanoshita to Lake Ashi. The treasure house is on the left as one enters the shrine precincts, at the top of the long flight of steps leading up from the road.

A small collection of sculpture, painting, calligraphy, armor, swords and sword fittings, and historical documents. The sculpture includes figures of priests, among them Mankan Shonin and Enno Gyoja, the latter the pioneer of the Buddhist mountaineer priests. The most famous painting is the *Hakone Gongen Engi,* of the Kamakura period, 14th century. (This scroll, however, is never on view; permission may be granted to see it if one has a proper introduction and writes in advance.)

The historical documents are interesting for the history of the Kamakura, Momoyama, and early Edo periods. Among them are documents of the Hojo family, including a letter by Hojo Soun, an edict of Hideyoshi, a letter from Ieyasu, and documents referring to Nobunaga.

37

One large sword among those shown belonged to Hojo Tokimune and another to Minamoto Yoritomo.

• COMMENTS • The quality varies; the display is fair. All objects, save for the above-mentioned scroll, are normally on view.

34. Hakutsuru Art Museum (Hakutsuru Bijutsukan), 1545 Ochiai, Sumiyoshi-cho, Higashinada-ku, Kobe, Hyogo-ken. Tel. Kobe 85-6001.

白鶴美術館　神戸市東灘区住吉町落合 1545 番地

Director: J. Nakamura, Curator. **Hours:** 10–5, Apr.–May; 10–4, Sept. 15–Nov. 15; closed Mon. and all summer and winter. (Check before going.) **Adm.:** ¥50. **Route:** From Kobe or Osaka, take local train on Hankyu line to Mikage station. The museum, a large two-story Oriental-style building, is in a walled garden, some 25 min. on foot uphill from the station. As the way is hard to find, it is advisable to take a taxi.

A superb collection of early Chinese bronzes and ceramics, plus a few Japanese objects. Many of the bronzes date from the Yin to the early Chou dynasty. There are no less than seven *yu,* of which one is square, several have heavy flaring flanges, and one is bird-shaped. An extraordinary *kuang* has a lid in the shape of an elephant's head. There are a number of *ting,* one with a lid and a bulbous body covered with the thunder and *t'ao-t'ieh* motives. Several fine covered *lei* and a number of heavier *tsun* are also in this group. Chariot fittings date from the early Chou dynasty and from the period of the Warring States. A tall *hu* is dated 9th century B.C. on the basis of its highly stylized bird-and-dragon design. A large *chien* has the entwined pattern one associates with the Warring States period, and a *hu* of the Han dynasty has a cloud pattern inlaid in gold and silver.

The T'ang mirrors include four with designs in high relief of birds and animals among vines and four more with designs of birds and flowers, of which two have mother-of-pearl inlay and two have gold and silver inlay. Also from this period are earrings, hairpins, and a fine group of small vessels in silver gilt with repoussé floral and hunting designs on a tooled ground.

The few early Chinese ceramics include such pieces as

a painted dish and a painted vase, both of the Han dynasty, and a very rare inkstone of the Six Dynasties. From the T'ang dynasty are a fine glazed ewer with a phoenix head at the lip and medallions in low relief on the body and a dish with a decoration of a duck among lotus leaves. A group of *temmoku* bowls of the Sung dynasty have oil-spot, leaf, hare's-fur, and tortoise-shell markings. The celadons are both plain and decorated with designs in relief. The cream of this section is a superb Tz'u-chou vase with a three-clawed dragon in black on a white ground. Large Ming-dynasty jars and vases, in blue-and-white, five-color enamel, and red-and-gold, are also among the treasures.

The collection includes some miscellaneous items, such as a jade *pi* of the Warring States period and two paintings from Tun-huang showing a Buddha surrounded by Bodhisattvas with donors below. There are also a few Japanese paintings (notably an album of the *Eight Views of the Hsiao and the Hsiang,* by Shokei, and screens by Kano Motonobu), as well as Japanese lacquer objects, sutras (note a Heian-period section of the *Hokke-kyo*), swords, and *magatama*.

• COMMENTS • The quality is very fine and the installation good. About 50 pieces are on view at any one time; objects not on view can be seen on request. An illustrated booklet on the Chinese bronzes and ceramics and an illustrated pamphlet, both in Japanese, are available. The museum should not be missed.

35. Hamamatsu Municipal Local Museum (Hamamatsu Shiritsu Kyodo Hakubutsukan), Hamamatsu-jo, Motoshiro-machi, Hamamatsu, Shizuoka-ken. Tel. Hamamatsu 3-3872.

浜松市立郷土博物館　静岡県浜松市元城町浜松城

Director: Kin'ichi Suzuki. **Hours:** 8:30–5, Apr.–Oct.; 9–4, Nov.–Mar.; closed Dec. 29–31. **Adm.:** ¥20. **Route:** The museum is in the castle tower. Take bus to Shiyakusho-mae (the city hall). The entrance to the grounds of the castle, which lies behind the city hall, is from the first road to the right.

A small collection of local archaeology, historical documents, objects pertaining to the history of the city, and one statue, housed in the newly rebuilt tower of Hamamatsu Castle.

Among the Jomon finds from Shijimizuka are many stone implements, fragmentary figurines, and a huge pottery vessel. There is a group of Yayoi pottery and wooden vessels (some of which contain the original seeds and nuts placed in them) from Iba, and from nearby tumuli of the Kofun period are mirrors, small crude figurines, and fragmentary metal bells and swords.

The single statue is a wooden Yakushi Nyorai of the Heian period. The local objects include a few costumes, some firearms, and a number of historical documents. Among the latter are letters written by Tokugawa Ieyasu, letters by the 16th-century local daimyo, and poems written in the 19th century by his descendants.

• COMMENTS • The quality is good, the display well done, with a few English labels. Only a small percentage of the archaeological material is on view. The exhibition is changed about twice a year. There are two illustrated pamphlets, both in Japanese.

Note: The museum maintains a godown at Shijimizuka (the Shijimi shell-mound site), a short distance outside the city. Take the city bus, Shijimizuka line, to Shijimizuka Jutaku-mae; or the Toetsu bus, Irino line, to Iseki-mae. The archaeological area, a large open space in which several houses have been reconstructed, is a short distance from both stops. The godown, a small new ferroconcrete building, is in one corner of the area and contains the larger part of the Jomon pottery, stone implements, and bone objects found on the site. It is open during the same hours as the museum but is closed on Mondays and the day after a national holiday.

36. Hatakeyama Museum (Hatakeyama Kinenkan), 67 Saru-machi, Shiba Shirogane, Minato-ku, Tokyo. Tel. Tokyo 447-5787.

畠山記念館　東京都港区芝白金猿町 67 番地

Director: Senjin Sakai. **Hours:** 10–4, Apr., May, Oct., Nov.; closed Mon. (Check before going.) **Adm.:** ¥200. **Route:** From Tokyo Central Station take Yamate line to Gotanda; then bus for Tokyo-eki Yaesu-guchi. Get off at Shirogane Saru-machi and ask for the Hannyaen, a famous restaurant. The museum, a handsome new two-story building in the contemporary Japanese style, lies in wooded grounds behind the garden of the Hannya-en; the entrance is through a small gate on the right side of the road leading downhill past the restaurant's garden.

A very beautiful collection of Chinese and Japanese paintings, calligraphy, sculpture, metalwork, and ceramics, as well as Korean ceramics and Japanese lacquer and tea-ceremony objects.

The Japanese paintings include a landscape attributed to Shubun, a bird on a branch by Sesshu, enchanting scrolls of flowers and poems of the four seasons—the joint work of Koetsu and Sotatsu—a fan by Koetsu, a duck and lotus flower by Sotatsu, a Hotei and a small landscape by Korin, and autumn flowers by Kenzan. Two large characters were written by Daito Kokushi.

The distinguished group of Japanese ceramics consists largely of items for the tea ceremony. There are an Old Seto tea caddy, a painted Shino *mizusashi,* an elaborate Oribe cake dish, and some Old Bizen bottles. One tea bowl was potted by Koetsu, another by Chojiro, and three incense burners representing Mount Fuji at dawn, noon, and sunset are by Ninsei. Kenzan painted ten plates, a bowl with a high rim, a small sauce pot, and a *futaoki.* There are also tea-ceremony spoons associated with the tea master Sen no Rikyu and iron teakettles and metal flower vases.

Among the fine lacquer pieces are a *tebako* of the Heian period and another of the Kamakura. The Noh robes of the Edo period are very striking.

The earliest Chinese piece is a fine bronze *yu* of the Yin dynasty. The Sung paintings include *Evening Bell at the Distant Temple* attributed to Mu Ch'i, *Insects and Bamboo* by Chao Ch'ang, *Pu Tai* by Liang K'ai, and *Zen Dialogue* by Yin T'o-lo. There are also samples of calligraphy assigned to the Sung dynasty. In the Chinese ceramic group are a glazed figure of a lady and a blue, white, and green plate (both of the T'ang dynasty); Sung celadons; and considerable Ming blue-and-white and five-color ware. A small stone Buddhist stele dates from the Northern Wei dynasty.

The Korean ceramics are mostly tea bowls from the early part of the Yi dynasty.

· COMMENTS · The quality is excellent, the installation

very well done, with some labels in English. There is a different exhibition each spring and autumn, accompanied by an illustrated catalogue; items are not changed during the exhibition, and about ten percent of the collection is on view at any one time. There is a tea-ceremony room on the upper floor. This is one of the most pleasant museums in Tokyo.

37. Hirado Castle Tower (Hirado-jo Tenshukaku), Iwanoue-cho, Hirado, Nagasaki-ken. Tel. Hirado 2201.

平戸城天守閣　長崎県平戸市岩上町

Director: Mayor of Hirado. **Hours:** 8:30–5, winter; 8:30–6, summer; closed Dec. 30–31. **Adm.:** ¥50. **Route:** The island of Hirado is 15 min. by ferry from Hiradoguchi on Kyushu. From the ferry landing, walk left around the small harbor, turn left over the first bridge, and fork right on the road leading up the hill on which the castle stands; turn left again by the parking lot. The tower is above and to the left of the gateway to the fortress (about 20 min.).

A small collection of arms and armor, largely from the nearby Kameoka Shrine, whose treasure house no longer exists, housed in the newly built castle that replaces the one pulled down by Hideyoshi.

One very large sword is said to be Chinese and to have been brought to Japan in the Kofun period. Most of the armor is of the Edo period. There are guns, cartridge cases, small hand grenades, saddles, and stirrups. A white silk kimono worn by the emperor Meiji as a child is also on view.

In a second, and far smaller, building just beyond the tower are samples of Hirado ware, some Dutch ceramics, and a few pieces of Imari. There are also Christian images (Hirado having been a center of Christianity), including a very provincial painting of the Madonna and Child.

• COMMENTS • The quality is good of its kind and the display well done and unchanging. The castle is worth visiting if one is on Hirado, and the view from the top of the tower is magnificent.

38. Hirado Kanko Historical Hall (Hirado Kanko Shiryokan), Okubo-cho, Hirado, Nagasaki-ken. Tel. Hirado 2813.

平戸観光資料館　長崎県平戸市大久保町

Director: Teruyo Yamaga. **Hours:** 8:30–5. **Adm.:** ¥40. **Route:** The island of Hirado is reached by ferry in 15 min. from Hiradoguchi. From the ferry landing, walk to the street parallel to the one along the water-front, turn right, and then take the fourth path on the left leading up-hill by a flight of stone steps; turn right on the path at the top of the steps. The museum, a small ferroconcrete building, is to the left of the path and occupies the original site of the Dutch factory at Hirado.

A small collection of arms, armor, ceramics, paintings, calligraphy, and Christian relics. The objects are all on loan from families living on Hirado.

Generally on view are a few suits of armor, swords, samples of Nakano and Arita wares and Karatsu tea bowls, Korean dishes assigned to the late 16th century, some 17th-century Dutch pottery, a charming painting by Basho, some good Edo lacquer, and a scroll illustrating the physiognomy of foreigners and the curious objects be-longing to them. Christian relics include such items as a small crucifix and figures of the Madonna and recall the period in the late 16th and early 17th centuries when Hirado was a center of Christianity. A touching item is a Christian child's letter written to his aunt on Hirado after his exile to Java.

• COMMENTS • The quality varies, the display is ade-quate. The armor, swords, and paintings are occasionally changed, but the other objects are on more or less per-manent display. While not in the same category as the Matsuura Museum (No. 105), this collection is worth see-ing during a visit to Hirado.

39. Hiraide Archaeological Museum (Hiraide Koko Hakubutsukan), Hiraide, Soga-ku, Shiojiri, Nagano-ken. Tel. Shiojiri 22.

平出考古博物館　長野県塩尻市曾我区平出

Director: Kazuo Kamijo. **Hours:** 9–4; closed Mon. **Adm.:** ¥50. **Route:** The museum, which is housed in an unpretentious building standing on wooded ground, lies to the south of Shiojiri station. A bus from the station passes near the museum, or it can be reached in 5 min. by taxi over dirt roads.

A very interesting collection of the finds from Hiraide, a site which was continuously inhabited from the middle Jomon through the Heian period.

There are good and quite large pieces of pottery and a group of stone implements of the Jomon period; some small Sue-ware bowls (probably of the 6th century); and Haji-ware dishes with high feet and ash-glazed bowls of the Nara period. There are also a large *dotaku* of the Yayoi period and a fine green-glazed water pitcher of the Nara period. Photographs of the site make an interesting complement to the exhibition.

• COMMENTS • The quality is excellent, and although the installation is crowded all the objects are easily visible. Ten percent of the finds are normally on view; the exhibition seldom changes. There is an illustrated pamphlet in Japanese. The collection is of great interest to any student of Japanese archaeology. The site itself lies not far from the museum.

40. Hiroshima Castle Museum (Hiroshima-jo Haku-butsukan) 1 Moto-machi, Hiroshima-jo, Hiroshima, Hiroshima-ken. Tel. Hiroshima 21-7512.

広島城博物館　広島市基町1番地　広島城内

Director: Yukihiko Murakami. **Hours:** 9–5, Apr.–Sept.; 9–4:30, Oct.–Mar.; closed Dec. 29–Jan. 2. **Adm.:** ¥100.　**Route:** Take either bus or tram for Kamiya-cho; get off at Kencho-mae (the prefectural office). The castle (built recently to replace the one destroyed in World War II) is to the right of a shrine and easily visible; the entrance to the grounds is through a *torii*.

An interesting display of Japanese archaeology, arms and armor, and material relating to the history of Hiroshima, shown on the first and third floors of the castle.

The archaeological display is very small, containing but a few pieces of Sue ware and some stone implements. The armor collection (some items of which are on loan) is far more extensive, and includes suits from the Muro-machi and Edo periods. There are also many helmets and banners. A feature of the collection is the standard of a commander carried during Hideyoshi's invasion of Korea. There is a large group of sword guards and other pieces of sword furniture, as well as a number of swords and a display on the technique of swordmaking.

In the historical section are the signatures of many of the daimyo of Hiroshima, a screen showing the topography of Hiroshima in the Edo period, some Meiji furniture, and a group of prewar photographs of the city.

The second floor houses the natural-history collection, and the fourth floor is used for special exhibitions, some four of which take place every year.

• COMMENTS • The quality is good, the display well done, with a few English labels. The exhibition does not change. There is a folder in English. Visitors to Hiroshima will find the museum interesting.

41. Hokkaido University Ainu Museum in Memory of Dr. John Batchelor (Hokkaido Daigaku Nogakubu Fuzoku Hakubutsukan Bachiera-kan), Botanical Garden, Nishi 8-chome, Kita Sanjo, Sapporo, Hokkaido. Tel. Sapporo 25-8010.

北海道大学農学部付属博物館　バチェラー館
札幌市北三条西8丁目　植物園内

Director: Hisashi Abe. **Hours:** 9–4, Apr. 29–Nov. 3. **Adm.:** ¥30 for garden, ¥10 for museum. **Route:** The Botanical Garden is in the northwestern section of the city. Walk straight ahead for 2 blocks down the main street leading away from the station; turn right and walk for 3 blocks to the edge of the garden, then left to the entrance. The museum, a small frame building in the Victorian style, is the second on the right of the central path leading from the entrance.

An excellent collection of Ainu material, largely gathered by and displayed in honor of the late Dr. John Batchelor, the American missionary who became the first scholar of the Ainu language and culture. The collection was installed in its present setting in April 1964.

The clothing on display includes cloth, fur, and skin garments, as well as ceremonial headdresses. There is also a very good selection of necklaces, pendants, earrings, pouches, and swords. Among the items for household use are lacquer vessels, boxes, and chests; wooden spoons; and birch-bark ladles. Bows, arrows, quivers, harpoons, traps, and a boat show something of the hunting and fishing habits of the Ainu. The religious practices are illustrated by a large selection of *inau,* animal skulls wreathed in wood shavings (such animals having been ritually killed), libation wands, and a special exhibition of objects set up for a religious ceremony. There are also agricultural implements, snowshoes, skis, and a group of special clubs used for physical punishment. Models of houses and photographs of dwellings and people complete the display.

• COMMENTS • The quality is excellent, the installation good. Half the collection is usually on view, and the material in storage may be seen if advance notice is given. This is the best public exhibition of Ainu material in Hokkaido and should not be missed by anyone interested in the subject.

Note: This museum and the nearby Natural History Collection (No. 42) are both under the general direction of the Department of Agriculture of Hokkaido University. The university itself has a very extensive collection of Ainu material, the property of Professor Kodama, housed in a large room in one of the buildings of the Department of Medicine. It is not open to the public, however, and may be seen only on previous application made in writing.

42. Hokkaido University Natural History Collection (Hokkaido Daigaku Nogakubu Fuzoku Hakubutsu-kan), Botanical Garden, Nishi 8-chome, Kita Sanjo, Sapporo, Hokkaido. Tel. Sapporo 25-8010.

北海道大学農学部付層博物館　札幌市北三条西 8 丁目
植物園内

Director: Takashi Tagawa. **Hours:** 9–4. **Adm.:** ¥30 for garden, ¥10 for museum. **Route:** The Botanical Garden is in the northwestern section of the city. Walk straight ahead for 2 blocks down the main street leading away from the station; turn right and walk for 3 blocks to the edge of the garden, then left to the entrance. The museum, a wooden building in the Victorian style, is the first on the right of the central path leading from the garden entrance.

The museum contains, on its upper floor, one row of wall cases devoted to the local archaeology, consisting of pottery, stone and bone implements, and *magatama* of the Jomon,

Zoku-Jomon, and Satsumon cultures. Only the best display pieces are on view, with much additional material held in storage.

There is also a small display of Burmese clothing and lacquer vessels. All the rest of the space is devoted to natural history.

• COMMENTS • The quality is fair, the display adequate. The exhibition, which does not change, is of interest only to the specialist.

Note: This museum and its neighbor, the Ainu Museum in Memory of Dr. John Batchelor (No. 41), are both under the general direction of the Department of Agriculture of Hokkaido University.

43. Homma Art Museum (Homma Bijutsukan), 12 Hamabata-machi, Sakata, Yamagata-ken. Tel. Sakata 1429.

本間美術館　山形県酒田市浜畑町 12 番地

Director: Yusuke Homma. **Hours:** 9–4:30; closed Mon., Dec. 15–Apr. 1, and when exhibition is being changed. **Adm.:** ¥50. **Route:** Follow the main street from the station and bear right at the first large street. The museum, a Japanese-style house set in a large garden, is on the right of the street, more than halfway down the block. There is no bus, but the walk takes only about 10 min.

A most interesting and extensive collection of Japanese painting and calligraphy, Chinese and Japanese ceramics, and Japanese swords, contemporary prints (about 300), and children's paintings (about 2,000).

Among the early paintings are a scroll of portraits of thirty patriarchs of the Tendai sect, two scrolls of Buddhist subjects by Shokado, a portrait and a painting of weasels by Okyo, and a screen by Buson. There are also a few sketches by Hokusai.

The calligraphy includes a Kamakura copy of the *Ise Monogatari,* a fragment of writing attributed to Tofu, a 14th-century copy of the *Bupongyoshu-kyo* written in honor of the parents of the emperor Komyo, a 16th-century treatise on the *Ise Monogatari*, and samples of Buson's poetry in his own handwriting.

In the ceramic section are a Sung celadon incense burner, Korean bowls of the Yi dynasty, and an Annamese jar in underglaze blue, as well as examples of Japanese Old Seto, Raku, Kakiemon, and Takatori wares.

A long sword is signed by Kanenaga of the Tegai school of Nara (mid-Kamakura) and a short one by Kunimitsu of the Rai school of Kyoto (late Kamakura). There are also two boxes for holding short swords, presented by Hideyoshi to Date Masamune.

· COMMENTS · The quality of the early material (much of which belongs to individual members of the Homma family rather than to the museum) is good. The display is well arranged; at most, five percent of the collection is on view. Even this small amount has to give way to some dozen temporary exhibitions held throughout the year. There is an illustrated pamphlet, and a booklet listing the important cultural properties of Yamagata Prefecture illustrates several of the Homma family possessions; both publications are in Japanese.

44. Hommyo-ji Treasure House (Hommyo-ji Homo-tsukan), Hommyo-ji, Hanazono-cho, Kumamoto, Kuma-moto-ken. Tel. Kumamoto 2-0630.

本妙寺宝物館　熊本市花園町　本妙寺内

Director: Giho Ikegami, Chief Priest. **Hours:** 9–5. **Adm.:** ¥30. **Route:** Take bus from station to Hommyo-ji (20 min.). The treasure house is in the temple precincts, almost opposite the bus stop.

An interesting collection of paintings, calligraphy, swords, armor, ceramics, lacquer, and documents, housed in a Japanese-style building. Many of the articles, such as the ceramics and lacquer, were the personal possessions of Kato Kiyomasa, the daimyo of the old Higo Province, founder of the temple, builder of the castle, and one of the generals in Hideyoshi's invasion of Korea. There are also portraits of Kiyomasa and other members of the Kato family and examples of his calligraphy as well as portraits of priests of the temple.

Other paintings include a fourfold screen ascribed to Kano Eitoku and two albums of portraits of the Thirty-six Poets ascribed to Tosa Mitsuoki.

· COMMENTS · The quality is good. The installation is adequate, though the lighting is poor. Ninety percent of

48

the collection is normally on view, but the swords are shown only on rare occasions, and many of the documents and examples of calligraphy are kept in storage. The treasure house is worth visiting.

45. Hoppo Bunka (Northern Culture) **Museum** (Hoppo Bunka Hakubutsukan), Soumi, Yokogoshi-mura, Nakakambara-gun, Niigata-ken. Tel. Yokogoshi 1.

北方文化博物館　新潟県中蒲原郡横越村沢海

Director: Bunkichi Ito. **Hours:** 9–5; closed for New Year season. The gardens are closed when it rains. **Adm.:** ¥70. **Route:** The museum, in the small village of Yokogoshi southeast of Niigata, can be reached directly from Niigata by bus (about 1 hr.), or by taxi (about 35 min.). It is housed in a rambling Japanese building set in a series of beautiful gardens and enclosed by a high wall and is the most prominent feature of the village.

A good collection consisting largely of Chinese sculpture and ceramics and Japanese painting, sculpture, ceramics, lacquer, folk art, and archaeology. Most of these objects are shown in adjoining rooms on the ground floor of what was formerly the residence of the local daimyo, but the Japanese archaeology and some of the folk arts are shown on the upper floor.

The Chinese section contains neolithic jars from Kansu, Han pottery vessels, a T'ang three-colored glazed vase and two glazed figurines, fragments of Sung Chun and Chien ware and of Yueh ware of the Liao dynasty, large Ming blue-and-white dishes and three-colored plates, and Ming celadons. There are also Han bronze mirrors and several small sculptures of the 6th century and the T'ang dynasty.

Among the Japanese items are fragments of Jomon and Yayoi pottery, a few large *haniwa,* lacquer saddles and stirrups, a few Buddhist paintings (some of which are assigned to the Kamakura period), a screen by Tosa Mitsuoki, a Dainichi Nyorai in wood (Heian period), and some small Buddhist figures from the Kamakura and Muromachi periods.

The folk arts include Ainu costumes and jewelry, textiles and pottery from the Ryukyu Islands, a selection of modern folk pottery, peasant lanterns, and peasant lacquered vessels.

There are also two pieces of Gandhara sculpture and a medieval Indian figure.

• COMMENTS • The quality is good to excellent, and the display is quite well arranged. All of the collection is normally on view. There is an illustrated pamphlet in Japanese and English. Much of the charm of the museum lies in the combination of a good collection, a handsome house, and beautiful gardens.

Note: There are two annexes to this museum. One, the Niigata Bunkan (Niban-cho, Minami Hamadori, Niigata; tel. Niigata 22–2262; 9–5; closed Mon. and New Year season; ¥30), is near the university. Take a taxi, since it is hard to find. This museum exhibits, in the pleasant rooms of a Japanese house, the calligraphy and poems of Dr. Yaichi Aizu, a native of Niigata and a professor at Waseda University, Tokyo. The material is changed four times a year. The contemporary paintings once shown here are now occasionally shown at the Hoppo Bunka Museum. There is a charming garden behind the house.

The other branch museum, the Shimizuen (Shimizudani, Shibata-shi; tel. Shibata 2659; 9–5; closed Mon. and Dec. 1–Mar. 15; ¥60), consists of the house and garden of the daimyo of the Shibata clan. Take a train to Shibata, on the Uetsu line of the national railways and 16 miles from Niigata; then a taxi, since the route, though less than 10 min. on foot, is complicated. The godown has been renovated for use as a gallery for local historical material.

46. Horyu-ji Treasure House (Horyu-ji Daihozoden), Horyu-ji, Ikaruga-machi, Ikoma-gun, Nara-ken. Tel. Ikaruga 2555.

法隆寺大宝蔵殿　奈良県生駒郡斑鳩町　法隆寺内

Director: Ryoken Saheki. **Hours:** 8–5, Apr.–Nov.; 8–4, Dec.–Mar. **Adm.:** ¥80. **Route:** The Horyu-ji, 7 miles southwest of Nara, is a short distance north of the Horyuji station on the Kansai main line of the national railways. There is also a bus from Nara. The treasure house, consisting of two rectangular buildings in ferroconcrete joined by a corridor, lies to the east of the Kondo. Turn right after passing through the Nandaimon (south main gate) and continue straight ahead to the end of the road.

The treasure house contains a number of the large statues and shrines that formerly stood in the Kondo, as well as masks, bronze statues, miniature wooden pagodas, and other objects, all the property of the temple. The collection is of the greatest importance for the study of early Japanese painting and sculpture.

Among the best-known objects are the Kudara Kannon (so called because it was once thought to have been brought from Kudara, an early name for the Korean kingdom of Paekche), the Tamamushi Shrine (from the beetle *tamamushi,* the iridescent wings of which were once set into the openwork metal edging) with its enchanting paintings of scenes from the life of the Buddha on the walls and doors, and the shrine of Lady Tachibana (the donor) with its Amida triad in bronze set against a lovely bronze screen. The first two items are of the Asuka period; the third is Nara, early 8th century.

The collection is almost as noted for some other bronze figures, especially a small seated Buddha with one attendant (the other is missing) placed against a large *mandorla* (Asuka period), a rather thickset medium-sized Kannon of the same period, and the graceful standing Yumetagae Kannon (Dream-Changing Kannon) of the early Nara period.

The Bugaku wooden dance masks of the Asuka and Nara periods are equally well known, as are the miniature wooden stupas containing printed copies of charms.

The sculpture also includes two seated Fujiwara Amida, a Fujiwara statue of Shotoku Taishi in a shrine, a Kamakura standing statue of Shotoku Taishi, three medium-sized bronze and three gilt-wood Bosatsu of the Asuka period, and a group of wooden angels from the canopy in the Kondo.

Also in the collection are some Nara documents, some Kamakura printing blocks, a Kamakura *keko,* some 6th- to 8th-century pottery found under the To-in, a Nara bronze bottle and some bronze bowls, a Heian *kei,* an Asuka textile fragment, a Fujiwara painting of Shotoku Taishi, and a screen of Rakan from the same period.

· COMMENTS · The quality is excellent, but the installation is only fair, since the lighting is poor. There are some labels in English. All the important objects are normally on view, and the exhibition never changes. There is a small illustrated pamphlet in English describing the temple and the treasure house.

Note: A number of bronze statues, masks, and other objects from the Horyu-ji are now in the Tokyo National Museum (No. 184).

47. Ibaraki Prefectural Art Museum (Ibaraki Kenritsu Bijutsukan), Bunka Senta, Semba-machi, Mito, Ibaraki-ken. Tel. Mito 3-6266.

茨城県立美術館　茨城県水戸市千波町

Director: Under direction of Board of Education, Mito. **Hours:** 9:30–5; closed Dec. 28–Jan. 4. **Adm.:** free (¥30 for special exhibitions). **Route:** The museum is housed in a large gallery on the second floor of the left-hand section of the Bunka Senta (Cultural Center), a new concrete building overlooking Semba Lake. A bus runs every hour from the station to the center. A taxi takes 5 min.

The museum owns a collection of paintings by local artists and one archaeological object of great importance: a large gilt-bronze crown topped with a row of horse-shaped plaques. The crown, from Sammaizuka in Ibaraki Prefecture, is of the Kofun period and probably 6th century. The collection also includes a few Kofun arrowheads and a pair of gilt-bronze ornaments, found with the crown. The paintings, numbering about 100, are mostly oils of the late 19th and 20th centuries.

· COMMENTS · The gallery is well arranged, save for the inadequate lighting of the floor cases. The archaeological items are always on view; these are supplemented with loans which change four times a year, the more important pieces being borrowed in the spring and autumn. In May 1966, the paintings were in storage, but it is planned to show some of them across the hall from the museum in a gallery that is under the direction of the Cultural Center; the dictates of the exhibition schedule for that gallery will determine which paintings will be on view at any time. The museum continues, on a small scale, to purchase paintings by local artists. Only a specialist in archaeology would journey to Mito to see the crown alone, but if the standard of the loan show of archaeology on view in the spring of 1966 is maintained, the museum will be worth visiting by anyone interested in Japanese art.

48. Ichijo-ji Treasure House (Ichjjo-ji Homotsukan), Sakamoto, Hojo-machi, Kasai-gun, Hyogo-ken. Tel. Shimo-zato 2261.

一乗寺宝物館　兵庫県加西郡北条町坂本

Director: Chief Priest. **Hours:** Open on request made in writing or by telephone several days ahead. **Adm.:** ¥50. **Route:** The temple lies deep in the countryside, a long way from Hojo. There is no bus to the temple, but one from Himeji station runs to Hokke Sanguchi (40 min.), and from there it is a 40-min. walk west along a country road across the valley and up into the hills. It is easier to take a taxi from Himeji to the Ichijo-ji (½ hr.). The treasure house, a small white building in the Japanese godown style, is to the left of the long flight of steps leading up to the Kondo.

A small but interesting collection of Japanese sculpture and painting. The pride of the collection is a fine gilt-bronze standing figure of Sho Kannon, of the Hakuho period. From the Heian period are another standing Sho Kannon and an Amida Nyorai. There are wooden statues of priests of the Kamakura period and two temple masks.

A copy of the *Hannya-kyo* in gold characters on dark-blue paper is assigned to the Kamakura period, and there are a number of paintings of Buddhist divinities assigned to the Muromachi period.

• COMMENTS • The quality varies from good to excellent, and the display is adequate. There is little or no change in the exhibition. A pamphlet describing the temple lists some of the objects in the treasure house.

Note: The best paintings owned by the temple are on loan at the Nara National Museum (No. 119).

49. Idojiri Archaeological Hall (Idojiri Kokokan), Shinano Sakai, Fujimi-machi, Suwa-gun, Nagano-ken. Tel. Fujimi 37.

井戸尻考古館　長野県諏訪郡富士見町信濃境

Director: Naoji Kobayashi. **Hours:** 8:30–5:30; closed Sun., national holidays, Jan. 15–16, and Dec. 28–Jan. 3. **Adm.:** ¥30. **Route:** Take train on Chuo line leading from Kamisuwa to Shinano Sakai (about 40 min.). Walk down the road leading away from the station for about 200 yards and turn left. The museum is in the municipal office, a two-story frame building about 50 yards along the road and on the left.

An excellent medium-sized collection of archaeology from the local area known as Idojiri (Ido, Shindo, and Sori are three of the sites from which the objects have come), housed in the left-hand side of the ground floor of the Municipal Office Building.

The major part of the material dates from the middle Jomon period, and the vessels of this period are noted for their variety, their size, and their excellent condition. There is one case that usually contains some of the finest pieces: seven large jars and one small figurine. Particularly fine are a narrow-waisted vessel with four square handles, another topped with wild swirls and loops, and a third with an overall impressed geometric pattern. There are other cases with chipped and polished stone implements and many other Jomon vessels, all complete. Further cases have fragments of pottery, a number of stone grinding vessels, more figurines, and some circular pottery earrings. There is a small amount of early-Jomon ware, including a fine vessel with an elaborate hatched design. The earrings and some of the figurines are late Jomon. A chart and maps complete the display.

• COMMENTS • The quality is excellent, the display adequate. About sixty percent of the material is on view; changes are made in the exhibition once a year, and as the excavations continue new objects are added. There are a pamphlet on the museum and two booklets on the excavations, all in Japanese. The quality of the middle-Jomon material is such that this museum is worth visiting even by one who is not a specialist.

50. Ii Art Museum (Ii Bijutsukan), Hikone-jo, Konki-machi, Hikone, Shiga-ken. Tel. Hikone 552.

井伊美術館　滋賀県彦根市金亀町彦根城

Director: Masahiro Ii. **Hours:** 9–4; closed Mon. **Adm.:** ¥50, plus ¥30 for adm. to castle precincts, in which museum is located. **Route:** The museum, in the gatehouse of Hikone Castle, which sits on an eminence surrounded by moats, is at the end of the main street leading north from the national railway station. It can be reached on foot in about 15 min.

An interesting collection of Japanese and Chinese paintings

and of Japanese calligraphy, ceramics, lacquer, masks, costumes, furniture, armor, swords and sword fittings, and musical instruments. They are chiefly the belongings of the Ii family, the former daimyo of Hikone Castle, and almost all date from the Edo period. An exception to this dating is a pair of screens of the *Four Seasons,* attributed to Dasoku, of the second half of the 15th century. There is also the well-known *Hikone Byobu,* a handsome sixfold screen of the very early *ukiyo-e* school. The collection is very rich in musical instruments, and there is considerable lacquer ware on view, ranging from sets of miniature vessels to game-boards, writing boxes, saddles and stirrups, and even a palanquin.

In the ceramic section are many pieces of the local ware called Koyo (after the eastern shore of Lake Biwa). Tea caddies, teakettles, bamboo vases, Noh masks and costumes, and arms and armor complete the display collections. There are also documents concerning local history, including a description of Commodore Perry's arrival written by the daimyo of that time.

· COMMENTS · The quality is good and the installation well done. There is a brief illustrated folder in Japanese describing the collections.

Note: Although the Hikone Castle Collection, which contains the arms, armor, and furniture of the Ii family, is still referred to as being separately housed in the Hikone Castle Tower (Hikone-jo Tenshukaku), it is now actually in the above museum.

51. Ikeno Taiga Art Museum (Ikeno Taiga Bijutsu-kan), 57 Matsuobankoku-cho, Ukyo-ku, Kyoto. Tel. Kyoto 38-2832.

池大雅美術館　京都府右京区松尾万石町 57 番地

Director: Yoneyuki Sasaki. **Hours:** 9–5. **Adm.:** ¥50. **Route:** From Shijo Omiya, take the Keifuku Electric Railway, Arashiyama line, to Arashiyama. The museum, a Western-style building of indifferent character, is on the right-hand side of the street leading to the Saiho-ji (the "Moss Temple").

The collection consists of about 80 paintings and examples of calligraphy by Taiga (1723–76), one of the foremost painters of the *bunjinga,* which show him in all his variety. It is rare in Japan that one artist can be studied so extensively in one place; for this reason, as well as for the paintings themselves, a visit to this museum is worthwhile.

• COMMENTS • The installation is adequate, with the paintings hung close together in the long continuous vitrines that line the walls. The labels are in English as well as Japanese, and almost all of the collection is permanently on display. There is a check list of the paintings in Japanese.

52. International Christian University Archaeological Collection (Kokusai Kirisutokyo Daigakuin Kokokan), Kokusai Kirisutokyo Daigaku, Osawa, Mitaka-shi, Tokyo. Tel. Mitaka 3-3131.

国際基督教大学院考古館　東京都三鷹市大沢
国際基督教大学内

Director: Professor J. Edward Kidder. **Hours:** Open on request made in advance by telephone. **Adm.:** free. **Route:** Take national railways Chuo line from Shinjuku station to Mitaka (22 min.) and bus from Mitaka to the university (10 min.). The collection is housed in a small exhibition room on the third floor of the university's main building, which is a short distance beyond and to the right of the bus stop.

A small, good collection of Japanese archaeology, chiefly from the excavations conducted on the university's own grounds. The majority of the display pieces are of the middle Jomon period. A workroom, containing much additional though largely fragmentary pottery from the site, adjoins the gallery.

• COMMENTS • The quality is good, the display well done, with labels in Japanese and English. All the important items are on view. Changes are made in the exhibition as new pieces from the excavations are added.

53. Ishibashi Art Museum (Ishibashi Bijutsukan), Ishibashi Bunka Senta, Nonaka-cho, Kurume, Fukuoka-ken. Tel. Kurume 4701.

石橋美術館　福岡県久留米市野中町　石橋文化センター内

Director: Kan'ichiro Ishibashi. **Hours:** 9–5:30, Apr.–Sept.; 9:30–5, Oct.–Mar.; closed Dec. 28–Jan. 1. **Adm.:** ¥60. **Route:** Take bus to the Bunka Senta-mae stop (10 min.). The museum is in the central building of the group, set in a small park, which comprises the Ishibashi Cultural Center.

The museum has no permanent collection and generally exhibits items belonging to the parent museum, the Bridgestone Gallery in Tokyo (No. 11). It also houses loan exhibitions of various types, such as a show in 1962 of ancient Chinese and Korean ceramics; others have been devoted to contemporary sculpture and paintings by artists belonging to various local societies.

• COMMENTS • The display is well arranged. The exhibitions change every month, and the special loan shows are held in the spring and autumn. The museum publishes an illustrated annual report.

54. Ishikawa Prefectural Art Museum (Ishikawa Kenritsu Bijutsukan), 37, 1-chome, Dewa-machi, Kenrokuen, Kanazawa, Ishikawa-ken. Tel. Kanazawa 31-7580.

石川県立美術館　石川県金沢市出羽町 1 丁目 37 番地
兼六園内

Director: Mamoru Takahashi. **Hours:** 9–4:30; closed Mon., day following a national holiday, for New Year season, and when exhibitions are being changed. **Adm.:** ¥100. **Route:** Take tram to Dewa-machi Kokuritsu Byoin-mae, the stop by the National Hospital on Dewa-machi. The museum, a handsome new building in the International style, is a 2-min. walk from this stop and lies just inside the Kenrokuen park.

A good collection of Japanese painting, lacquer, textiles, swords, metalwork, and ceramics, with the accent on Kutani ware, since the Kutani kilns are not far from Kanazawa. There are also some historical documents.

Among the paintings are a pair of sixfold screens by Morikage showing the agricultural pursuits of the four seasons, a painting by Sesshu of the West Lake at Hangchow, a self-portrait and inscription by the Zen priest Takuan, and two paintings by Sotatsu.

An incense burner in the shape of a pheasant, a water jug by Ninsei, and a large Old Kutani plate with a picture of Hotei are considered the outstanding ceramic pieces. The great interest of the ceramic section lies, however, in its large group of Old Kutani and its examples of the more recent Kutani productions, such as the Kasugayama, Yoshidaya, and Wakasugi wares and the products of the Miyamotoya factory.

• COMMENTS • The quality of the collection and the display are both very good. There is an illustrated pamphlet in Japanese, and some idea of the museum's group of Kutani ware can be had from the catalogue of an exhibition held at the Takaoka Municipal Museum in the autumn of 1964. There are about ten special exhibitions a year, during which only a portion of the regular collection is shown in one room on the upper floor, the special exhibition occupying all the rest of the space. The main collection is generally on view in midsummer and midwinter. Some of the loan shows are of very high quality and are accompanied by good illustrated catalogues in Japanese. The museum is well worth visiting.

Note: On deposit at the museum is a good collection of Japanese painting, calligraphy, ceramics, metalwork, tea-ceremony objects, and lacquer, all the property of the Yamakawa Fine Arts Foundation. It includes paintings by Doan, Morikage, Tsunenobu, and Yasunobu; calligraphy by Koetsu; a screen by Sotatsu; Chinese Swatow-ware bowls; a bowl by Kenzan; Shino, Iga, Bizen, and Raku wares; a lacquer box by Korin; a fine lacquer reading stand; flower baskets; and bamboo vases. There is an illustrated catalogue that accompanied the exhibition of the objects from this collection held in the spring of 1963.

55. Itsukushima Shrine Treasure House (Itsukushima-jinja Homotsukan), Itsukushima-jinja, Miyajima-machi, Hiroshima-ken. Tel. Miyajima 36.

厳島神社宝物館　広島県宮島町　厳島神社内

Director: Motosada Nosaka, Chief Priest. **Hours:** 8–5. **Adm.:** ¥100 (additional ¥30 for adm. to shrine itself). **Route:** The treasure house, a ferroconcrete building in Japanese style, is at the far side of the shrine (the side away from the ferry landing and the main part of town), opposite the covered passage connecting the shrine with the land. It is most easily approached by walking through the shrine, but it can also be reached by a road which passes behind the shrine.

A varied collection of objects dedicated to the shrine. Foremost among them are the famous sutras known as the *Heike Nokyo,* which were offered to the shrine by the Taira (or

Heike) family between 1164 and 1167. In the elegance of the paintings at the beginning of each scroll and of the written text, they show Heian art at its most refined. (The originals, however, are never on view, and excellent copies, some partially open, others rolled up, take their place in the vitrines.)

The Heian sutra box, decorated with clouds and dragons in gold and silver and made to contain the *Heike Nokyo,* is generally on view together with a 17th-century lacquered chest (made to contain the sutra box) and a small lacquered chest dated 1183. The shrine also owns two fans—one painted, the other with calligraphy—of the Heian period, superb Heian and Kamakura suits of armor, Noh and Bugaku masks (many of the latter from the Heian period), musical instruments used for Bugaku performances, Noh costumes of the Momoyama period, court costumes, swords, a wooden horse (Muromachi period), wooden dogs (Heian and Kamakura periods), portable Buddhist shrines and objects used in Buddhist services (Kamakura period), and paintings of the Edo period (including one by Rosetsu of a witch). There is also a group of toys that belonged to the child emperor Antoku.

• COMMENTS • The quality of the collection varies from superb for the early pieces to fair for the later ones; the display is only fair. As little as two percent of the collection is on view at any one time; part of the exhibition is changed twice a year. There is an illustrated pamphlet in Japanese and English on the shrine and the treasure house. The treasure house is well worth visiting, and the shrine itself is one of the great sights of Japan.

Note: Many Noh costumes are on display in April, when Noh performances are given at the shrine.

56. Itsuo Art Museum (Itsuo Bijutsukan), 1965 Tateishi-cho, Ikeda-shi, Osaka. Tel. Ikeda 5-3865.

逸翁美術館　大阪府池田市建石町 1965 番地

Director: Rihei Okada. **Hours:** 10–4; closed Mon., New Year season, and for about 1 week when exhibitions are being changed. (New exhibitions usually open in Mar., Jun., Sept., and Dec.) Check before going. **Adm.:** ¥50. **Route:** Take Hankyu line from Umeda station,

Osaka, for Takarazuka and get off at Ikeda. The museum, a Western-style house set in a garden, is about a 20-min. walk northeast and uphill from the station; since it is hard to find, it is advisable to take a taxi.

A large and very choice collection of Japanese painting, calligraphy, and lacquer; Chinese sculpture; and Japanese, Chinese, Korean, and Western ceramics.

The best-known scrolls are two from the Kamakura period of the story of the goblins on Mount Oe (*Oe-yama Ekotoba*). From the same period are several portraits of the Thirty-six Poets and *kakemono* of Amida Nyorai, Fudo, and Jizo. Five scrolls of the *Ashibiki Emaki* (The Story of a Priest and His Minions) date from the Muromachi period. The collection is also noted for the large group of paintings and illustrated texts by Buson and Goshun; in no other place can these two artists be better studied. There are paintings by other Edo artists such as Hoen, Hoitsu, Keibun, Okyo, Oju, Ozui, and Sosen. An interesting historical document is a portrait of Hideyoshi attributed to Sotatsu. Korin and Kenzan are represented by some charmingly painted fans. A pair of screens by Ganku show a dragon and a tiger; two flower screens are further decorated with poems written by well-known Edo-period calligraphers; and other screens depict the popular life of this same period.

The calligraphy is very fine. It includes sutras dating from the Nara and Heian periods and many fragments from the *Iseshu,* the *Kokinshu* (or *Kokinwakashu*), and the *Man'yoshu,* as well as other works attributed to such notable calligraphers of the Heian and Kamakura periods as Gyosei, Kinto, Kosei, Tofu, Saigyo, Tsurayuki, and Tameie. Calligraphy of artists and tea masters of the Muromachi and Edo periods is also well represented.

The Japanese ceramic collection is both large and distinguished, with pieces from nearly all the well-known kilns. To be especially noted are a Seto bottle (called Kamakura) and, from the Momoyama period, a square Oribe tea plate, Yellow Seto bowls, a Shino dish with a handle, and Iga and Tamba vases. A Shigaraki dish with a handle is early Edo, while a "Korean" Karatsu bottle and some Bizen dishes, vases, and bowls range from the Momoyama to the mid-Edo period. Among the pieces by famous potters are a black Raku tea bowl by Chojiro, a tea bowl by Koetsu, a squarish bowl and six small dishes and a water holder by Kenzan, and other bowls by Dohachi and Eiraku Hozen. There are also many tea bowls by 18th- and 19th-century Raku potters.

In the field of Chinese porcelains are *ying-ch'ing* and Ting bowls, a variety of celadons, and several samples of Chun ware, all of the Sung dynasty. There are many small bowls in underglaze blue and overglaze enamels of the Ming dynasty and a few bowls, also decorated in overglaze enamels, of the Ch'ing dynasty. Other Chinese objects include several Chou-dynasty bronzes, two gilt-bronze Kuan Yin on a single stand (dated 589), and a small seated gilt-bronze Buddha of the T'ang dynasty.

The Korean section has a group of tea bowls, mostly with monochrome glazes, of the Yi dynasty. The European porcelains include English, French, and German examples of the 17th to the 20th century. The Near Eastern pottery dates from the 12th to the 14th century.

Among the Japanese lacquer pieces are an incense burner of the Muromachi period, writing boxes of the Momoyama period, and a Momoyama chest and a circular box to hold the Host, both inlaid with mother-of-pearl.

There is a teahouse in the garden.

• COMMENTS • The quality is excellent and the installation as good as the house permits. The labels are complete in Japanese, scant in English. The most important items are apt to be on display during April, May, October, and November; the summer show is usually devoted to ceramics, while the winter one is of a general nature. About 75 of the total of 3,500 objects are on view at any one time. Each exhibition is accompanied by an illustrated catalogue or a check list, in Japanese only.

57. Iwakuni Municipal Museum (Iwakuni Chokokan), 358 Yokoyama, Kikko Koen, Iwakuni, Yamaguchi-ken. Tel. Iwakuni 4-0452.

岩国徴古館　山口県岩国市吉香公園横山 358 番地

Director: Tsuneto Morimoto. **Hours:** 9–4:30; closed Tues. a.m., day after a national holiday, and Dec. 28–Jan. 4. **Adm.:** free. **Route:** Take bus (30 min.) to Kintai-bashi (Kintai Bridge), a charming five-arched construction. Walk over the bridge and proceed straight ahead through the park as far as the road allows; then turn right, then left, then left again as the road bends. The museum, a heavy gray Western-style building, is on the left, standing back from the road.

A collection of local paintings, photographs, maps, records, documents, coins, folk-art material, and finds from local archaeological sites. It is shown in two rooms and the entrance hall of the ground floor. The most interesting items are the drawings, paintings, and sketches of the Kintai Bridge, ranging all the way from 1673, the date of its original construction, to the present. Other paintings are by local artists working in both the Japanese and the Western manner. The maps show the considerable change that industrialization has recently made in the local topography. Fragments of the original bridge are installed in the entrance hall.

 • COMMENTS • The artistic quality is mediocre, but the material is historically informative and interesting. The display is fair. The exhibition changes once a month, and about two percent of the collection is apt to be on view at any time. There is a pamphlet, not illustrated and in Japanese only.

58. Iwata Archaeological Collection (Iwata Shuzoko), Chuo-cho Iwata, Shizuoka-ken. Tel. Iwata 2-2111.

磐田収蔵庫　静岡県磐田市中央町

Director: Under direction of Iwata Board of Education. **Hours:** 8:30–5, Sat., Sun.; 8:30–12, Mon. **Adm.:** free. **Route:** The museum, a small ferroconcrete godown, lies on the edge of the town. Take a taxi (5 min.), since it is hard to find.

The museum, finished in 1962, houses a good collection of local archaeological material. There are a few Jomon pieces, and much Yayoi and Sue ware, the latter including vessels with ash glaze. There are also Kofun *magatama* and two huge *haniwa* cylinders, as well as quite a number of other *haniwa* pieces. The collection includes tiles of the Nara period and three Chinese bronze mirrors. Almost all the material is either from the excavation site at Doyama-kofun or from Kokubunji.

 • COMMENTS • The quality is good, the display adequate. Half the collection is on display, the remainder being stored in drawers and cupboards along the walls. Excavations are continuing, and as new items are added to the collection the exhibition changes. The specialist will find this museum very interesting.

59. Izumo Taisha Treasure House (Izumo Taisha Homotsuden), Izumo Taisha, Taisha-machi, Shimane-ken. Tel. Taisha 650.

出雲大社宝物殿　島根県大社町　出雲大社内

Director: Mitsuhiko Senkei, Chief Priest. **Hours:** 8–4:30. **Adm.:** ¥50. **Route:** A bus runs from Taisha station to the shrine. The treasure house, a new ferroconcrete building the design for which was inspired by the tall racks on which the rice sheaves are dried in the nearby fields, is in the precincts of the shrine, to the left as one enters through the great bronze *torii*.

A miscellaneous collection of objects belonging to the shrine. Among the antiquities are a large *magatama* and a bronze *ko* of the Kofun period and a number of mirrors. The earliest and best known of the suits of armor usually on view is a splendid one of the Muromachi period with red and white lacings, given to the shrine by the Ashikaga shogun Yoshimasa. The shrine also owns some 80 swords, one of which belonged to Hideyoshi.

A superb lacquer *tebako,* with a design of birds, deer, and autumn grasses, is dated Kamakura, 13th century; another lacquer box is dated 1667. There is also a 19th-century painted *biwa* and its box, a map of the shrine precincts and the surrounding area of the early Edo period, a model of the main building of the shrine, and a lion mask. The many documents include letters of the emperor Godaigo and an account of a religious ceremony of 1248.

• COMMENTS • The few important pieces are very fine, the display sparse. The exhibition changes periodically, but there is no set schedule. There is a pamphlet in Japanese.

60. Japan Folk Art Museum (Nihon Mingeikan), 861 Komaba-cho, Meguro-ku, Tokyo. Tel. 461–8742.

日本民芸館　東京都目黒区駒場町 861 番地

Director: Shoji Hamada. **Hours:** 10–4; closed Mon. and all of Jan., Feb., and Aug. **Adm.:** ¥100. **Route:** Take train from Shibuya station to Komaba (the third stop after Shibuya) on the Inogashira line of the Keio Teito Electric Railway. Bear left from the station exit and continue straight ahead until the road bends (5 min.). The museum, a two-story building in Japanese style, is immediately on the right.

The earliest and most important collection of Japanese folk arts, largely assembled by the former director, Soetsu Yanagi, it contains Japanese painting, pottery, porcelain, prints, lacquer, masks, textiles, furniture, toys, metalwork, and costumes, as well as articles from the Ainu in Hokkaido and from Okinawa, Korea, North America, and Europe. All are either examples of ancient folk-art traditions or objects made by contemporary artists working in the folk-art manner.

In the Japanese painting section, and dating from the Edo period, are Otsu-e done in bright pigments on a slip-covered coarse brown paper; *ema* depicting horses, birds, fish, and genre scenes; and *namban* paintings of Europeans and the ships in which they first came to Japan.

The ceramic collection is a large one, containing less sophisticated examples of such well-known wares as Imari, Karatsu, Satsuma, Seto, Tamba, and Shigaraki and examples from kilns that served a small local population, such as that at Kimura in Kumamoto Prefecture, whose products are known as Shodai ware—to name but one type. There are also fine pieces made by famous contemporary potters working in the folk tradition.

Among the prints are some Buddhist ones for popular use, while the lacquer objects include cake boxes, trays, and bowls. The masks are generally the heavy wooden ones used in festivals. In the textile and costume field are cotton bedding and printed cotton curtain materials, embroidered cotton kimono and aprons, linen ceremonial hoods, leather coats, straw raincoats, shoes, and tobacco pouches.

The furniture includes wooden seamen's chests bound with metal. There are also carpenters' tools, locks and other hardware; iron teakettles, flower vases, and stands for kettles; and a great variety of dolls and toys.

There are an excellent group of textiles from Okinawa and many objects illustrating the crafts of the Ainu people. Korea is represented by pottery of the Yi dynasty, Europe by a variety of pottery, and North America by folk pottery and basketry, including pottery of the Indians of the Southwest.

· COMMENTS · The quality is the best of its kind, and the installation is good. The exhibition changes four times a year, with about ten percent of the collection normally on view. An illustrated catalogue with English subtitles, prepared for an exhibition of objects from the museum held at the Daimaru Department Store, gives a good idea of the range of the collection. One room of the museum is used as a salesroom for contemporary Japanese handicrafts.

61. Japan Handicraft Museum (Nihon Kogeikan), 619, 3-chome, Shinkawa, Naniwa-ku, Osaka. Tel. Osaka 641-6309.

日本工芸館　大阪市浪速区新川 3 丁目 619 番地

Director: Chuichi Miyake. **Hours:** 10–5; closed Mon., Dec. 26–Jan. 5, and when exhibition is being changed. **Adm.:** ¥50. **Route:** The museum is a little to the southwest of the Takashimaya Department Store and the terminus of the Nankai Electric Railway at Namba, which is also a stop on the subway line. The building is an interesting example of contemporary architecture that retains a strong Japanese flavor, with white-plastered walls and a steep-pitched gray roof, set back from the street behind a low wall in a pebbled enclosure. Since it is hard to find, it is advisable to take a taxi.

A medium-sized collection of Japanese folk pottery, basketry, paper, and textiles, plus pottery by present-day artists working in the folk tradition. There is also some Ainu material.

The folk pottery dates largely from the early and middle Edo periods and consists in part of household jars for storing oil, tea, pepper, and pickles and of bowls and bottles.

· COMMENTS · The quality is very good of its kind, and the display, though rather crowded, is adequate. The exhibition is changed four or five times a year. The museum has a small illustrated folder in Japanese and publishes a monthly periodical *Nihon no Kogei* (Handicrafts of Japan).

Note: There is a sales shop, displaying chiefly pottery, in an annex at the rear of the main building.

62. Jingu Museum of Antiquities (Jingu Chokokan), Kuratayama, Ise, Mie-ken. Tel. Ise 8-2644; 8-5030.

神宮徵古館　三重県伊勢市倉田山

Director: Kiyoshi Tanaka. **Hours:** 8:30–4:30, Mar.–Nov.; 8:30–4, Dec.–Feb. **Adm.:** ¥50. **Route:** Take bus for Dogunaigu and get off at Chokokan-mae (5 min.). Walk up the long driveway on the right. The Museum of Antiquities is in the left wing of a large two-story E-shaped building in the Western style.

A large collection of Japanese paintings, calligraphy, prints and documents, ceramics, lacquer, masks, arms and armor; Chinese and Japanese archaeological material; and objects of Shinto ceremonial use. These are all shown on the ground floor, with Japanese contemporary paintings, sculptures, and ceramics on the upper floor.

The most famous painting is a Kamakura scroll, the *Ise Shin Meisho Uta-awase Emaki* (Story of a Poetry Contest on Ten Famous Scenic Spots in Ise), in which the poems alternate with the scenes that inspired them. The paintings, in fine lines and pale colors, are attributed to Fujiwara Takasuke. On another plane are amusing *kakemono* and fans by the 18th-century priest Gessen. Among the books and documents are a Kamakura copy of the Chinese *Book of History,* poems and other writings of the Shinto priest Moritake (1473–1549), an imperial order of the emperor Gonara dated 1551, another order given by Hideyoshi exempting the land of the shrine from a survey, and poems by the emperor Sakuramachi. Many of the prints depict visitors to the shrine.

A suit of armor is dated in the Muromachi period, while the Heian period is represented by a sword worn by a member of the Fujiwara family and a stirrup with a handsome openwork design of leaves. Another sword is signed Arikuni and is assigned to the Kamakura period.

In the archaeological section are a Jomon-period figurine and, from the Kofun period, an elaborate vessel on a very high pierced foot and an unusual tripod (both Sue-ware pieces), some *haniwa,* and metal mirrors. There are also Chinese swords of the Han dynasty and T'ang-dynasty pottery figurines.

The collection of objects used in the Shinto ceremonies includes implements for lighting the sacred fire and holding the sacred water, as well as ceremonial robes. Objects dedicated to the shrine include a handsomely painted box and shells for the game of matching shells, globes, and fans given by Tokugawa Iemitsu.

The large and varied contemporary section contains, among many others, a good still life in oil by Sotaro Yasui and, in the Japanese manner by Seto Maeda, charming views of the ceremonies attending the most recent moving of the shrine.

• COMMENTS • The quality is good, the display adequate. The historical material and the Shinto ceremonial objects are most interesting and make this museum worth visiting, but the most important object in Ise is the *naigu* or main shrine itself.

Note: A small building called the Rekishi Kaigakan (Historical Painting Hall), opposite the footbridge leading to the *naigu,* contains large paintings of recent date illustrating events in Japanese history and legend.

63. Kagoshima Municipal Art Museum (Kagoshima Shiritsu Bijutsukan), 134 Yamashita-machi, Kagoshima, Kagoshima-ken. Tel. Kagoshima 2-5513.

鹿児島市立美術館　鹿児島市山下町 134 番地

Director: Goji Taniguchi. **Hours:** 9–4:30; closed Mon., national holidays, and for New Year season. **Adm.:** ¥20. **Route:** Take tram to the Asahidori stop, then turn right and walk for two main blocks. The museum, a Western-style building of rather Victorian aspect, is on the second cross street, set in open ground well back from the street.

A collection of paintings in both the Western and the Japanese style, local ceramics, and local folk arts. The museum is best known for its group of paintings by Seiki Kuroda (1866–1924), who introduced the Impressionist style to Japan during his many years of teaching in Tokyo. A room on the upper floor is set aside for his paintings and some of his personal possessions.

Other Japanese paintings in the Western style are exhibited in a room on the ground floor to the left of the entrance. A large room to the right usually contains Japanese-style paintings by artists from Kagoshima Prefecture. Among them are several scrolls by Kimura Tangen, a Kano artist of the 18th century.

The folk arts, displayed in galleries in the center of the building, include farmers' tools, baskets, lacquer vessels, and a collection of toys. There is also a large group of Satsuma ware, with examples from, among others, the Hirasa, Kochosa, and Ryumonji kilns, and many pieces of Satsuma glass. For the foreigner, the Satsuma ware is particularly interesting, as it is very different and aesthetically much finer than the highly decorated type so popular in the West.

• COMMENTS • The quality of the ceramics is good, and the paintings and the folk arts are interesting. The display is fair. About seventy percent of the some 1,000 objects is normally on view. The folk-arts and ceramics exhibits almost never change. There is a small pamphlet in Japanese. Temporary loan shows, generally of contemporary art, are held frequently in a new wing to the right of the main building.

64. Kaisendo Museum (Kaisendo Hakubutsukan), 277 Tanaka, Tokamachi, Kaminoyama, Yamagata-ken. Tel. Kaminoyama 155.

蟹仙洞博物館　山形県上山市十日町田中 277 番地

Director: Kenzo Hasegawa. **Hours:** 9–5, Apr.–Oct.; 9–4, Nov.–Mar.; closed in Feb. and whenever there is no electricity. **Adm.:** ¥50. **Route:** Walk left from the station and left again across the railroad tracks (about 10 min.). The museum, a white-plastered two-story building with a recessed entrance, is to the left of the entrance to the first large compound on the right side of the street. Ring at the museum entrance for admission.

A very interesting medium-sized collection of lacquer (chiefly Chinese) and some Japanese armor, swords, and sword furniture. The lacquer is shown on the ground floor; some of the armor, swords, and sword furniture is on the ground floor, the rest on a narrow balcony that runs around the room.

The Ming and Ch'ing carved red (cinnabar) lacquer forms the largest group, but there are also examples of carved yellow lacquer and painted and incised lacquer. The objects include large boxes (rectangular, circular, and lobed), trays and plates, small incense boxes (one of which is designated Yuan), picnic boxes, vases, and low tables.

A Korean box with mother-of-pearl inlay and a few pieces of Japanese lacquer of the Muromachi and Edo periods are also on view. The swords range from the Fujiwara to the Edo period; several are of the Osafune school of the Kamakura period. The sword guards and other pieces of sword furniture are of good quality, though largely of the Edo period. Local archaeology is represented by a bronze sutra box and an iron sword, both excavated at Yonezawa.

• COMMENTS • The quality is very good, and the display, which never changes, is well done. There is a small illustrated pamphlet in Japanese. The collection is well worth a visit, especially for the Chinese lacquer, which makes the Kaisendo unique among the smaller museums of Japan.

65. **Kaitokukan Historical Collection** (Kaitokukan), Marunouchi, Kochi Koen, Kochi, Kochi-ken. Tel. Kochi 2-2772.

懐徳館　高知市丸内　高知公園内

Director: Chief of Department of Social Culture, Kochi Prefectural Government. **Hours:** 8:30–5; closed Dec. 27–Jan. 1. **Adm.:** ¥30. **Route:** The museum is in the castle. Take tram for Sambashi; get off at Koen-mae (7 min.) and walk a block and a half to the north. The entrance to the castle grounds is through a gate on the left, and the castle is on a high mound, approached by several flights of steps.

A small collection of local archaeology, painting, calligraphy, ceramics, armor, and folk arts.

Among the archaeological pieces are a few fragments of Jomon pottery, stone tools, stone arrowheads, and a small pottery figurine. There are also a few fragments of Yayoi ware and some good Sue-ware pots and fragments of Kofun metalwork.

The paintings are by such artists as Koyo and the local painter Chikugen; the calligraphy, by the last daimyo of Kochi. There is a good selection of the charming local pottery, called Oto or Nosazan ware. Guns, spears, several suits of armor, and even a 17th-century Portuguese felt hat are also on view. In the folk-arts section are oiled-paper and straw umbrellas, clothing (including special *geta* for the rice fields), baskets, lanterns, toys, and puppets.

• COMMENTS • The quality is fair to good, the display adequate. About half the collection is usually on view, and changes in the exhibits are made twice a year. The collection has some interest for its local paintings and handicrafts. The castle is very handsome.

66. Kakurin-ji Treasure House (Kakurin-ji Homotsukan), Kakurin-ji, Kakogawa-machi, Kakogawa, Hyogo-ken. Tel. Kagogawa 2-2563.

鶴林寺宝物館　兵庫県加古川市加古川町　鶴林寺内

Director: Jitsunen Yoshida, Chief Priest. **Hours:** Open on request. **Adm.:** ¥100. **Route:** The temple lies a short distance south of Kakogawa. Take local train on Takasago line to Kakurinji, the second stop, which is beside the temple grounds. The treasure house, a smallish one-story wooden building, is on the west side of the precincts. (A taxi from Kakogawa station takes about 10 min.)

A very interesting group of paintings, sculpture, pottery, and other objects.

The finest piece of sculpture on view is a Juichimen Kannon of the early 9th century. There is also a small wooden statue of one of the Shi Tenno, of the Kamakura period, and some Muromachi wooden *mandorlas*. A Fujiwara copy of the *Kongo Hannya-kyo,* written in gold on dark-blue paper, is also on view. Three Muromachi paintings illustrate the life of Shotoku Taishi (who is said to have founded the temple); other paintings, perhaps of this period, depict the Sixteen Rakan and the death of the Buddha. Portraits of priests complete the group. The other objects include wood blocks for printing sutras, Seto tea caddies, and a Korean bronze temple bell of the Koryo period.

• COMMENTS • The quality runs from good to excellent; the installation is adequate. There is a brief folder in Japanese. In all, the treasure house owns some 200 items, of which about 50 are usually on view, including some of the most important pieces. The exhibition is changed occasionally.

Note: A number of the finest possessions of the temple are usually on loan at the Nara National Museum (No. 119). Among these are apt to be the Fujiwara portraits of Shotoku Taishi and the priest Jikei, eight Muromachi scrolls of the life of Shotoku Taishi, and a gilt-bronze Hakuho Kannon. In the spring of 1966 a new treasure house had been built, but the collection had not yet been installed.

67. Kamakura National Treasure House (Kamakura Kokuhokan), 1034 Yukinoshita, Kamakura, Kanagawa-ken. Tel. Kamakura 2-0753.

鎌倉国宝館　鎌倉市雪の下 1034 番地

Director: Jiro Shibue. **Hours:** 9–5; closed Mon., national holidays, and Dec. 28–Jan. 1. **Adm.:** ¥30. **Route:** The museum, a ferroconcrete building in Japanese style, is on the right-hand side of the precincts of the Tsurugaoka Hachiman-gu. From the Kamakura station on the Yokosuka line, turn left down the main street, cross a busy intersection, and pass under a *torii*. Then turn right on the first wide and straight dirt road, then left on a paved walk.

The museum is primarily an exhibiting gallery for many of the most important objects—all largely from the Kamakura and Muromachi periods—owned by the temples, shrines, and private collectors of the Kamakura district. The items on view include Japanese sculpture, Japanese and Chinese painting and ceramics, and Japanese metalwork, lacquer, furniture, and prints.

The best-known sculptures are the Kamakura seated portrait in wood of Uesugi Shigefusa and the wooden statue of the nude Benzaiten, dated 1266 and shown dressed in a kimono. There are also wooden statues of the ten chief disciples of Shaka Nyorai carved in 1258, several Kamakura painted wooden statues of Jizo, a stone Yakushi dated 1296, a Fujiwara Fudo in wood, one of the Ju O dated 1251, a lacquered wood Shaka (Kamakura), a fine Amida and two attendants dated 1175, and several colored wooden masks (also Kamakura).

A number of very good Japanese scrolls are on deposit at the museum, including two 13th-century scrolls of the *Taima Mandara Engi* (Legends of the Taima Mandara) and a 14th-century scroll of the *Jodo Goso Eden* (Biographies of the Five Jodo Patriarchs), all three lent by the Komyo-ji. There are also two 14th-century scrolls of the *Hoyake Amida Engi* (Legend of the Hoyake Buddha), lent by the Kosoku-ji.

The largest group of Japanese paintings, however, are Kamakura and Muromachi *kakemono* of Buddhist subjects and portraits of priests. Among the former are a Taima *mandara,* a Kokuzo Bosatsu, and an Amida (all of the Kamakura period), a Shoki by Yamada Doan, and two paintings of the Sixteen Rakan attributed to Mincho. In the second group are a portrait of the priest Tao-lung Lan-

71

chi dated 1271, another of the priest Muso (Kamakura period), and several Muromachi portraits, among them one of the priest Kiko attributed to Shokei. From the early Edo period is a fine *View of Fuji* by Tan'yu.

The Chinese paintings consist largely of Buddhist subjects, such as the Five Hundred Lohan, the Eighteen Lohan, and Kuan Yin and Sakyamuni, attributed respectively to Chang Ssu-kung and Lu Hsin-chung of the Sung dynasty and to Yen Hui of the Yuan dynasty, artists better known in Japan than in China.

Among the Chinese ceramics are fine celadon incense burners and vases of the Sung dynasty. Japanese ceramics are represented by vases from the Seto kilns and Kamakura-period pots of Tokoname ware excavated locally.

The Kamakura lacquer pieces include quivers, a writing box inlaid with mother-of-pearl, and some rare pieces of furniture, such as a carved wooden desk, a chair, a table, and a large altar. There is also a large Momoyama set of dishes, bowls, and trays.

• COMMENTS • The quality is excellent. The display is quite adequate, with some labels in English. About ten percent of the museum's contents (of which only about five percent belong to the museum) is normally on view at any one time. Changes are made in the exhibition every month, and objects not on show may be seen if enough advance notice and proper introduction are given. There is a small guide in English, listing the most important pieces housed in the museum, and a series of illustrated catalogues, in Japanese, of the occasional special loan exhibitions. It is essential for the student of Japanese art to see this collection.

68. Kamegaoka Archaeological Collection (Kamega-oka Kokokan), 8 Aza Kameyama, Oaza Tateoka, Kizukuri-machi, Nishi Tsugaru-gun, Aomori-ken. Tel. Tateoka 1.

亀ヶ岡考古館　青森県西津軽郡木造町大字館岡字亀山 8 番地

Director: Under the direction of the Kizukuri-machi Branch Office. **Hours:** 9–4, Apr.–Nov.; closed Mon. and day after a national holiday. **Adm.:** ¥20. **Route:** Take express bus from Aomori bus terminal opposite Matsukiya Department Store for Goshogawara (1 hr.), then local bus for Jusan, and get off at Kameyama (50 min.). The museum, a small one-room white-plastered building, is just beyond the bus stop, on the left.

This museum serves as a repository for finds, owned by members of the community, from the nearby Kamegaoka late-Jomon site and shell mound.

A medium-sized figurine and a shallow red lacquered bowl are perhaps the most unusual pieces in this collection. After these come two shards with red and black decoration, another with gray and red decoration, a number of small red pottery vessels, and several high-stemmed cups. Many other shards and small but complete pottery jars show characteristic late-Jomon decoration.

There are also many stone arrowheads, knives, small clubs, and beads, as well as a few hooks and pins of bone.

• COMMENTS • The quality is good to excellent, the display fair. There is a small pamphlet in Japanese. Only the specialist will find the long trip to this museum rewarding.

69. Kanagawa Prefectural Museum of Modern Art
(Kanagawa Kenritsu Kindai Bijutsukan), 1051 Yukino-shita, Kamakura, Kanagawa-ken. Tel. Kamakura 2-5000.

神奈川県立近代美術館　鎌倉市雪の下 1051 番地

Director: Kyosaku Murata. **Hours:** 9–4, Tues.–Fri.; 9–4:30, Sat., Sun.; closed Mon. and for short periods when exhibitions are changed. **Adm.:** ¥30. **Route:** The museum, a largish white building in the contemporary Western style, is on the left in the precincts of the Tsurugaoka Hachiman Shrine. It can be reached in 10 min. on foot from the Kamakura station (Yokosuka line) by turning to the left down the main street, crossing a busy intersection, and passing under a *torii*.

This is primarily an exhibiting gallery, with about ten different shows a year, varying from contemporary art to the ancient culture of China and Japan. The museum also owns a small but growing collection of contemporary Western and Japanese art—paintings, sculpture, prints, and handicrafts—which is displayed as the exhibition schedule permits. Most of the sculpture, however, is always on view, since it is shown outside the entrance to the museum and in the interior courtyard. Japanese painting in the Western manner and Japanese and Western prints predominate.

• COMMENTS • The exhibitions are well shown in ample, airy, and well-lighted galleries. Each exhibition is accompanied by a catalogue, and there is also a check list of the museum's own collection; both are in Japanese only.

Note: A new annex was opened in June 1966 and has given additional exhibition space.

70. Kanazawa Bunko Museum (Kanazawa Bunko), 27 Kanazawa-machi, Kanazawa-ku, Yokohama, Kanagawa-ken. Tel. Yokohama 70-9069.

金沢文庫　横浜市金沢区金沢町 27 番地

Director: Masao Kumahara. **Hours:** 9–4:30; closed national holidays, last day of every month, and Dec. 25–Jan. 7. It may also be closed last 10 days of June and first 10 days of July. **Adm.:** ¥ 20. **Route:** Take Keihin Kyuko Electric Railway from Yokohama to Kanazawa (20 min.) and then bus to the Shomyo-ji (5 min.). The museum and the library are housed in a two-story Japanese-style ferroconcrete building that lies above a large pond beyond and to the left of the second temple gate.

A collection of sculpture, painting, calligraphy, and historical documents, and a large library of the Chinese and Japanese classics, Buddhist sutras, and Zen writings. The collection and the library owe their origin to the Hojo family, who founded the Kanazawa Bunko in 1260 and supported it until the Kamakura shogunate fell in 1333.

Among the sculptures are figures of Aizen Myo-o, Juichimen Kannon, Shaka Nyorai, the Ju Dai Deshi, and Sogyo Hachiman. The paintings include a large *kakemono* of the Juni Shinsho and a most important scroll of the 14th century giving a topographical view of the Shomyo-ji buildings and grounds. The remarkable feature of the collection is its group of some 50 portraits of members of the Hojo family and of priests of the Shomyo-ji, which offers a unique opportunity for the study of Kamakura portraiture. The collection also contains some Han and T'ang pottery and Sung celadon.

A few of the important holdings of the library are usually included in the museum exhibit. The most valuable items are the Chinese Buddhist writings and the Sung editions of the classics; there is also a scroll of *waka* which is the earliest known text to be written in *kana*.

• COMMENTS • The quality is excellent, the display adequate. The sculpture is always on view; the paintings and documents are occasionally changed.

71. Kanshin-ji Treasure House (Kanshin-ji Reihokan), Kanshin-ji, Teramoto, Kawachi Nagano, Osaka. Tel. Kawachi Nagano 2134.

観心寺霊宝館　大阪府河内長野市寺元　観心寺内

Director: Gyozen Nagashima, Chief Priest. **Hours:** 9–5. **Adm.:** ¥20. **Route:** The temple is 2½ miles from the station of Kawachi Nagano, which is 30 min. on the Nankai line from Osaka. Take bus for Kobuka, which leaves once an hour, and get off at Kanshin-ji-mae, the entrance to the temple precincts. The treasure house is near the entrance, on the left.

A very interesting collection of Japanese paintings, sutras, documents, sculpture, armor, and altar fittings, housed (in the autumn of 1965) in a small narrow godown. The earliest statues are a remarkable group of four small bronze Buddhist figures of the Hakuho period. There is an equally fine group of large wooden statues of the Heian period, including a Jizo, a Sho Kannon, a Juichimen Kannon, two guardians, a seated Miroku, a delicate Nyoirin Kannon, and a portrait of a priest in a shrine. A small metal halo is dated 658.

Among the paintings is a representation of a seated eight-armed Bosatsu and some fifteen scrolls of the *Chusonji-kyo,* all dating from the Heian period. The documents include an inventory (compiled in 883) of the property of the temple, letters by the faithful follower of the emperor Godaigo, Kusunoki Masashige, and a directive written by the emperor Gomurakami.

• COMMENTS • The quality is very good, but the display is barely adequate. About one-third of the collection is on view. There is an illustrated booklet, in Japanese, on the temple and treasure house, which lists all the objects and describes some of them, but without any dates. The treasure house is worth visiting.

Note: A large new concrete treasure house with a tile roof has been built to the left of the Kondo. It is expected that it will open in the autumn of 1966 and that more of the collection will then be on view.

72. Kasuga Shrine Treasure House (Kasuga Taisha Homotsukan), Kasuga Shrine, Kasugano-machi, Nara, Nara-ken. Tel. Nara 22-7788.

春日大社宝物館　奈良市春日野町　春日大社内

Director: Chief Priest. **Hours:** 8:30–4:30, Apr.–Oct.; 9–4, Nov.–Mar. **Adm.:** ¥30. **Route:** The buildings of the Kasuga Shrine are at the upper end of Nara Park, on the slopes of Mount Mikasa, in the eastern section of the city. The treasure house is a little below and to the left of the shrine's main buildings. It is most easily reached by taxi.

A collection of masks, armor, swords and sword fittings, bows and arrows, drums, mirrors, lacquer objects, and calligraphy, all the property of this Shinto shrine.

The masks for Bugaku dances, many of which date from the 12th century, are excellent, and the armor and swords are equally fine and of great interest to the specialist. The two sets of red-laced armor of the Kamakura period and a pair of *kote* are among the most important pieces of their kind in Japan. One sword is of the Heian period, and several date from the Kamakura period. One mirror, made in China in the T'ang dynasty, was given to the shrine by the emperor Godaigo; other mirrors have dates of the late Heian period.

In the lacquer section is a 12th-century large black lacquered box on its wooden stand. The musical instruments include several *koto* and two huge drums, while a long scroll, dated 1236, lists the performances of sacred music at the shrine. Shinto priests' robes complete the exhibition.

• COMMENTS • Much of the material is very important. It is adequately shown in one large room, with a few labels in English. Occasional changes are made in the display. There is a booklet about the shrine, in Japanese and English, illustrating some of the objects in the treasure house and listing, in Japanese only, the important items. The treasure house is well worth visiting.

73. Kawaguchi Tibetan Collection, Tohoku University (Tohoku Daigaku Kawaguchi Chibetto Shiryoshitsu), Tohoku Daigaku, Kitahiro-cho, Sendai, Miyagi-ken. Tel. Sendai 23–6073 (home of Professor Kameda).

東北大学河口チベット資料室　仙台市北広町　東北大学内

Director: Professor Tsutomu Kameda. **Hours:** Open on request. **Adm.:** free. **Route:** Take tram labeled Tohoku Daigaku Byoin (Tohoku University Hospital). Get off at Tohoku Daigaku-mae (Tohoku University). Go through the main gates, turn right on the first broad street, and go as far as the next to last building on the left (before reaching the side gates of the campus). The collection is in the building behind this one, in a room on the third floor front, to the right of the stairway.

An extensive study collection of Tibetan objects, plus a few pieces of Indian and Nepalese sculpture. Among the former are paintings and priests' robes, reliquaries, prayer wheels, *vajra,* skull cups, bells, drums, saddles, swords, and one mask. The paintings and priests' robes are usually stored in trunks; a selection of the other items is shown in cases.

There are three Nepalese bronzes, while the Indian sculptures include a head and a small section of a balustrade of the Mathura period and a number of small medieval figures, mostly Pala.

• COMMENTS • The quality is good, the display adequate. About ten percent of the more than 1,500 items in the collection is apt to be on view. This collection is arranged for and is of interest primarily to students.

Note: It is planned to place this collection, together with the university's archaeological collection, in a new building when the university is moved to new quarters.

74. Kibi Archaeological Collection (Kibi Kokokan), 183 Jitokatayama, Yamate-mura, Soja, Okayama-ken. Tel. Soja 433.

吉備考古館　岡山県総社山手村地頭片山 183 番地

Director: Kiyomi Miyaoka. **Hours:** 8–4. **Adm.:** ¥40. **Route:** Take train from Kurashiki on Hakubi line or train from Okayama on Kibi line to Nishi Soja; then bus to Yamate-mura, and there ask for the Shinto shrine, to the right of which lies the museum. If the building is locked, ask for the key at the house across the road and to the left of the main building of the shrine. (By taxi from the station to the museum takes about 10 min.)

An extensive archaeological collection housed in a frame building. It consists largely of Jomon pottery and stone implements, Yayoi ceramics, Kofun ironwork and ceramics, and Heian roof tiles. Save for a good Kofun coffin, the pieces are mostly fragmentary, but they are interesting for the variety and extent of the local sites which they represent.

• COMMENTS • The display is very crowded. All the collection is normally on view. The museum is valuable only to the specialist.

Note: Some of the best display pieces belonging to the collection are shown in a museum (under the same director and with the same name; 9–5; free) housed in one room on the stairway of the ropeway to the Kyoyama Amusement Park in Okayama. (A bus runs from Okayama station to the ropeway terminus.) There are also photographs of the sites where the pieces were excavated. The display is well done, and the specialist will find the collection worth visiting as much for its material as for its rather surprising location. The director has made a worthy attempt to interest the general public in the local archaeology.

75. Kikusui Handicraft Museum (Kikusui Kogeikan), 2911 Komatsu, Kawanishi-machi, Yamagata-ken. Tel. Kawanishi 10.

掬粋巧芸館　山形県川西町小松 2911 番地

Director: Shoshichi Inoue. **Hours:** 9–4; closed last 3 days of every month and Dec. 1–Apr. 15. **Adm.:** free. **Route:** On leaving the station of Unzen Komatsu (which is on the Yonesaka line, not far from Yonezawa), take the first main street to the right and walk for about 15 min. until the street makes a sharp turn to the right. The museum, a godown-type building approached through a garden along a straight path, is on the left side of the street just beyond the turn. (By taxi, the trip takes only a few minutes.)

A collection of about 500 pieces of Chinese, Japanese, and Korean ceramics, with a few additions from Thailand and Annam. The main part of the collection is shown in the godown described above; there is also some material on display in a Western-style house to the left of the path leading to the museum.

The Japanese section begins with a Kofun vase and continues with two Kamakura vases; Muromachi examples of Tokoname, Bizen, Yellow Seto, and Shigaraki wares; and a piece of gray Shino and a Bizen jar of the Momoyama period. The remainder of the large Japanese section is chiefly of the Edo period, and contains many Old Kutani, Seto, Karatsu, Tamba, Oribe, Satsuma, Shino, and Bizen pieces, as well as a good selection of Imari, Nabeshima, Kakiemon, and Hirado porcelain. There are also a few contemporary copies of older Chinese wares.

In the Chinese group are a black pottery vase of the Chou dynasty, Han pottery grave figurines, models of buildings, and some vessels. There are also tomb figurines and pottery vessels of the Six Dynasties and the T'ang dynasty (many from the latter period are blue-glazed), and a few pieces of Yueh ware assigned to the Six Dynasties. From the Sung dynasty are Tz'u-chou vases, more examples of Yueh ware, Chun vessels (plus a number of fragments), pillows, Ting ware, a Hsiu-nei-ssu vase, Chien bowls, celadons (including two of *kinuta* shape), and a small white-glazed vase called Hsing-chou. The Yuan dynasty is represented by a very rare large blue-and-white vase of gourd shape. The large Ming group contains many pieces decorated in underglaze blue and in colored overglaze enamels, some bearing the reign marks of Chia-ching, Wan-li, and T'ien-ch'i. The Ch'ing porcelains, few in number, are mostly blue-and-white.

There is a handsome group of Korean celadons, generally small in size, of the Koryo dynasty. Many are decorated with inlaid designs. The Yi-dynasty group is somewhat larger and contains, among others, many blue-and-white pieces, white-bodied vessels with designs in iron red, brown, and cobalt blue, and light-greenish celadons with incised decoration.

• COMMENTS • The quality is very good, and the installation, though crowded, is adequate. There are occasional English notes on the labels. All objects are normally on view. There are a short illustrated pamphlet and a catalogue, both in Japanese.

76. Kinreitsuka Archaeological Collection (Kinreitsuka Ibutsu Hozonkan), Otayama Koen, Ota, Kisarazu, Chiba-ken. Tel. Kisarazu 3676.

金鈴塚遺物保存館　千葉県木更津市太田山公園

Director: Tokumatsu Ikeda. **Hours:** 8:30–4:30; closed Mon. afternoon, Tues., day after a national holiday, and Dec. 29–Jan. 3. **Adm.:** ¥20. **Route:** Kisarazu may be reached from Tokyo either by train from

Ryogoku station or by hydrofoil from Shibaura. From Kisarazu station, take bus No. 5 to Hozonkan-mae; then the first road to the left and the path up the hill to the museum, a new one-room ferroconcrete building which can be seen on the hill above the bus stop.

A small but excellent collection of Kofun material from Kinreitsuka, a large burial mound in the immediate vicinity. Particularly notable are four quite complete iron swords in their gilt-bronze scabbards, each with its gilt-bronze pommel in perfect condition. There are many other pommels and some more swords, the latter in rather fragmentary condition. One of these swords has a *t'ao-t'ieh* mask on its handle and is presumed to have been brought from China.

The collection also includes fine gilt-bronze horse trappings, rectangular gilt-bronze plaques presumed to be from a suit of armor, iron armor, an iron helmet, high-stemmed bronze cups complete with covers and resting on cup stands, mirrors, gilt-bronze bells, and two sections of a saddle. The high-stemmed Sue-ware dishes and the Sue-ware jars are noted for their unusual shapes and fine condition. Silver bow tips are a rare item, as is a gilt-bronze perforated plaque that served as a ceremonial fan.

A map of the Kofun sites in Japan, a model of the excavated burial mound, and a reproduction of a tomb complete the exhibition.

• COMMENTS • The quality is excellent. The display is good, with a few labels in English. Special care has been taken to preserve the iron objects. About half the collection is on view, and no changes are made in the exhibition. There is an illustrated pamphlet in Japanese. The museum is well worth visiting, not only by the specialist but also by anyone with a general interest in Japanese archaeology.

77. Kinsuien Art Museum (Kinsuien Bijutsukan), 1006-1 Matogahama Kaigan, Beppu, Oita-ken. Tel. Beppu 3-1213.

錦水園美術館　大分県別府市的ケ浜海岸 1006-1

Director: Kiku Yokoyama. **Hours:** 9 a.m.–10 p.m. **Adm.:** ¥150, 9–5; ¥200, 5–10 p.m. (no minors allowed at any time). **Route:** The museum is on the ground floor of the Kinsuien Ryokan, a Japanese inn that can be reached from the station by bus (Nakamadori stop) or on foot by going down the main street leading to the waterfront, turning left along the waterfront on the street with double car tracks and continuing a short way beyond the Nakamadori bus stop. The inn, an attractive complex of Japanese-style buildings, is on the left.

A miscellaneous collection of Chinese, Japanese, and Korean objects, shown in several rooms on the ground floor to the right of the main entrance of the inn. The Chinese items include a T'ang stone Bodhisattva and three large and several small T'ang pottery figurines. The Japanese section, which is by far the largest, contains Kamakura wooden sculptures of a lion and an elephant, a screen attributed to Kano Eitoku, and many paintings of the women of the gay quarters by Toyokuni, as well as prints by him and other artists of the 19th century.

There is an extensive arms-and-armor section that contains a few Kofun swords and many Edo suits of armor, swords, arrows, quivers, sword fittings, and guns. Lacquer furniture, Noh costumes, *inro,* tobacco pipes, clocks, weights and measures, feudal money, and some Korean armor round out the exhibition. A special feature is a room full of gourds.

• COMMENTS • The quality varies enormously. The display is adequate. The exhibition, which is made up of all the items that can be shown publicly, changes every few years, but only to make way for new acquisitions.

78. Kitano Temman-gu Treasure House (Kitano Temman-gu Homotsuden), Kitano Temman-gu, Kitano Bakuro-cho, Kamikyo-ku, Kyoto. Tel. Kyoto 44-0005.

北野天満宮宝物殿　京都市上京区北野馬喰町
北野天満宮内

Director: Daiken Kasai, Chief Priest. **Hours:** 9–4, on 25th of every month if it is not raining. It may also be seen at other times if request is made in writing 3 days in advance. **Adm.:** ¥30. **Route:** Tram No. 10 goes directly to the shrine, which is in the northwest section of the city. The treasure house is the first building on the right after the main gate.

An important collection of paintings and calligraphy, with some pieces of sculpture, lacquer, metalwork, and a few costumes, all the property of the shrine. It is especially noted for the scrolls of the *Kitano Tenjin Engi* (Life of Sugawara Michizane and the Origin of the Tenjin). Nine of these (the Shokyu version) are attributed to Fujiwara Nobuzane, Kamakura period, 13th century; two more (Koan version) are attributed to Tosa Yukimitsu of the next century; three are by Tosa Mitsunobu, Muromachi, 15th century; and Tosa Mitsuoki painted yet another three in the 17th century. Of all these scrolls, four of the first group are usually on display.

Among other objects on view are a pair of dragon screens by Yusho, calligraphy of the emperor Sanjo and of the Tokugawa shoguns Ieyasu and Iemitsu, a poem by the emperor Reigen, a fragment of a sutra said to have been written by Tofu, and topographical paintings of the shrine from the Muromachi period. Lacquer, metalwork, inkstones, and court costumes complete the exhibit.

• COMMENTS • The quality is excellent, the display good. The exhibit is seldom changed. There is a pamphlet describing the shrine, with a brief mention of the treasure house.

79. Kobe Municipal Art Museum (Shiritsu Kobe Bijutsukan), 35, 1-chome, Kumauchi-cho, Fukiai-ku, Kobe, Hyogo-ken. Tel. Kobe 22-3043.

市立神戸美術館　神戸市葺合区熊内町 1 丁目 35 番地

Director: Shinsei Arao. **Hours:** 9–4:30, 1st–25th of every month; closed Mon., all of Aug., and New Year season. **Adm.:** ¥20. **Route:** The museum, a small Western-style building of several floors, is in the upper part of the town, away from the waterfront and northeast of Sannomiya station. The No. 2 bus stops at the museum, or it can be reached in 5 min. on foot from the 1-chome Kumauchi-cho tram stop.

A very interesting collection of *namban* art: screens, paintings, prints, and lacquer objects by Japanese artists of the late 16th, 17th, and 18th centuries showing foreigners and foreign objects in Japanese surroundings. Also of the same period are paintings by Japanese artists in the Western manner and relics of Christianity in Japan.

Among the screens are a pair of sixfold ones showing the arrival and departure of Portuguese in their ships; a fourfold screen of armed Europeans and Near Eastern warriors in combat; and a pair of sixfold screens of European genre scenes. The last two are copied from European originals.

The paintings include scenes of the Dutch trading establishments and of Dutch ships by the Nagasaki artists Genkei, Shuseki, and Yushi; in the Western manner are works by Aodo Denzen, Denki Gennai, Shiba Kokan, and Tairo —all artists of the 18th and early 19th centuries. Prints made in Nagasaki depict the foreigners and their ships; other prints by well-known printmakers of the 18th and the early 19th century show Japanese using foreign objects.

• COMMENTS • The artistic standard of these works, measured against the finest products of Japanese art, is admittedly not high; their great interest lies in the fact that they are the first Japanese representations of Westerners and that they show the beginning of the influence of Western culture, trade, and religion on Japan. For anyone interested in this field, the museum is enthralling. The display is quite good, though the labels in English are scant. The exhibition changes every month, and the percentage of the entire collection (some 4,500 items, of which about 500 are display pieces) shown at any time depends on the type of the exhibition. There is a small illustrated booklet in Japanese with English captions.

80. Kofuku-ji Treasure Hall (Kofuku-ji Homotsukan), Kofuku-ji, 59 Noborioji-cho, Nara, Nara-ken. Tel. Nara 22-7755.

興福寺宝物館　奈良市登大路町 59 番地　興福寺内

Director: Chief Priest. **Hours:** 9–5. **Adm.:** ¥70. **Route:** The grounds of the Kofuku-ji lie a very short distance east of the Nara station of the Kinki Nihon Railway. Walk uphill and turn right, opposite the new prefectural offices. The treasure hall, a new Japanese-style fire- and earthquake-proof building, is to the north of the pagoda.

A collection of some of the finest sculptures in Japan. Among the early pieces are a superb bronze head of Yakushi Nyorai from a figure cast in 685 and destroyed in 1411; the Tenryu Hachibu Shu, a famous group that was made for the original Saikondo (erected in 734) and includes the appealing Ashura represented as a youthful six-armed, three-faced figure; a group of six of the Shaka Ju Dai Deshi in hollow dry lacquer of the Tempyo period; and the Shi Tenno, dated 791, in lacquer over a wood core. A second group of the Shi Tenno, in wood, dates from the early Heian period, and a remarkable set of the Juni Shinsho, in wood carved in low relief, is assigned to the late Heian period. A seated Yakushi Nyorai, of lacquered and colored wood, is dated 1013.

The sculpture of the Kamakura period is also remarkable. It includes a very large Fukukensaku Kannon in gilt wood; portrait statues of the patriarchs of the Hosso sect; two Nio; a Senju Kannon; a Monju Bosatsu; another set of the Juni Shinsho; a standing Bonten carved by Jokei in 1202 and a Yuima Koji, also by Jokei; the famous statues of Muchaku and Seshin by Unkei; a seated Miroku by a follower of Unkei; and figures of Tentoki and Ryutoki, sometimes said to be by Koben, the third son of Unkei.

Among the few paintings are a portrait of the priest Jion and a Hosso *mandara,* both of the Kamakura period, and a scroll, the *Nihon Ryoiki* (Record of Miracles), dated 904. The collection also includes an elaborate bronze *kagen-kei,* said to have been made in China in the T'ang dynasty.

• COMMENTS • The quality is superb, and there are many pieces which are essential to the study of Japanese sculpture. The display is good, and there are a few labels in English. About ninety percent of the collection is normally on view. Illustrated handbooks and pamphlets in Japanese and English are available.

81. Kokubunji-machi Archaeological Gallery (Kokubunji-machi Bunkazai Hozonkan), 1631 Kokubunji-machi, Kitatama-gun, Tokyo. Tel. Kokubunji 21-0420.

国分寺町文化財保存館　東京都北多摩郡国分寺町 1631 番地

Director: Ryosho Hoshino. **Hours:** 8–5; closed national holidays. **Adm.:** ¥10. **Route:** Take national railways Chuo line from Shinjuku station to Kokubunji, then bus for Tachikawa. Get off at Tetsudo Gakuin-mae and turn left on the first paved road beyond the bus stop. The grounds of the Kokubun-ji, where the museum is located, are a short way down this road and on the left, beside a graveyard. The museum, a small one-room wooden building, is on the right as one enters the precincts.

A small collection of Japanese archaeology from local sites and a group of documents concerning local history. The outstanding items are several excellent middle-Jomon pieces, especially a large urn with a narrow waist and broad shoulders topped with heavy coils. There are also Jomon stone arrowheads, chipped and polished stone implements, two *sekibo,* a stone vessel for the grinding of grain, some pieces of Yayoi pottery, and an iron sword. Two cases contain circular and curved tiles of the Nara period from the original site of the Kokubun-ji, and two more contain fragments of tiles incised with the names of individuals and districts contributing to the building of the temple. Among the documents is a permission for trade with China issued by the third Tokugawa shogun, Iemitsu.

• COMMENTS • The quality of the Jomon pieces is excellent. The display is only fair. The exhibition does not change, and material not on view is stored in boxes under the cases. There is no pamphlet. This is a collection primarily for the specialist.

82. Kokugakuin University Archaeological Collection (Kokugakuin Daigaku Kokogaku Shiryoshitsu), Kokugakuin Daigaku, 9 Wakagi-cho, Shibuya-ku, Tokyo. Tel. Tokyo 401-3101.

国学院大学考古学資料室　東京都渋谷区若木町9番地
国学院大学内

Director: Uji Kato. **Hours:** 9–5; closed Sun. and national holidays. **Adm.:** free. **Route:** Take No. 53 bus from Shibuya station bound for Nisseki Byoin and get off at the stop at the corner of the university grounds. The museum is on the second floor of the second building on the left of the main entrance to the university.

An excellent collection of Japanese archaeological material from the pre-Jomon period to early historical times, plus a few objects of similar epochs from China, Korea, and North America. Nearly all the Japanese items come from known sites. There are stone artifacts of the pre-Jomon period, a large group of Jomon pottery of the second through the fifth stages (including some quite fine large vases and jars), as well as polished stone and shell ornaments. The Yayoi period is represented by pottery and other materials; the Kofun period by a fine lot of *haniwa* (including a horse, figures of warriors, and a house), a large coffin, metal mirrors, *magatama,* metal jewelry, and a rare stone pillow, plus Sue pottery vessels and other objects. There are also fragments of pottery, stone tools, bronze weapons, and a few grave figurines from China and stone arrowheads and pottery from North America. A feature of the exhibit is a cross section of a shell mound.

The collection also contains Japanese burial urns, roof tiles, and small stone pagodas of the Nara and later periods.

• COMMENTS • This collection provides an excellent opportunity to study Japanese archaeology, especially since the provenance of nearly every object is known. The exhibits, shown in new cases in a large well-lighted room, are arranged chronologically; the labels, though in Japanese only, are very full. Less than fifteen percent of the collection is normally on view, and even so the cases are crowded; however, the objects are clearly visible. Study rooms adjoin the main hall. There is an illustrated handbook to the collection, in Japanese.

Note: On the first floor is a large room devoted to the display of objects used in Shinto ceremonies and festivals, including costumes, banners, musical instruments, and drums. This is a most unusual exhibition and one of great interest to every student of the Shinto religion.

83. Komatsu Municipal Museum (Komatsu Shiritsu Hakubutsukan), Ashiki Koen, Komatsu, Ishikawa-ken. Tel. Komatsu 22-4111, ext. 394.

小松市立博物館　石川県小松市足木公園

Director: Tadayasu Ogawa. **Hours:** 9–6, Apr.–Oct.; 9–5, Nov.–Mar.; closed Mon., national holidays, and Dec. 29–Jan. 3. **Adm.:** free. **Route:** Take bus for Kanazawa, get off at Kyo-machi, and turn left. The museum, a nondescript Western-style building, stands opposite the municipal office.

A rather small collection of archaeology, folk art, and other material, displayed on the ground floor of the museum. The archaeological section contains samples of Jomon, Yayoi, and Kofun pottery, Kofun swords and metal objects. There are also a few Nara tiles and some ceramics of the Heian period, as well as a group of lacquer *tebako* and some of the large lion masks used in temple festivals. The folk arts include farm tools and farmers' clothing.

Natural-history material occupies the upper floor.

• COMMENTS • The quality is fair, the display adequate. The regular exhibit may at times be pushed aside to make room for loan shows, some eight of which are held each year; the percentage of the collection normally on view depends on the size of the temporary loan show. The museum is hardly worth a special visit.

84. Korekawa Archaeological Hall (Korekawa Koko-kan), 6, 6-chome, Aza Nakai, Oaza Korekawa, Hachinohe, Aomori-ken. Tel. Hachinohe 2-6484.

是川考古館　青森県八戸市大字是川字中居6丁目6番地

Director: Yoichiro Ohashi. **Hours:** 9–4, Apr.–Nov.; closed Mon. and day after a national holiday. **Adm.:** ¥30. **Route:** The museum, a small new two-story boxlike building, is in the country, some distance to the southwest of Hachinohe. Take bus from terminal in Yakamachi, Hachinohe, for Korekawa and get off at Kokokan-mae. The building is set back from the road, on the right. (By taxi, the ride is 10 min. from Hachinohe over rough country roads, or 20 min. from Shiriuchi.)

A medium-sized and very interesting collection of late-Jomon objects from the Korekawa site in the immediate vicinity of the museum. (The objects were excavated by Mr. Izumiyama and given by him to the city of Hachinohe.) Of great interest and rarity are a number of small pottery vessels with an elaborate openwork design on top, resembling incense burners of a much later date. Of equal interest are many other small vessels with ovoid bodies, broad flaring lips, and small spouts. The excavations also brought to light a number of small red pottery vessels and one jar decorated in red and white, as well as a large number of the more usual Jomon pottery items.

Other rare pieces are wooden bows, fragments of red lacquered combs, and cleats made of wisteria vines to go under straw sandals. There is also a considerable group of small figurines with masklike faces.

Stone tools, bone hooks and needles, and shells from a shell mound complete the display.

• COMMENTS • The quality is excellent, the installation adequate. The exhibition changes four times a year, with the same type of objects always shown. About ten percent of the collection is on view; the remainder, kept in an adjoining storeroom, may be seen on request. There are a pamphlet and an illustrated booklet describing the site and the finds. The archaeologist will find this collection fascinating. The building is a good example of the archaeological-site museum becoming so frequent in Japan.

85. Koryu-ji Treasure Hall (Koryu-ji Reihoden), Koryu-ji, Futohata Hachigaoka-machi, Ukyo-ku, Kyoto. Tel. Kyoto 86-1461.

広隆寺霊宝殿　京都市右京区太秦蜂岡町　広隆寺内

Director: Eiko Kiyotaki, Chief Priest. **Hours:** 9–5. **Adm.:** ¥60.
Route: The temple is in the western part of the city, close to the Uzumasa stop on the Arashiyama line of the Keifuku Electric Railway. Bus No. 11 from Keihan Sanjo stops nearby. The treasure house is beyond the Kondo.

A most important collection of Japanese sculpture, calligraphy, documents, and costumes, all the property of the temple.

The best-known sculpture is the Asuka wooden Miroku Bosatsu in the *hanka shiyui* pose (seated, with the right foot crossed over the upper part of the left leg, the right elbow resting on the right knee, and the right hand raised to the face). It is, perhaps, the most appealing statue in Kyoto. Another figure of Miroku, behind and to the right of the one above, is also of the Asuka period, while a third one, to the left, is of the same date but is made of clay, a rare material for Kyoto statues.

Among the other sculptures are a superb group of nine of the Juni Shinsho carved by Chosei and dated 1064. (The other three from this group are divided between the national museums in Kyoto and Tokyo.) A second set of statues, the Shi Tenno, dates from the Heian period. From the early Heian (Jogan) period are a standing Sho Kannon, a figure of Jizo, a Bishamonten, and a Kisshoten. There are many single statues from the later Heian period, among them a seated Fudo, a seated Dainichi Nyorai, and a Kisshoten. A figure of Aizen is from the Kamakura period. At the entrance is a huge Senju Kannon, somewhat damaged and dated 1012.

Two of a set of paintings of the Juniten of the early Kamakura period, said to be by members of the Takuma family, are generally on view. Among the documents is a temple inventory of the 9th century. There is also a copy of the *Hannya Shin-gyo,* said to be by Kobo Daishi.

The costume section has an interesting display of 19th-century coronation robes.

• COMMENTS • The quality is excellent. The display is adequate, and there are a few labels in English. All objects are normally on view, except the scrolls, and the exhibit almost never changes. There is a very brief leaflet in English. The treasure house should be seen by every visitor to Kyoto and must be seen by every student of Japanese sculpture.

86. Kotohira Shrine Museum (Kotohira-gu Hakubutsukan), 892 Kotohira-machi, Kagawa-ken. Tel. Kotohira 2121.

金刀比羅宮博物館　香川県琴平町 892 番地

Director: Mitsushige Koto-oka, Chief Priest; Sadaichi Osaki, Curator. **Hours:** 9–4:30. **Adm.:** ¥30. **Route:** The museum, a two-story concrete building with a Japanese-style roof, is in the shrine precincts, halfway up and to the right of the very steep and long flight of steps leading to the main shrine building. On leaving the station, turn right, then left on the next main street, then right again on the street lined with souvenir shops that brings one to the steps leading to the shrine. The climb to the museum takes about 20 min.

A fairly large collection of Japanese painting, calligraphy, sculpture, metalwork, arms and armor, masks, and musical instruments, all owned by the shrine.

The paintings include a good 14th-century Kamakura scroll of the *Nayotake Monogatari,* a fine painting of a carp by Rosetsu, a Kannon attributed to Sesshu, a charming sketch of a radish by Sesson, a screen illustrating the *Genji Monogatari* by Tosa Mitsumoto, a landscape by Taiga, and a pair of screens of deer by Kansai. Three Buddhist paintings are bravely assigned to the priest Mincho. There are also a figure of a warrior by Niten and twelve views of Mount Zozu by Yasunobu. Among the writings are a copy of the *Hannya-kyo* said to be by the emperor Sutoku, *shikishi* by Fujiwara Teika, and calligraphy of the emperors Godaigo, Goyozei, Gohanazono, and Sutoku.

The armor is largely of the Edo period. The earliest piece of metalwork is a *dotaku.*

• COMMENTS • The quality is fair to good, the installation adequate. Parts of the exhibit are occasionally changed. There is a booklet in Japanese on the shrine and a pamphlet on the museum. The collection is worth a visit.

Note: A second museum in the shrine precincts, the Kotohira Kakugeikan, lies lower down, nearer the town and in front of the shrine library. (Same director, hours, and admission fee as the main museum.) From the town, take the small street to the right of the main street and walk for 10 min. uphill along the path at the end of this street. The museum contains an odd mixture of Sue ware, *ema,* toys, modern calligraphy, and paintings in oil by some of the Japanese pioneers in this medium. The display is adequate. About seventy percent of the material is on view, and changes are made in the exhibit once a year. There is a pamphlet in Japanese. Only specialists in contemporary or votive painting or in toys will be interested.

What is called the third shrine museum lies above the main one and was originally one of the shrine buildings. It now serves, in part, as an office; has excellent screens by Okyo, Jakuchu, and Gantai; and is well worth visiting.

87. **Koyasan Treasure House** (Koyasan Reihokan), Koyasan, Koya-machi, Wakayama-ken. Tel. Koyasan 32.

高野山霊宝館　和歌山県高野町高野山

Director: Shinkai Hotta. **Hours:** 8–5, summer; 8:30–4, winter. **Adm.:** ¥70. **Route:** To reach Koyasan from Osaka, take Koya line of Nankai Railway from Namba station to the end of the line, then connecting cable car to the top of the mountain. From Kyoto or Nara, take Japanese National Railways to Hashimoto and change there to Nankai Railway. The bus from the cable-car terminus at the mountaintop to the Daimon passes in front of the Reihokan, which stands a little way back from the left-hand side of the street, almost opposite the Kondo of the Kongobu-ji.

This museum, a large building in the Japanese style, was erected in 1921 to preserve and display the important art objects owned by the temples on Koyasan. The treasure house contains some 5,000 items, of which there are generally on view some 40 pieces of sculpture, about 20 paintings, several sutras, about 20 pieces of calligraphy, and an equal number of Buddhist ritual objects.

The famous Heian *raigo* triptych, showing Amida surrounded by music-making Bosatsu, is practically never shown; in its place is a good Meiji copy. A copy also takes the place of the portrait of Kobo Daishi, who founded the Kongobu-ji on Koyasan. The Red Fudo Myo-o of the early Heian period, belonging to the Myo-o-in, is also almost never shown, and the same seems to be true for the paintings of the Go Dairiki Bosatsu of the same period and for the *Death of the Buddha* dated 1086.

There is always on view, however, an interesting selection of original paintings—Buddhist in subject matter: Buddhist deities, *mandara,* and portraits of priests—of the Kamakura and, occasionally, of the Muromachi period. Copies of the *Issai-kyo,* in gold and silver on dark-blue paper, are generally on view, and sometimes the writings of Kobo Daishi, letters of Yoritomo and Yoshitsune, a prayer written by the emperor Godaigo, orders written by the emperor Goshirakawa, and many other pieces of Kamakura and Namboku-cho calligraphy held by the Kongobu-ji.

The sculpture usually on view dates from the Heian to the Kamakura period. Among the Heian pieces are two fine seated Amida Nyorai, one with a pedestal and *mandorla* carved with flying Bosatsu, and a seated Shaka Nyorai, also with a pedestal and *mandorla.* From the Kamakura period are a Yakushi Nyorai, a Jizo, and a Nyoirin Kannon, all with pedestals and *mandorlas;* an Amida triad; and many single figures of monks and of the Hachi Dai Doji (some of the last by Unkei). There are also some good Kamakura lion-dogs.

Among the Buddhist ritual objects are alms bowls, incense burners, *vajra* (some the property of Kobo Daishi), and the Heian Ryokai *mandara* carved on wooden plaques and housed in a shrine.

• COMMENTS • The quality is of the highest order; the display is adequate, with occasional English labels. Though the sculpture seldom changes, the paintings and calligraphy are changed about twice a year. There is also a special exhibition of paintings from August 8 to 14. An illustrated booklet, in Japanese only, describes some of the finest pieces owned by the various temples and sometimes exhibited in the treasure house, which is one of the richest in Japan and should be seen especially by anyone interested in Buddhist art.

88. Kozo-ji Museum (Kozo-ji Hakubutsukan), Kozo-ji, Setoda-machi, Hiroshima-ken. Tel. Setoda 6018.

耕三寺博物館　広島県潮声田町　耕三寺内

Director: Kozo Kosanji. **Hours:** 7–5. **Adm.:** ¥100. **Route:** The temple is at the port of Setoda on the island of Ikuchijima in the Inland Sea and can be reached by boat from Onomichi or Mihara on Honshu or from Imabari on Shikoku. From the landing, walk along the main shopping street for about 10 min. The grounds of the recently built temple are on the right.

A large and varied collection of Chinese and Japanese art, housed in five buildings. Two of these, rectangular in design, are on either side of the entrance; two, resembling temple structures, are on either side of the pagoda; the fifth, also in temple style, is to the right of the main complex.

Among the Chinese pieces are several bronze vessels of the Chou and Han dynasties, Han pottery vessels and figurines, large glazed and smaller unglazed T'ang figurines, many small T'ang gilt-bronze Buddhist figures, rather fragmentary Buddhist sculpture of the 6th century, and a small white marble sculpture of the same period. There is a large sword dated 3rd century A.D., while a few celadons belong to the Sung and Yuan dynasties. Ink sticks and inkstones of a much more recent date are also shown.

In the early Japanese group are swords and many gilt-bronze horse trappings, several *haniwa,* some Sue and Haji vessels, and *magatama* of the Kofun period. There is a large body of Buddhist sculpture, which includes five guardian figures of the Heian and Kamakura periods, a Shaka Nyorai of the Jogan (early Heian) period, a Kamakura pair of lions, a seated Amida attributed to Kaikei, and a good seated Amida of the Heian period. A miniature shrine containing the Jodo *mandara* carved in wood and a lovely bronze mirror decorated with birds and flowers are also of the Heian period.

A large painting, *The Death of the Buddha,* is assigned to the Muromachi period, and there are Kamakura paintings of single Buddhist deities in gold and colors. There is also a charming *View of a Waterfall* by Okyo and a *Duck* by Goshun. Other paintings are by such recent artists as Gyokudo Kawai and Kiyokata Kaburagi. There is also a large group of contemporary paintings and sculpture, almost all of Buddhist subjects. The documents and calligraphy include a copy of the *Daihannya-kyo* assigned to the Tempyo period, a poem by the emperor Fushimi, calligraphy by the priest Ikkyu and the tea master Sen no Rikyu, and a letter by Hideyoshi.

Japanese ceramics are represented by an Iga vase, Raku tea bowls, and a square Oribe dish. A rare item is a group of textile fragments of the Asuka period.

• COMMENTS • The quality varies from fair to excellent. The display is fair, being marred (as of November 1965) by the lack of proper lighting and the helter-skelter arrangement of the material, with Chinese and Japanese objects of widely different date and type shown in the two lower buildings and in the one to the left of the pagoda. The building to the right of the pagoda contained the Japanese Buddhist art, and the fifth building the contemporary objects. Changes are made in the exhibit about twice a year. There is an illustrated booklet on the temple and its collection which lists many of the important items without, however, giving provenance or date. Despite such drawbacks the museum is well worth visiting.

89. Kumamoto Municipal Museum (Kumamoto Shiritsu Hakubutsukan), Kumamoto-jo, Kumamoto, Kumamoto-ken. Tel. Kumamoto 2-5879.

熊本市立博物館　熊本市熊本城

Director: Seiji Moritaka. **Hours:** 8:30–5; closed Mon. **Adm.:** ¥50. **Route:** Take bus to Kumamoto-jo-mae (Kumamoto Castle stop). The castle is approached by a long winding uphill footpath.

An interesting collection, consisting chiefly of local ceramics and archaeology and some historical documents, well installed in a newly rebuilt large and handsome castle tower.

On the ground floor are objects relating to the history of the castle and some very fine examples of the local ceramics, including pieces of Shodai ware, Old Shodai ware, and Old Kodai ware.

The second floor is devoted to historical documents, while the third floor has the archaeological exhibits, which consist of fragments of Jomon pottery, huge Yayoi jars, and

Kofun swords, armor, *magatama,* beads, and excellent metal-work (the horse trappings and sword pommels are of particular interest). There are also some Nara tiles.

• COMMENTS • The quality is good, the display very good. The exhibition changes in part once or twice a year, with generally about two-thirds of the items on display belonging to the museum and the remaining material on loan. The museum is worth visiting.

Note: The main office of the museum is in the center of the city (Hana-batake-machi; tel. 2-5879; 9–5, except Mon.; ¥20). The Karashima-machi tram stop is on one side of the building. There is a collection of folk arts, farm implements, lamps, natural history, and science exhibitions. Aesthetically, the display has little interest; the installation is fair. There is an illustrated pamphlet in Japanese.

90. Kumano Hayatama Shrine Treasure House
(Kumano Shimpokan), Kumano Hayatama Shrine, Shin-gu-machi, Shingu, Wakayama-ken. Tel. Shingu 02-2533.

熊野神宝館　和歌山県新宮市新宮町　熊野速玉大社内

Director: Chief Priest. **Hours:** 8–5, Apr.–Oct.; 9–4, Nov.–Mar. **Adm.:** ¥50. **Route:** Take bus for Katsuura and get off at Gongen-mae. The treasure house, of ferroconcrete and externally in the Japanese style, is to the right of the path leading from the *torii* to the main shrine building.

A good small collection of local Japanese archaeology and an excellent collection, almost all of the Fujiwara and Kamakura periods, of small sculptures, metalwork, ceramics, lacquer, and fans.

There are prehistoric chipped stone tools, a middle-Jomon vase and fragments of pottery from the sites of Omi-zusaki and Wasa, Yayoi pottery from Ota and Onaka, and a good *dotaku* and a large spear of the same period. An elaborate Sue-ware vessel of the Kofun period comes from the Tomeki site.

From the Heian period are mirrors, metal and pottery sutra boxes, small Chinese porcelain boxes from the sutra mound of Shinkurayama at Shingu, and pottery jars from this and the Kahodo mound, also at Shingu. These same mounds, and that of Anshuiko, have yielded a number of single Buddhist figures and *kakebotoke* from the Heian to the Muromachi period. Also found at Shingu was a large

Seto baluster-shaped vase of the late Heian or early Kamakura period.

The cream of the collection, however, consists of objects listed in the shrine inventory of 1390 and a few that were added shortly afterwards. Among these are ten fans of cypress wood painted with charming landscapes and flower designs in the Yamato-e manner, a lacquer box holding a scepter, a sword, bows, a quiver full of arrows, artificial flowers used as hair ornaments, long strands of hair for the use of court ladies, an amulet box, lacquer *tebako,* a square pillow, shoes, sachets, two pendants to be hung from the canopy of a Buddhist shrine, metal spindles, a bowl to hold the ball of thread when spun and a lacquer frame around which to wrap it as it was spun.

A large and elaborate portable shrine and a smaller one resting on a boat round out the exhibition.

• COMMENTS • The quality is excellent. The installation is adequate, as are the labels, though they are in Japanese only and give few dates. No changes are made in the exhibition, save for the objects on the inventory list, half of which are usually shown at any one time. There is an illustrated handbook in Japanese.

91. Kunozan Tosho-gu Treasure House (Kunozan Tosho-gu Homotsukan), Kunozan, Shizuoka, Shizuoka-ken. Tel. Shizuoka 85-5612.

久能山東照宮宝物館　静岡市久能山

Director: Chief Priest. **Hours:** 8–5, Apr.–Sept.; 8–4, Oct.–Mar. **Adm.:** ¥50. **Route:** The shrine lies at the top of Kunozan, a hill 6 miles southeast of Shizuoka. Take bus from Shizuoka station to Nihon Daira (about 40 min.), a neighboring peak to that on which the shrine is situated; then the ropeway to the shrine (6 min.). The treasure house is 50 yards to the right and downhill from the ropeway station.

A very interesting collection of armor, swords, costumes, lacquer, paintings, guns, and objects of personal use, in large part the property of Ieyasu, the first Tokugawa shogun, and left by him to the shrine. (He was first buried here, before his remains were transferred to Nikko.)

Perhaps the most interesting pieces are two suits of armor worn by Ieyasu, a portrait of him by Tan'yu, two

Bizen swords used by Hidetada and Iemitsu (the second and third Tokugawa shoguns), and a suit of armor worn by Iemitsu. Among the other items given to the shrine by Ieyasu and his successors are many suits of armor and the coats worn over the armor, swords, spears, arrows, quivers, war fans, guns and pistols, and lacquer boxes for both hats and food. Ieyasu's personal possessions include a cloak made in Spain in 1581, his spectacles, scissors, and compass. His handwriting is shown in the large character for "tiger" and in some moral precepts. There is also a print of his hand, as well as prints of the hands of many of the other Tokugawa shoguns and of Hideyoshi, Nobunaga, and Kato Kiyomasa.

• COMMENTS • The collection is very good of its kind and offers a fascinating picture of military and domestic life in the late 16th and the 17th century. The display is crowded, with one-third of the collection normally on view. There is an illustrated folder in Japanese describing the treasure house; another illustrated booklet, in Japanese and English, describes the shrine and its surroundings.

92. Kuon-ji Treasure House (Minobusan Homotsukan), Kuon-ji, Minobu-machi, Yamanashi-ken. Tel. Minobu 2, 3, 142.

身延山宝物館　山梨県身延町　久遠寺内

Director: Hishizu Fujii. **Hours:** 8–4:30. **Adm.:** ¥30. **Route:** Bus from Minobu station (which is on the Minobu line from Kofu to Fuji) takes 20 min. to the main temple gate at the bottom of the long uphill path to the temple itself. (A taxi goes, by a rough road, direct to the treasure house in about 15 min.) The treasure house, a Victorian-style wooden building, is to the left as one faces the main temple buildings.

A collection of painting, sculpture, calligraphy, lacquer, masks, and metalwork. Among the items is a landscape in color on silk assigned to the Sung dynasty, a copy of the *Book of Rites* printed in the Sung dynasty, paintings in ink attributed to Motonobu, and a landscape by Tsunenobu. There are pieces of calligraphy by Nichiren and other priests of the sect (the Kuon-ji is the headquarters of the Nichiren sect of Buddhism, and Nichiren is buried here), and by the emperors Goyozei and Reigen. The collection also includes a fine pair of calligraphic screens by Koetsu, screens illustrating temple dances, paintings of the death of the Buddha and of Nichiren, copies of the *Hokke-kyo,* Noh masks and masks for temple dancers, wooden figures of temple guardians, recent portraits and statues of Nichiren, and lacquer tobacco sets and incense burners. A few pieces of Siamese Buddhist sculpture complete the display.

• COMMENTS • The quality varies widely; the installation is adequate. About half the collection is apt to be on view, and the exhibition is changed once a year. A few postcards are available. The treasure house is worth visiting as much for the beauty of its setting as for the collection.

93. Kurashiki Archaeological Museum (Kurashiki Kokokan), 1015 Maegami-cho, Kurashiki, Okayama-ken. Tel. Kurashiki 22-1542.

倉敷考古館　岡山県倉敷市前神町 1015 番地

Director: Kesshin Takeuchi. **Hours:** 9–4; closed Mon., Mar. 23, Apr. 29, Sept. 23, and Dec. 30–Jan. 4. **Adm.:** ¥50. **Route:** Walk straight ahead from station and turn left just before the International Hotel. Follow this street, which is soon bordered on the left by a canal. The museum, one of the converted Edo-period godowns in this section of Kurashiki, is on the left side of the canal, just as the canal bends to the right, and is reached by an arched bridge.

An interesting medium-sized collection of Chinese and Japanese archaeology, plus some Gandhara heads and pieces of pre-Columbian pottery from Peru. The Chinese section has two neolithic painted pottery vessels, a variety of Han pottery grave figurines and other objects (the majority of them with a green glaze), a Han stone tomb slab, a number of T'ang grave figurines and pottery vessels, a stone head of a Buddha from Lung-men, and small steles from the Northern Wei through the T'ang dynasty. The earliest Japanese artifacts are stone tools from the neolithic period. These are followed by a few Jomon wares of the early, middle, and late periods and shell and cylindrical stone ornaments. From the Yayoi period come a *dotaku,* swords, spearheads and arrowheads, and considerable pottery. The Kofun period is represented by *haniwa,* iron swords, mirrors, large and small Sue and Haji vessels, a coffin, *magatama,* and bracelets. All these objects have been excavated from recorded sites in the vicinity.

In the small early-Buddhist section are pottery sutra cases, tiles, a mortuary urn, and other mortuary vessels.

· COMMENTS · The quality is good; the display is adequate, with a few brief labels in English. About half the collection is normally on view, and the exhibition sometimes changes. There is an illustrated pamphlet in Japanese. The museum is a worthy member of the group of institutions centered in this part of town.

94. Kurashiki Folk Art Museum (Kurashiki Mingeikan), Maegami-cho, Kurashiki, Okayama-ken. Tel. Kurashiki 22-1637.

倉敷民芸館　岡山県倉敷市前神町

Director: Kichinosuke Tonomura. **Hours:** 9–4; closed Mon., Mar. 23, Apr. 29, Sept. 23, and Dec. 30–Jan. 4. **Adm.:** ¥50. **Route:** Walk straight ahead from station and turn left just before the International Hotel. Follow this street, which is soon bordered on the left by a canal, until it bends to the right after passing the Ohara Museum (No. 134). The museum, about 20 yards beyond the bend and on the right, is in a series of connected godowns of the Edo period that are grouped around a small courtyard.

A large and important collection of Japanese and Western folk art, the latter including American Indian ceramics and baskets and European peasant ceramics and metalwork.

The museum shows the entire gamut of Japanese folk and peasant arts: glazed and unglazed pottery bowls, jars, braziers (some old, some by contemporary potters working in the folk tradition); a large variety of textiles; objects made of bamboo and bamboo leaf; lamps; smoking and kitchen utensils; wooden tables, chests, and lunch boxes; lacquered vessels; Ainu clothing; straw raincoats, hats, and snowboots; baskets of straw and reed; oiled-paper umbrellas; samples of paper. The objects come from all regions of Japan and from the Ryukyu Islands. Several rooms are fitted up with furniture, one with a spinning wheel and loom, another with a hearth and its kettles from a farmhouse.

There are also some Chinese and Korean ceramics and bamboo objects from China and Taiwan.

• COMMENTS • The quality is very good. The installation is charmingly and instructively arranged, with some English labels to describe the Western material. The collection has about 8,000 items, of which about ten percent are on view at any one time. Sixty percent of the exhibit is changed four times a year. There is an illustrated folder in Japanese. The museum is well worth visiting.

95. **Kushiro Municipal Museum** (Kushiro Shiritsu Kyodo Hakubutsukan), 3 Tsurugadai Koen, Kushiro, Hokkaido. Tel. Kushiro 2-5809.

釧路市立郷土博物館　釧路市鶴ケ岱公園3番地

Director: Hiroyuki Masatomi. **Hours:** 10–5; closed Mon. and Dec. 29–Jan. 4. **Adm.:** ¥20. **Route:** The museum, a two-story ferroconcrete building in Western style, is on the edge of Tsurugadai Park. Take Harutori line bus via Shiroyama and get off at Hakubutsukan-dori, the stop near the entrance to the park.

A large collection of Ainu material and a considerable group of local archaeological objects, housed on the ground floor of the museum. The archaeology, from local sites, is shown in rooms to the left of the entrance. The display pieces are mostly Jomon-ware vessels, many fragmentary, and some stone implements.

The Ainu material, shown to the right of the entrance, is very extensive. Among the articles of clothing are coats with the characteristic Ainu decoration, straw sandals, and leather boots. The utensils include lacquer bowls, pitchers, and boxes; pot holders; libation wands; and tobacco pouches and pipes. There are also swords, bows and arrows, quivers, and a large variety of jewelry, including many necklaces with metal roundels. The cult objects include *inau* and accessories for the bear ceremony; there is also a scroll depicting this ceremony. A loom, a wooden boat, models of houses, and photographs of Ainu life complete the display.

Part of the museum is occupied by a large natural-history collection.

• COMMENTS • The quality is good, the display adequate.

There are some 20,000 items in the collection, of which five percent are on view at any one time. The exhibit is changed about once every two or three years, the change usually being made to accommodate new archaeological material, as the museum continues to excavate. There is no pamphlet, but the monthly bulletin, in Japanese, contains much information on the collections. The museum is of interest to the specialist in either archaeology or the culture of the Ainu.

96. Kyoto City Art Museum (Kyoto-shi Bijutsukan), Okazaki Koen, Sakyo-ku, Kyoto. Tel. Kyoto 77-4107.

京都市美術館　京都市左京区岡崎公園

Director: Michio Shige. **Hours:** 9–5; closed Dec. 28–Jan. 1. **Adm.:** depends on exhibition. **Route:** The museum, a large brick building, is in the southeast corner of Okazaki Park, which lies in the eastern section of the city and is best known as the site of the Heian Shrine. Take tram No. 6 from the station and get off at Higashiyama Niomon; walk right (east) for about 250 yards to the entrance to the park. The museum is on the right.

This is primarily an exhibiting center for the shows of the local art societies and traveling exhibitions. For example, in November 1963 it housed two large shows: one of the paintings of Chagall, the other of the work of the Society for the Creation of National Painting. In October 1965 there was the splendid loan show of the objects from the tomb of Tutankhamen.

The museum does, however, own a small group of contemporary Japanese paintings in both the Western and the Japanese manner, some Japanese sculpture and handicrafts, and a few contemporary Western paintings. The Japanese paintings predominate.

· COMMENTS · The permanent collection is seldom on view. The building is reasonably adapted to the demands of the constantly changing exhibits.

97. Kyoto National Museum (Kyoto Kokuritsu Haku-butsukan), Higashiyama Shichijo, Higashiyama-ku, Kyoto. Tel. Kyoto 56-0054.

京都国立博物館　京都市東山区東山七条

Director: Zenryu Tsukamoto. **Hours:** 9–4:30, weekdays; 9–5, Sun. and holidays (no admission during last ½ hr.); closed Mon., New Year season, and when exhibition is being changed. **Adm.:** ¥50 (¥150 for special exhibitions). **Route:** The museum is in the southeastern section of the main part of the city. Take any tram from the station, get off at the first stop, change to tram No. 8 eastbound, and get off at Higashi-yama Shichijo. The collections are housed in a large new building, set well back from the street.

This museum, like the one in Nara, was built to preserve and exhibit the art objects owned by the temples in the region. It now contains some 1,200 items on loan from temples, plus another 2,000 from private collectors; about two-thirds of this material is on more or less permanent deposit, with the balance on short-term loans. The museum has also built up a collection of its own and now has about 2,000 pieces, of which some 1,300 are occasionally on display; the remainder are never on view, usually because of their fragile condition. Given the special nature of this museum, it is impossible to predict in any detail what may be on view at any time, but almost any exhibition will be made up of material on loan and the items belonging to the museum.

The material on loan includes very fine early Japanese Buddhist paintings, narrative scrolls of the Heian and Kamakura periods, all forms of Japanese painting from the Muromachi through the Edo period, Chinese paintings, Japanese and Chinese calligraphy, some superb Japanese Buddhist sculpture, an excellent array of Japanese archae-ology, and good examples of Japanese metalwork, lacquer, ceramics, Noh robes, and kimono. There are also Chinese ceramics and some Chinese bronzes and sculpture.

One of the most important Japanese paintings owned by the museum is a Heian *senzui byobu* (landscape screen) of the 11th century, used in the initiation ritual of the Esoteric Buddhist sect. There are also a 12th-century album of cal-ligraphy containing fragments of poems by several of the Thirty-six Poets and excerpts from the *Kokinwakashu* and the *Man'yoshu*. From the same period comes a scroll of the

Gaki Zoshi, while a Yamahara *mandara* dates from the 13th century, as does another scroll, the *Kuge Retsuei Zukan* (Portraits of Courtiers). Sesshu's famous landscape of Ama no Hashidate is here, as well as a painting of birds and flowers by Shokei, and a 17th-century screen of willows and a bridge. An interesting scroll of sketches is by Tan'yu.

The museum also owns a considerable group of late Chinese paintings—works by Ch'en Shun, T'ang Yin, and Wen Pi of the Ming dynasty and by the four Wangs, Wu Li, and Yun Shou-p'ing of the Ch'ing dynasty—as well as many examples of Ch'ing calligraphy. In addition, there is a good selection of Chinese ceramics from the neolithic period through the Ming dynasty, including a piece of 10th-century Yueh ware that was excavated at Uji.

In the Japanese section there is much Yayoi pottery and a *dotaku,* Kofun Sue-ware vessels, cinerary urns of the 7th and 8th centuries, Muromachi lacquer writing boxes, and Edo Noh robes and kimono.

The museum also holds a group of Chinese and Japanese sutras that is one of the finest in the world. The Japanese ones date from the Nara through the Kamakura period, and dates ranging from the T'ang through the Yuan dynasty are given to the majority of the Chinese ones.

• COMMENTS • The quality is excellent. Since this guidebook went to press before the collections were moved into the new building (scheduled to open in October 1966), no comment can be made on the actual installation; but a view of the interior in April 1966 showed well-designed cases and pedestals, good lighting, and a generally pleasing background, all of which augured well for a handsome and up-to-date arrangement. The new building also has considerably more space than the old one, making it possible to show more of the collections.

It has been the policy to hold special loan exhibitions in the autumn—in 1963, a large show of Japanese archaeology; in 1964, an exhibition of Noh masks and costumes; in 1965, views of daily life in Kyoto—during which time most of the regular collections, except for the sculpture, were not on view. A small folder in English describes the museum; catalogues of the special exhibitions are available in Japanese.

Specific objects not on display can be seen if proper introductions and advance notice are given.

98. Kyoto Prefectural Exhibition Hall (Kyoto Furitsu Sogo Shiryokan), Hangi-cho, Shimogamo, Sakyo-ku, Kyoto. Tel. Kyoto 78-9101.

京都府立総合資料館　京都市左京区下鴨半木町

Director: Seiichi Nishimura. **Hours:** 9–4:30; closed Mon. and for a week when exhibition is being changed. **Adm.:** depends on exhibition. **Route:** The building, a large new one in the International style, is in the northern part of the city, on the edge of the Botanical Garden. Take the city bus No. 4 and get off at Sogo Shiryokan-mae in Hangi-cho. The entrance to the exhibition gallery is on the north side of the building, facing Kitayama-dori.

A large new building, designed for the study and exhibition of industrial and folk arts and the traditional handicrafts of Kyoto, it contains a library, a lecture hall, a conference room, and a large exhibition hall. Loan exhibitions are held throughout the year, each lasting somewhat over a month. Large special exhibitions take place each spring and autumn. The shows of objects made of wood and bamboo, held in 1965, and of textiles, in 1964, were excellent.

• COMMENTS • The installation is very good. Handsome, well-illustrated catalogues accompany the major exhibitions. The visitor to Kyoto would do well to include this exhibition hall in his itinerary.

99. Kyoto University Faculty of Letters Archaeological Collection (Kyoto Daigaku Bungakubu Chinretsukan), Kyoto Daigaku, Yoshidamoto-machi, Sakyo-ku, Kyoto. Tel. Kyoto 77-8111, ext. 81.

京都大学文学部陳列館　京都市左京区吉田元町　京都大学内

Director: Professor Kyoichi Arimitsu. **Hours:** Open on request. **Adm.:** free. **Route:** Take bus No. 6 to Higashi Ichijo, walk north for half a block and turn into the university campus by the footpath on the right side of the street. Turn left at the first crosswalk. The collection is in a room at the back on the ground floor of the second building on the left. Ask at the office in the left rear corner of this building for someone to open the exhibition room.

A large and very good collection of Chinese, Japanese, and Korean archaeology. There is a good range of Chinese ceramics, from the neolithic age through the T'ang dynasty, as well as of early Chinese bronzes and jades. Particularly of note are the helmet from Anyang, the Han mirrors, and the Shang-dynasty jades. There are also some small pieces of Chinese Buddhist sculpture and a few pieces of Han-dynasty lacquer.

The Jomon pottery runs from the rare earliest period to the final stage, and the Yayoi period is equally well represented with some good *dotaku* and other metal pieces in addition to the pottery. From the Kofun period come some large *haniwa,* Sue-ware vessels, an enormous *magatama,* Chinese mirrors found in tumuli, and many pieces of armor, including that for a horse. Most of the items are from known sites.

From Korea come ceramics and bronzes of the Silla period.

· COMMENTS · The quality is excellent, but no attempt is made at display. All of the collection is visible, if one includes the storage drawers under the cases. Volumes I and III of the illustrated catalogue of the collection are in print, in Japanese and English; volumes II and IV are in preparation. The specialist will find this collection very important.

100. Lake Biwa Cultural Hall (Biwa-ko Bunkakan), Uchidehama, Otsu, Shiga-ken. Tel. Otsu 2-8179.

琵琶湖文化館　滋賀県大津市打出浜

Director: Osamu Fukushima. **Hours:** 9–5. **Adm.:** ¥70. **Route:** The museum, a large new building in pseudo-castle style, is situated on the edge of Lake Biwa, not far from the center of Otsu. On leaving the station of the Keihan Electric Railway, turn left towards the lake, then right on the street running parallel to the shore. The cultural hall is on the left, about 400 yards down the street.

A good collection of Japanese archaeology from local excavations, painting, and sculpture, housed on the three upper floors of the building. (The ground floor contains an aquarium, and there is a handsome botanical garden to the left of the building.)

Among the objects on the first two exhibition floors may be found pottery and stone tools of the Jomon period; Yayoi pottery and *dotaku;* Kofun armor, mirrors, and stone objects for personal adornment; Nara tiles; Nara to Heian pottery vessels (including a sutra box); a small Miroku and a slightly larger Yakushi of the Nara period; wooden Heian and Kamakura sculptures (the Heian figures including a Juichimen Kannon, a Sho Kannon, a Jizo, and a large Yakushi); Heian Bugaku masks; and a Buddhist *mandara* of the Kamakura period. Unusual items are Kamakura figurines of wrestlers and Heian and Kamakura Shinto figures. There are also a few Chinese porcelains and some Japanese ceramics and metalwork (note particularly a fine *keman* and two *keko*).

The third floor is given over to paintings. Among them are a *kakemono* by Yusho; a screen of animals by Togan; scrolls by Hoitsu, Jakuchu, Tsunenobu, and Watanabe Shiko; a pair of flower screens; and an album of scenes from the *Genji Monogatari*, all of the Edo period. There is also some 19th-century calligraphy.

A large gallery for temporary loan shows adjoins the exhibition halls on the first floor.

• COMMENTS • The quality is very good. (The archaeological objects and the paintings of the Edo period belong to the museum; most of the other items are on loan, the sculptures coming from various local temples.) The display is very well arranged. The archaeology and the sculpture are seldom changed; a few of the paintings change every month. There is a brief pamphlet in Japanese. The museum is well worth visiting.

101. Matsumoto Folk Arts Museum (Matsumoto Mingeikan), Shimoganai, Matsumoto, Nagano-ken. Tel. Matsumoto 3-2520 (director's house).

松本民芸館　長野県松本市下金井

Director: Taro Maruyama. **Hours:** 10–4, on 3rd, 13th, and 23rd of every month from Apr. through Oct. **Adm.:** free. **Route:** The museum lies on the eastern outskirts of Matsumoto. Take the bus for Utsukushigahara Onsengo and get off at Shimoganai-guchi. The museum, a small two-story building of the godown type that now seems standard for Japanese folk-art galleries, is within 200 yards of the bus stop.

A good collection of Japanese and Korean folk arts, charmingly installed in an informal manner. There are rubbings of wayside stone images carved in low relief (many of them of Dosojin), a large variety of pottery jars, bowls, and plates (among them, many examples of Shinshu ware), lacquer vessels for household use, iron kettles, lampstands, tobacco pouches, *geta,* cotton garments, and wooden chests (note particularly the fine Korean ones).

• COMMENTS • The quality is good; the display is well done. There is no pamphlet, but No. 142 of *The Mingei,* a monthly publication on folk arts, is devoted to the museum and contains photographs of the display. The museum is one of the best of those devoted to the folk arts.

102. Matsumoto Municipal Museum (Matsumoto Shiritsu Hakubutsukan), 3-chome, Ninomaru-machi, Matsumoto, Nagano-ken. Tel. Matsumoto 2-0133.

松本市立博物館 長野県松本市二の丸町3丁目
松本市中央公園内

Director: Iwao Tanaka, Chairman of the Board of Education. **Hours:** 8:30–4:30; closed Sun., and Dec. 29–Jan. 3. **Adm.:** ¥30. **Route:** Take bus for Asama Onsen and get off at Oshiro-mae (about 10 min.). The museum, a wooden frame building, is to the right of the entrance to the castle and beside a ferroconcrete godown.

A medium-sized collection consisting largely of Japanese archaeology from local sites, plus some armor, costume accessories, folk arts, and ethnological material. There is also a group of Western-style oil paintings by a local artist, Hakutei Ishii, as well as a natural-history collection, and a group of objects relating to mountaineering.

On the ground floor there are some early-Jomon pieces, quite a number of middle-Jomon pottery vessels, and some Yayoi and a little Kofun pottery. On the upper floor is more Kofun material, including an iron helmet, swords, horse bits, a mirror, and some more pottery. There is also a very fine *kei* (generally kept in the godown) of the Kamakura period. In the same room are several suits of armor of fairly recent date, bows, guns and truncheons, hairpins and combs, *geta,* straw shoes, dolls and other toys, wooden sakè containers, lamps, a spinning wheel, farm implements, tiles from the castle, signboards, and fire-fighting equipment. Of special interest is a fascinating group of carved wooden animals dedicated to a local shrine and a Dosojin.

• COMMENTS • The collection is interesting for its archaeological and ethnological material and is worth visiting if one is in the region. The display, which seldom changes, is old-fashioned but adequate. There are special exhibitions in the spring, summer, and autumn. About ten percent of the archaeological material is normally on view, but items from the collection which are kept in the godown are visible on application to the director.

Note: A new building to house the collection is being planned. Also under the same director is the Nakayama Archaeological Museum (No. 118), 4 miles southeast of Matsumoto. The Matsumoto Castle has been restored and is a very interesting example of the architecture of the Momoyama period.

103. Matsunaga Memorial Hall (Matsunaga Kinen-kan), 943 Itabashi, Odawara, Kanagawa-ken. Tel. Odawara 22-2962.

松永記念館　神奈川県小田原市板橋 943 番地

Director: Ario Saji, Curator. **Hours:** 10–4, for about 1 week in spring and 1 in autumn. The collection can also be seen by special appointment on presentation of proper documents. Telephone the Tokyo branch office (Otemachi Building, Chiyoda-ku, Tokyo; tel. Tokyo 201-7035) for exact details. **Adm.:** free. **Route:** The building lies on the outskirts of the town, well beyond the far, or inland, side of the railway. Take bus No. 7, get off at Itabashi, turn right, and ask for further directions. (It is easier to take a taxi.)

A very distinguished collection of Japanese painting, calligraphy, sculpture, metalwork, ceramics, lacquer, and armor; Chinese bronzes, jades, sculpture, painting, calligraphy, and porcelain; Korean ceramics; and a few examples of Iranian ceramics, Egyptian sculpture, medieval Indian and Gandhara sculpture, and Sassanian silverware.

The earliest Japanese painting is a fragment of the *Inga-kyo* of the Nara period. From the Heian period there is a scroll of the *Hokke-kyo* on fan-shaped paper, a painted wooden panel from the Daigo-ji, Kyoto, portraying the deity Emma, and a very large and very beautiful (and very seldom shown) 11th-century *Kinkan Shutsugen*. The items from the Kamakura period include a section of the *Jigoku Zoshi,* a section of the *Yamai no Soshi,* and a scroll of the *Heike Kindachi Soshi.* A Kasuga *mandara* dates from the late Kamakura or the early Muromachi period. Sesshu is represented by a landscape and a painting of Toshimi. There are a picture of Hotei by the Ashikaga shogun Yoshimochi, a landscape by Kantei, *Hotei Looking at Fighting Cocks* by Niten, and three paintings by Kenzan: *Eggplant, Willows,* and the delicious and often-reproduced *Flower Baskets.*

In the field of Japanese calligraphy there are examples of the writing of the tea master Sen no Rikyu, an introduction to the *Kongo Hannya-kyo* by Kobo Daishi, and a letter by Kokei Sochin. Sotatsu and Koetsu combined their talents for painting and calligraphy in a scroll of rare charm.

The sculpture includes a small seated bronze Kannon of the Asuka period, a Heian Taishakuten, and two Kamakura wooden figures: a Fujin and a Zochoten. Among the pieces of metalwork are an engraved bronze bowl, a sutra box, a *kei,* and a mirror with a design of birds and flowers, all of the Heian period. From the Kamakura period are a mirror with a design of fans and a lovely *keko* used in the Buddhist flower-strewing ceremony. There is also a gilt-metal incense burner, dated 1388, and an Old Ashiya teakettle.

Japanese ceramics are well represented and include pottery vessels of the Yayoi and Kofun periods; a jar and a bottle-shaped vase, both with natural ash glaze and both of the Heian period; a large Tokoname jar and a Seto glazed lion of the Kamakura period; an Old Seto bottle and bowl and a Shigaraki vase and jar, all of the Muromachi period; a Shino tea bowl and jar, a Bizen bowl and water jar, an Oribe square dish and tea bowl of the Momoyama period; a vase by Ninsei, an incense box by Kuchu (the grandson of Koetsu), and examples of Yellow Seto and Iga ware.

The lacquer items include a very delicate Heian tray with designs of birds; a Kamakura mirror box and an incense box, both with mother-of-pearl inlay; a lacquer tray (Momoyama or early Edo); and pieces of Negoro lacquer.

In the textile field are an embroidered hanging from the Horyu-ji showing *tennin* and a *kesa* from the end of the Muromachi or the beginning of the Momoyama period. Pieces of a boy's suit of armor are dated late Kamakura.

The Chinese section, though smaller, is equally fine. Among the bronzes are a *yu,* a *chueh,* and a *kuang* in the shape of a bovine animal, all of the Yin dynasty, a *kuei* of the middle Chou period, and a Han-dynasty *lien* of bronze inlaid with designs in gold. There is also a Yin jade dagger-axe, a *tou* in white pottery, and a *ts'ung* in white marble. A stone lion dates from the Six Dynasties and a stone bas-relief from the Han dynasty. A small stele is dated A.D. 557. Among the paintings are a *kakemono* by the Sung artist Mu Ch'i portraying the sixth Zen patriarch, Hui Neng; a very amusing figure painting by Liang K'ai; and *Rocks and Iris* by the Yuan artist Po Tzu-t'ing. Examples of calligraphy are from the Sung and Yuan dynasties. The ceramics include a Ju bowl and a celadon vase, both Sung, and several Ming pieces in underglaze blue and five-color overglaze enamel.

Korean celadons are represented by a vase and a bowl of the Koryo period, both with inlaid designs, and a "named" tea bowl from the early Yi dynasty.

• COMMENTS • The quality is excellent, the display good. Ten to twenty percent of the collection is visible at any one time, and completely illustrated pamphlets or catalogues, in Japanese only, accompany each exhibition.

104. Matsushima Museum, Kanrantei (Matsushima Hakubutsukan, Kanrantei), Matsushima-machi, Matsushima, Miyagi-ken. Tel. Matsushima 245.

松島博物館　観瀾亭　宮城県松島市松島町

Director: Under direction of Matsushima Tourist Association. **Hours:** 8 to about 5, closing time depending on the daylight. **Adm.:** ¥40. **Route:** Turn left on the main road. The entrance to the Kanrantei is just after the Park Hotel, on the right. The museum, a pleasant one-room building in contemporary Japanese style, adjoins the temple.

A collection consisting of some of the possessions of the Date family (the famous daimyo of Sendai), some archaeological material lent by Tohoku University, and a very complete representation of local marine shells.

Among the items belonging to the Date family (all of the Edo period, and giving an excellent idea of the possessions of a daimyo and his retainers) are lacquer vessels, tobacco sets, toilet sets, fans, *inro, netsuke,* painted shells for the game of matching shells, long-sleeved kimono, armor, stirrups, and spears (both for ceremonial use and for warfare). The archaeology consists of a case with pieces of Jomon pottery, bone implements, and bracelets. The marine shells are displayed in cases in the center of the room, and there is also a relief map of the region.

• COMMENTS • The quality is good, and the items are adequately displayed, with some scanty English labels. As of November 1964 about eighty percent of the Date collection was on view, and the exhibition does not change. The remaining objects—paintings and armor—will be shown when an extension to the museum is completed. There is an illustrated folder in Japanese.

Note: The Kanrantei (Wave Viewing House), a charming pavilion with screens attributed to Kano Sanraku, stands on a cliff overlooking the bay, just beyond the museum. It was a gift from Hideyoshi to Date Masamune, the founder of the Date family, and was moved from Hideyoshi's castle at Fushimi (in Kyoto) to Edo and then to its present site. It has been listed as housing the Date family possessions, but this collection is now in the above museum.

105. Matsuura Historical Museum (Matsuura Shiryo Hakubutsukan), 12 Kagamigawa-machi, Hirado, Nagasaki-ken. Tel. Hirado 2792.

松浦史料博物館　長崎県平戸市鏡川町 12 番地

Director: Ichiro Shiraishi. **Hours:** 9–4, winter; 9–5, summer; closed Dec. 29–Jan. 1. **Adm.:** ¥50. **Route:** The island of Hirado is 15 min. by ferry from Hiradoguchi on Kyushu. From ferry landing, walk left, then turn right on the second paved street; this brings one almost at once to the stairway leading up to the museum, which is in front of the gate at the top of the stairs.

A fascinating collection of about 5,000 items, including arms and armor, household objects, paintings, calligraphy, and ceramics, plus a group of some 25,000 documents, all once the property of the Matsuura family, the daimyo of Hirado. Given to the museum by the family, the collection is now housed in part of their former residence.

In the arms and armor section are banners, standards, war fans and drums, as well as swords, armor, guns, and cannon. The household objects of lacquer include an enormous service of bowls, dishes, and tables of the early 19th century in addition to a mirror stand, jewel boxes, *tebako,* clothes racks, and bookshelves. An especially charming item is the lacquer box for the volumes of the *Genji Monogatari.* There is also a collection of clothing and a set of early-19th-century dolls representing the twelve signs of the zodiac. A screen with lions in black on a gold ground is attributed to Kano Tan'yu. The ceramics include good pieces, mostly blue-and-white or white only, of the early Hirado wares (Nakano and Mikawachi), as well as Chinese blue-and-white of the Ch'ing dynasty and 17th- and 18th-century Dutch ceramics and glass.

For the Westerner, one of the most interesting parts of the exhibition is that relating to the early foreign trade of this area. There is a long scroll with pictures of Dutch ships dated 1795; another, of 1789, showing the Dutch establishment at Deshima; and a third, of 1808, showing the Chinese merchants in their establishments at Nagasaki. Figureheads from 17th-century European ships and celestial and terrestrial globes are, for Japan, unique items.

The documents include directives of the emperor Godaigo and others, but the main part of the large collection deals with the history of Hirado and its foreign trade.

• COMMENTS • The quality is good and the display well arranged, with some labels in English. There are generally about 400 items on view, and changes are made in the exhibits every two months. There is a pamphlet in Japanese, with a little English. The museum is very interesting.

106. Meiji University Archaeological Collection

(Meiji Daigaku Kokogaku Chinretsukan), Meiji Daigaku, 1-chome, Surugadai, Kanda, Chiyoda-ku, Tokyo, Tel. Tokyo 291-9474.

明治大学考古学陳列館　東京都千代田区神田駿河台１丁目
明治大学内

Director: Sosuke Sugihara. **Hours:** 10–5; closed Sun., all Jul. and Aug., and Dec. 27–Jan. 7. **Adm.:** free. **Route:** Take Chuo line from Tokyo Central Station to Ochanomizu. Leave by west exit and turn left. Enter the first gate of the old-fashioned building in the third block on the right and climb to the third floor. The museum is in the north wing of the building, facing the street.

A very good collection of Chinese and Japanese archaeological objects, with a few prehistoric pieces from the West.

The Chinese items date from the prehistoric period to the T'ang dynasty, and the Japanese from the pre-Jomon to the Kofun period. The major part of the Japanese objects were excavated by members of the university's archaeological staff.

The Chinese section contains pottery jars of the Yang-Shao neolithic culture; early Chinese stone implements from the sites of Chou-k'ou-tien (where Peking man was found) and Ting-ts'un; oracle bones from Hsiao-t'un at Anyang; several fine Yin-dynasty bronze vessels; a good middle-Chou tripod; Warring States vessels, chariot fittings, and weapons; Han pottery jars; tomb figurines from the Han to the T'ang dynasty; Han jades; and a good series of mirrors dating from the Warring States period to the Han dynasty.

From the Japanese pre-Jomon period are chipped stone implements. A fine series of pottery vases from all stages, several very interesting figures, ornaments, a clay object shaped like a tortoise, and a stone tablet give an excellent picture of the Jomon culture. Jomon stone implements are matched by rather similar polished tools from the West. The changes in the Yayoi pottery as it advanced from the early to the middle and late periods are well shown in a series of jars (note the large funerary jars with tall, occasionally bulbous necks). There are also Yayoi stone implements, ornaments, bronze swords, and large *dotaku*. These are followed by more pottery jars of the Kofun period, bronze mirrors (one with bells attached to the rim), weapons, stone and metal ornaments, an iron helmet and an iron cuirass, and good *haniwa* of men, horses, and a house. The Korean items include fragments of painted lacquer from Lo-lang. A special feature of the exhibition are models of Japanese tombs and photographs of excavation sites.

· COMMENTS · The quality is excellent, the display quite adequate, and the labels complete, though in Japanese only. About ten percent of the material is normally on view. The exhibition changes in part when newly excavated material is added. There is an illustrated handbook in Japanese.

Note: The collections are to be moved to quarters on the second floor of a newer building diagonally across the street from the south corner of the present building.

A PORTFOLIO OF
REPRESENTATIVE JAPANESE MUSEUMS

Kumamoto Municipal Museum, Kumamoto Castle, Kumamoto City

Nagasaki Prefectural
Art Museum,
Nagasaki

Hoppo Bunka Museum, Yokogoshi Village, Niigata Prefecture

To-ji Treasure House, Kyoto

Ryokan Memorial Collection, Izumozaki, Niigata Prefecture

Neiraku Museum, Nara

Sanuki Folk Art Museum, Takamatsu, Kagawa Prefecture

Ohara New Art Museum,
Kurashiki, Okayama Prefecture

Kanagawa Prefectural Museum of Modern Art, Kamakura

Yamato Bunkakan, Nara

Izumo Taisha Treasure House,
Taisha-machi, Shimane Prefecture

Kurashiki Folk Art Museum, Kurashiki, Okayama Prefecture

Goto Art Museum, Tokyo

Shimane Prefectural Museum, Matsue, Shimane Prefecture

Oyamazumi-jinja Treasure House,
Omishima Ehime Prefecture

Kurashiki Archaeological Museum, Kurashiki, Okayama Prefecture

Okayama Art Museum, Okayama City

Ishikawa Prefectural Art Museum, Kanazawa

Hatakeyama Museum, Tokyo

Gallery of Horyu-ji Treasures, Tokyo National Museum

107. Mie Prefectural Museum (Mie Kenritsu Haku-butsukan), Komyo-cho, Tsu, Mie-ken. Tel. Tsu 8-2283.

三重県立博物館　三重県津市広明町

Director: Hiroshi Matsushima. **Hours:** 9–4:30; closed Mon., national holidays, end of month, and Dec. 29–Jan. 3. **Adm.:** ¥50. **Route:** On leaving the station, turn right, then take the second street on the left. The museum, a fairly large Western-style building, is at the end of the street, on the edge of Kairaku Park (10 min.).

The small collection consists of paintings of the Edo period by local artists; Yayoi and Kofun pottery from local excavations; lacquer, masks, armor, swords, and sword fittings; and folk objects, chiefly Ainu, and Okinawan fishing and agricultural implements.

• COMMENTS • The quality is fair, the display adequate. As all the galleries are apt to be used for some temporary exhibition, such as that of contemporary painting from Mie Prefecture, the permanent collections are frequently off view. The museum is of interest only to the specialist in the archaeology of the locality (the excavations continue) or in the local paintings of the Edo period.

108. Mitsukuni and Nariaki Tokugawa Memorial Collection (Mitsukuni Nariaki Tokugawa Giretsukan), Tokiwa Koen, Mito, Ibaraki-ken. Tel. Mito 2-3586.

光圀斉修徳川義烈館　茨城県水戸市常磐公園

Director: Noriyuki Kashima. **Hours:** 8–4:30, Mar.–Oct.; 9–4, Nov.–Feb. **Adm.:** ¥30. **Route:** Take bus to Tokiwa Koen, the terminus of the line. The museum, a medium-sized Japanese-style building, is to the right of the newly built Shinto shrine which stands in the center of the park.

An interesting collection of the possessions of the Mito branch of the Tokugawa family. As the name of the museum indicates, the objects are largely those belonging to Mitsukuni, the second daimyo of Mito, and Nariaki, the ninth daimyo. Generally on view are a portrait of Mitsukuni, a painting by him, examples of his calligraphy, a copy of his history of Japan, some of his clothes, and 17th-century Dutch and German books from his library. From Nariaki's

113

hand are many charming paintings, calligraphy and even some tea bowls. His pipes, pistols, palanquin, and other personal belongings are also on display, as well as a photograph of him. The collection further includes a painting by the fourth daimyo, Munetaka, and calligraphy by the fifth and tenth daimyo, Munemoto and Yoshiatsu, as well as swords, armor, saddles and stirrups, storage chests, writing boxes, lacquer bowls, and the like. There are also contemporary paintings of Commodore Perry and his "black ships."

· COMMENTS · The quality is very good, the display adequate. Thirty percent of the collection is normally on view, while special shows are arranged two or three times a year. There is a brief leaflet in Japanese. The exhibition gives a fascinating idea of the life and tastes of this distinguished ruling family.

109. Miyazaki Prefectural Museum (Miyazaki Kenritsu Hakubutsukan), Higashi Shin'en, Jingu-machi, Miyazaki, Miyazaki-ken. Tel. Miyazaki 3-2738.

宮崎県立博物館　宮崎市神宮町　東神苑内

Director: Kokichi Yanagi. **Hours:** 9–4:30, closed Mon., first day of every month, national holidays, and New Year season. **Adm.:** ¥20. **Route:** The museum is in the precincts of the Miyazaki Shrine, in the northern part of the city. Take local train from main station to the Miyazaki-jingu stop; then walk straight ahead for 4 blocks to the east entrance of the shrine precincts. The museum, a large E-shaped building of ferroconcrete, is near the entrance. (From the main, or south, gate the museum is to the right of the walk leading to the shrine.) A taxi from the center of Miyazaki takes about 10 min.

An excellent collection of archaeological material plus a small group of local fine arts and historical objects.

The extensive archaeological finds, all from local sites, are shown in the galleries to the right of the entrance. From the Jomon period are many chipped and polished stone tools, stone arrowheads, pottery vessels (many of which are fragmentary), and some figurines. The Yayoi period is represented by polished stone implements, bronze arrowheads and spearheads, and a variety of pottery vessels. The

Kofun objects include *magatama,* tube-shaped beads, good bronze mirrors, Sue and Haji pottery vessels (the large Sue-ware pieces, showing traces of glaze, are very good), a few *haniwa,* swords (a Chinese sword of the Han dynasty is shown for comparison), harness trappings, and fragments of body armor and helmets. An excellent feature of the exhibition are the models of various tumuli.

The fine arts and historical sections occupy the left wing. Among the items usually on display are armor from the Shimazu family (the daimyo of Satsuma); 17th-century swords by Kunihiro, Kunisada, and Shinkai; samples of local pottery from the Maruyama, Komine, and Wakimoto kilns; Nara tiles; a Heian sutra box; a painting by Tamon of a country scene; and a scroll of the Edo period depicting the Mongol invasion.

• COMMENTS • The quality of the archaeological material is excellent; the other objects have a certain interest. The display is adequate. There are a brief illustrated pamphlet and a more complete illustrated booklet, both in Japanese. About one-fifth of the 5,000 pieces in the archaeological collection, including most of the important objects, is on display. Some changes in the exhibition are made during the year, and in the spring and autumn special loan shows are held.

Note: A number of the Jomon objects and all the large *haniwa* figures and models of houses are reproductions.

110. Morioka City Local History Hall (Morioka-shi Kyodo Shiryokan), 14, 1-chome, Atago-cho, Morioka, Iwate-ken. Tel. Morioka 2-6738; 2-9682.

盛岡市郷土史料館　岩手県盛岡市愛宕町 1 丁目 14 番地

Director: Under direction of Morioka Board of Education. **Hours:** 9–4:30; closed Mon., last day of month, national holidays, and Dec. 29–Jan. 3. **Adm.:** ¥20. **Route:** The museum, a large converted go-down, is in the grounds of the park that also contains the Morioka Kominkan (Citizens' Hall). Take bus for Yamakabashi and get off at Kominkan-mae. Walk ahead to the first entrance on the left leading into the park. The museum is the first building on the left.

An interesting collection of archaeology; local folk arts,

ironwork, and pottery; and objects belonging to the Nambu family, the former daimyo of Morioka.

The archaeology consists of a few middle-Jomon pottery vessels, two small figurines, stone tools, a huge Sue-ware jar, and an equally large jar of the Heian period. Among the Nambu family possessions are a lady's lacquered palanquin, a letter from Hideyoshi, and some scientific instruments. There are also suits of armor, headrests, lamps, a lacquered box holding shells for the game of matching shells, and weapons. An item of particular interest is a scroll of the *Chusonji-kyo* of the Heian period, in gold on dark-blue paper.

The folk arts include baskets, hats, shoes, and raincoats—all of straw—farm tools, cooking utensils, wooden chests, a loom, and spinning wheels. The local products on view are Morioka iron teakettles *(nambu tetsubin)* and a sampling of ceramics from Iwate Prefecture.

• COMMENTS • The quality is good of its kind, and the installation adequate though at times crowded. The exhibition does not change. There is an illustrated pamphlet in Japanese. The collection is worth seeing if one is in the vicinity.

111. Musashino Local Museum (Musashino Kyodo-kan), Koganei Koen, Koganei-shi, Tokyo. Tel. Koganei 8-1336.

武蔵野郷土館　東京都小金井市小金井公園

Director: Yasuhiko Makino. **Hours:** 9–4:30; closed Dec. 29–Jan. 1. **Adm.:** ￥20. **Route:** Take national railways Chuo line from Shinjuku station to Musashi Koganei and then a red bus bound for Amitaka. Get off at Koganei Koen-mae. The museum is in a large temple building in the park, approached by a broad road leading at right angles away from the bus stop.

A rather large collection mainly of local archaeology and local folk arts. The archaeological display opens with dioramas illustrating local life from prehistoric times through the Kofun period. This is followed by an exhibition of chipped stone implements and good examples of Jomon pottery vessels of all periods. To be noted are the pointed vessels of the earliest Jomon period and the elaborate vessels from Hachioji of the middle Jomon period. There are also a reconstructed shell-mound burial, bone objects from the Shomyoji shell mound (Yokohama), and pottery figurines from the Hirohata shell mound in Ibaraki Prefecture.

From the Yayoi period are pottery vessels (Asakayama Koen, Tokyo) and polished stone implements. The Kofun period is represented by *haniwa* of a horse and a sword in its scabbard, Sue-ware vessels (some with traces of ash glaze), and *magatama*. Charts, diagrams, and photographs of the excavations supplement the archaeological section.

Pottery roof tiles of the Nara period, many with names impressed on them, come from the nearby site of Kokubunji.

A figure of Shaka is assigned to the Nara period, while large pottery burial jars date from the Heian to the Muromachi period. There are small fragments of Chinese celadon of the Sung dynasty from the site of Hachioji Castle, sutra boxes from the pagoda of the Tenno-ji in Tokyo (which burned down in 1957), and Edo-period scrolls of religious festivals.

The folk-art section contains all the usual household utensils and farm tools, prints depicting trades and professions, and a large number of interesting *ema*.

In the grounds behind the museum are models of houses of the Jomon, Yayoi, Kofun, and Nara periods, a Kofun mound, and a farmhouse and water mill of the Edo period.

• COMMENTS • The quality is good, the display fair. There is a short guidebook, in Japanese but with English captions to the illustrations. All the objects are normally on view. The specialist in archaeology or folk arts will find the museum worth a visit.

112. Museum of Calligraphy (Shodo Hakubutsukan), 125 Negishi-cho, Ueno, Taito-ku, Tokyo. Tel. none.

書道博物館　東京都台東区上野根岸町 125 番地

Director: Heigoro Nakamura, owner. **Hours:** 10–4; closed Mon. and New Year season. **Adm.:** ¥100. **Route:** Take Yamate line to Uguisudani, the first stop beyond Ueno. The museum, a small two-story building on the grounds of a private house, is not far from the station but can be found only by diligent inquiry.

A small collection (made by the father of the present owner) of pottery, bronzes, jades, mirrors, swords, oracle bones, sculpture, stone steles, stone and pottery slabs, coins, rubbings, inkstones, ink sticks, seals, and brushes. It also includes a wooden stupa and prayer sheets from the Horyu-ji. Almost all the objects have inscriptions of some kind and were brought together to illustrate the history of calligraphy. The majority of the pieces are Chinese, the remainder Japanese.

The Chinese bronze vessels and the jades date from the Chou to the Han dynasty; the mirrors date from the period of the Warring States to the T'ang dynasty; and the weapons, from the period of the Warring States to the Han dynasty. Among the pieces of Chinese sculpture are a small gilt-bronze Buddha seated against a *mandorla* and dated 489 and a Maitreya in white marble dated 544.

• COMMENTS • The display is very crowded, and there are almost no labels. About fifty percent of the collection is normally visible. There is a catalogue of the collection, in Japanese and without illustrations. The museum contains no great display pieces, but its scope is unique, and hence it has considerable interest for the specialist.

113. Nagaoka Contemporary Art Museum (Nagaoka Gendai Bijutsukan), 2-chome, Sakanoue-machi, Nagaoka, Niigata-ken. Tel. Nagaoka 2-4467.

長岡現代美術館　新潟県長岡市坂の上町２丁目

Director: Jukichi Komagata. **Hours:** 10–5; closed Jan. 1–3. **Adm.:** ¥50. **Route:** Walk down the main street leading away from the station, turn right on the fourth cross street and enter the first office building on the left. The museum is on the ground floor, to the right of the entrance.

The collection, in the autumn of 1965, consisted of some 110 paintings in the Japanese style, about 200 oils by contemporary Japanese and Western artists, and a few prints. It is housed in a new museum, founded in 1964, which has a single well-designed and well-lighted gallery.

Shotaro Koyama, Shigeru Aoki, Chu Asai, and Tetsugoro Yorozu are among the older Japanese artists whose works are in the collection. Kazu Wakita, Sue Ono, Takashi Asada, Yoshishige Saito, Josaku Maeda, and Sadamasa Motonaga are a few of the present-day artists whose paintings have been purchased. The foreign artists represented include Hundertwasser, Miró, Léger, Picasso, Tamayo, and Zao Wu Ki.

The museum holds six shows a year; two or three of these contain some loan material, but otherwise the exhibition consists of the museum's collection. About 35 paintings are shown at any one time.

• COMMENTS • The quality, as in any contemporary collection, varies. The display is very well done. Catalogues or check lists accompany some of the shows and are in Japanese, though some of the artists' names are also given in English. The museum is a good example of the lively interest in contemporary art in Japan. Anyone in the region will find it worth a visit.

114. Nagaoka Municipal Natural Science Museum
(Nagaoka Shiritsu Kagaku Hakubutsukan), Yukyuzan Koen, Nagaoka, Niigata-ken. Tel. Nagaoka 2-0184.

長岡市立科学博物館　新潟県長岡市　悠久山公園内

Director: Goro Koshiba. **Hours:** 9–5, Apr.–Nov.; 9–4, Dec.–Mar.; closed Dec. 29–Jan. 3. **Adm.:** ¥30. **Route:** Take bus to the end of the line, Yukyuzan Koen (20 min.). Then, keeping the sports ground on the left, walk forward under a *torii* and uphill to a shrine, behind which lies the museum, a one-story frame building standing in an open space (about 10 min.). Signs in Japanese point the way. By taxi, one can go directly to the museum in about 20 min.

A good collection of local archaeology, housed in the rear room of a building otherwise devoted to natural history and science. It opens with an extensive group of early-Jomon chipped-stone implements and pottery, many of the finds coming from Senryu-ji and the Muroya cave. It then shows a superb group of middle-Jomon vessels and small figurines from Umataka. One vessel is a particularly splendid example of the type known informally as *kaen-toki* or "flame" ware. There is also a considerable amount of late-Jomon pottery and stone implements and a small number of vessels from the Yayoi period. Photographs and maps of the sites accompany the display.

• COMMENTS • The quality varies from good to excellent; the display is adequate. Twenty percent of the material is normally on view, and changes are made once a year in the exhibition. There is no pamphlet, but the museum is described in the illustrated guide to Niigata Prefecture put out by the Niigata Prefectural Museum Association. Those interested in Japanese archaeology will find the museum well worth a visit.

Note: The folk material relating to the local "snow culture," now in the Sekisetsu Kagakukan in the grounds of the Department of Engineering of Niigata University, will be transferred to this museum in the near future.

115. Nagasaki Municipal Museum (Nagasaki Shiritsu Hakubutsukan), Nagasaki Kokusai Bunkakan, 7-chome, Hirano-machi, Nagasaki, Nagasaki-ken. Tel. Nagasaki 4-0990.

長崎市立博物館　長崎市平野町 7 丁目　長崎国際文化館内

Director: Tsuneoki Ikematsu. **Hours:** 9–5. **Adm.:** ¥20 to Kokusai Bunkakan; adm. to museum depends on exhibition. **Route:** Take bus or tram for Nishi-machi; get off at Hamaguchi-machi (about 20 min.), cross the street, and walk along the road leading uphill to the six-story building of the Kokusai Bunkakan, which crowns the small hill. The museum occupies the third and fourth floors.

This museum owns some 200 relics of the early Christians of Nagasaki, thousands of documents referring to the Dutch and Chinese trade of the Edo period, and a very large group of Japanese paintings of which about 100 are oils and the remainder are of the Nagasaki school. There are also some Chinese paintings of the Ch'ing dynasty. However, the Christian relics are now kept at the prefectural library, and only a very few documents and paintings are ever shown, since the strong daylight in the galleries is unsuitable for such material. The objects in storage may be seen on request.

• COMMENTS • There are no outstanding works among the paintings, but the group as a whole is most interesting, particularly to the specialist. The display is adequate. A new building is planned to house the museum's collection. The museum holds one special loan exhibition each year.

116. Nagasaki Prefectural Art Museum (Nagasaki Kenritsu Bijutsukan), 2 Tateyama-machi, Nagasaki, Nagasaki-ken. Tel. Nagasaki 2-6700; 3-1883.

長崎県立美術館　長崎市立山町２番地

Director: Tamaki Hirayama. **Hours:** 9–5; closed Mon., Nov. 12, national holidays, and Dec. 28–Jan. 5. **Adm.:** ¥50 (more for special exhibitions). **Route:** Take bus for Shokaku-ji-shita and get off at Shiyakusho-mae (the municipal office); walk forward and take the first street to the left. The museum, a new building in the International style with a bas-relief in cement encircling the upper floor, is a short distance along this street, on the right.

The museum, opened in November 1965, is primarily an exhibiting center. Its own collection, at the inauguration, consisted of a single Japanese oil painting and about a hundred documents connected with Dr. von Siebold (the Dutch physician and surgeon who lived in Nagasaki in the 19th century), the *nanga* school of painting, and the Nagasaki foreign trade.

A new loan exhibition is held every month, generally of contemporary material. The museum hopes to build up a permanent collection in the next few years.

• COMMENTS • The display is well arranged in two rooms on the entrance floor and in the large gallery that occupies the entire upper floor. There is a folder in Japanese.

117. Nagoya Castle Treasure House (Nagoya-jo Homotsukan), 1, 6-chome, Minamisotobori-cho, Naka-ku, Nagoya, Aichi-ken. Tel. Nagoya 231-1700/2700.

名古屋城宝物館　名古屋市中区南外堀町６丁目１番地

Director: Zen'ichi Hasegawa. **Hours:** 9–4:30. **Adm.:** ¥50. **Route:** The museum is in the tallest of the towers that rise above the moat-encircled walls of the Nagoya Castle precincts, which lie northeast of the station. Take bus No. 116 and get off at Seimon-mae, the main gate of the castle.

The collection, which is housed on several floors of the tower (a replica, built in 1959, of the original that was destroyed in World War II), consists in large part of the painted wooden doors and sliding screens taken from the palace which was in the castle precincts and was also destroyed in the war. They are by members of the Kano school and date from the late Momoyama and early Edo periods. The wooden doors include a pair with designs of tigers and another of a flower cart. The sliding screens are mostly in black and white with faint touches of color and include such subjects as Chinese landscapes; fans floating on a stream; birds, flowers, and trees; and the diversions of the common people. A number of the screens have been set up in surroundings approximating their original setting, and they all provide an excellent idea of the Kano school at its best. There are also some roof tiles from the old castle, documents pertaining to the history of the castle, maps, portraits, and costumes.

Some of the space is taken up by temporary loan exhibitions. In the autumn of 1963 there was a show from the Tokugawa Library Collection of Chinese, Japanese, and Korean books, manuscripts, scrolls, and other material to illustrate the history of painting; in the autumn of 1965, a large exhibition of armor and swords.

• COMMENTS • The quality of the painting is excellent. The display is very handsomely arranged (except for the too-bright fluorescent lighting in the bottom of the cases), and the labels, in Japanese and English, are very full. About eighty percent of the collection is normally on view. There are an illustrated folder in English and an illustrated booklet in Japanese.

118. Nakayama Archaeological Museum (Nakayama Kokokan), Torinouchi, Nakayama-ku, Matsumoto, Nagano-ken. Tel. Nakayama 3822 (municipal office).

中山考古館　長野県松本市中山区鳥内

Director: Iwao Tanaka, Chairman, Matsumoto Board of Education. **Hours:** 9–4:30; closed for New Year season. (As it is apt to be shut at any time, it is advisable to telephone before going.) **Adm.:** ¥20. **Route:** Take the bus from Matsumoto station for Nakayama and get off at Kumiai-mae (Agricultural Association Building). Ask for the key to the museum at the Nakayama Municipal Office, which is across the street from the Agricultural Association Building. Walk back along the road towards Matsumoto and take the first fork to the right. The museum, a small white-plastered building, is about 100 yards down this road, on the left-hand side.

The museum, a branch of the Matsumoto Municipal Museum (No. 102), houses archaeological material excavated in the Nakayama area. The collection consists of a few fairly complete pottery vessels, some small figurines, and many fragments, mostly of the middle Jomon period, as well as chipped and polished stone implements and stone vessels. There are also Yayoi pottery jars and stone implements and, from the Kofun period, iron swords, horse bits, arrowheads, *magatama,* and Sue and Haji vessels, both whole and in fragments.

• COMMENTS • The quality is fair to good. Little attempt is made at display, and the scanty labels are in Japanese only. All the objects are on view, and, as the excavations continue, new material is added every so often. There is a pamphlet in Japanese. This museum is for the hardy specialist.

119. Nara National Museum (Nara Kokuritsu Hakubutsukan), 50 Noborioji-cho, Nara, Nara-ken. Tel. Nara 22-7771.

奈良国立博物館　奈良市登大路町 50 番地

Director: Kura Kurata. **Hours:** 9–4:30, Mar.–Oct.; 9–4, Nov.–Feb.; closed 1st and 3rd Mon. each month and for indeterminate periods at unscheduled times when exhibition is being changed. **Adm.:** ¥100.
Route: The museum, built in the Beaux Arts style, stands just inside Nara Park, on the right of the road leading uphill from the station of the Kinki Nihon Electric Railway and beyond the new prefectural offices.

This museum, like the Kyoto National Museum (No. 97), was built more to house and display the works of art belonging to temples and shrines in the Nara area than to exhibit any objects of its own, but it is in process of building up a collection and now owns some 50 paintings and 20 pieces of sculpture. The objects on loan include Buddhist sculpture from the Asuka through the Muromachi period, sutras and *mandara* from the Nara through the Kamakura period, and paintings of Buddhist deities and portraits of priests from the Heian through the Muromachi period. There are also many objects used in the Buddhist rites, as well as sutra boxes, mirrors, *kakebotoke,* and *keman,* chiefly of the Heian and Kamakura periods. An excellent series of roof tiles shows their development from the Asuka to the end of the Heian period. In general, these temple loans are made for three years, and the objects are shown once a year during that time.

Among the paintings owned by the museum are a *Jigoku Zoshi,* a Kasuga no Miya *mandara,* a portrait of the priest Shinran attributed to Joga, and *kakemono* of Buddhist deities, all of the Kamakura period. There is also a charming album of sketches by Chikuden. A seated wooden figure of Yaku-shi Nyorai dates from the Jogan period, and a portrait statue of Enno Gyoja from the Muromachi period. The museum also owns an extraordinary Nara embroidery showing the Buddha preaching, a traveling monk's axe *(nyoho ono)* of the Muromachi period, and Heian mirrors engraved with Buddhist subjects.

· COMMENTS · The quality is superb. The installation is as good as the rather old-fashioned building permits, and on occasion there are a few labels in English. Objects on view are generally changed once a month. There is a special show each autumn, when objects from the Shoso-in occupy all the exhibition space, and another in the spring, usually devoted to some aspect of Buddhist art. These special exhibitions are accompanied by illustrated catalogues in Japanese. There is also an illustrated guidebook in English which gives a brief history of Buddhist art. The percentage of the objects on deposit, as well as of the museum's own possessions, on view at any one time depends on the type of exhibition.

Given the special nature of this museum, it is not possible to provide a detailed account of what the museum may be showing; one can only say that the exhibitions usually contain examples of the best in Japanese art, especially of its Buddhist phase, and should on no account be missed.

120. Naritasan History Hall (Naritasan Shiryokan), Shinsho-ji, Narita, Chiba-ken. Tel. Narita 234.

成田山史料館 千葉県成田市新勝寺

Director: Sadakichi Takada. **Hours:** 9–4; closed Tues.; national holidays; Jul. 7, 8, 9; Aug. 13, 14, 15; and Dec. 25–30. **Adm.:** free. **Route:** Take Keisei line from Ueno station, Tokyo, to Narita (1 hr. by express); then the bus to the terminus of the line at Monzen (10 min.), the entrance to the precincts of the Shinsho-ji. Walk through the temple grounds and climb up the low ridge at the back. The museum, a white Western-style building, is on top of this ridge, to the right. (By taxi, it is 10 min. from Narita station to the museum.)

A collection of local archaeology, *ema,* prints, and folk arts, housed in part of the building.

The archaeological section includes several small figurines, bone and shell ornaments, many chipped and polished stone implements, and pottery vessels of the Jomon period; the Yayoi period is represented by only a few pottery vessels. From the Kofun period there are several good mirrors, *magatama,* tubular beads, a *haniwa* head, a stone headrest, and much Sue ware. There are also Nara tiles and a metal sutra box of the Muromachi period. The *ema,* dating mostly from the 19th century, are large in scale, done on wood, and heavily framed. Fudo saving devotees (Fudo is the patron deity of this temple), actors, horses, birds and flowers, and Chinese figures are among the subjects. Many of the prints, which are also of the 19th century, depict the temple precincts or show Fudo rescuing his believers. Kiyochika, Kunisada, Kuniyoshi, and Toyokuni are among the artists represented. The folk-art section contains farm tools, a loom, spinning wheels, *geta* for use in the rice fields, firemen's clothing, money boxes, and accountants' equipment.

• COMMENTS • The quality of the collection is fair. The display is adequate and is changed once a year. Very little of the archaeological material is on view; about 10 out of the 57 *ema* in the collection are visible and the same number of prints out of a total of 45 items. There is an illustrated booklet on the museum, check lists for the *ema* and the prints, and a catalogue of the archaeology; all are in Japanese only. The collection is of interest to the student of either archaeology or *ema.*

121. Nata-dera Treasure House (Nata-dera Homo-tsukan), Nata-dera, Nata-machi, Awazu, Komatsu, Ishi-kawa-ken. Tel. Awazu 65-1602.

那谷寺宝物館　石川県小松市淡津那谷町　那谷寺内

Director: Chief Priest. **Hours:** 8–5. **Adm.:** ¥100. **Route:** The treasure house is in the precincts of the Nata-dera temple at Nata-machi, some distance inland from Komatsu. Take bus from Komatsu station for Yamanaka Onsen and get off at Nata-dera (35 min. by express bus).

The collection of objects belonging to the temple is to be housed in the handsomely converted attic of the Fumon-kaku, a large 17th-century building that lies just inside the temple grounds to the left of the main entrance.

Among the items in the collection are Buddhist statues of the Heian and Kamakura periods, Kano-school paintings, Chinese porcelains that were the gift of the emperor Gomi-zuno-o, and a large Ming passport consisting of characters embroidered on cloth.

• COMMENTS • In the spring of 1966 no objects were on view, nor was it known when the installation would be finished. The empty room was both unusual architecturally and very handsome and gave every indication of providing a good background for the temple's possessions.

Note: The main floor of the Fumonkaku is used for tea ceremonies.

122. National Museum of Modern Art (Kokuritsu Kindai Bijutsukan), 11, 3-chome, Kyobashi, Chuo-ku, Tokyo. Tel. Tokyo 561-0823.

国立近代美術館　東京都中央区京橋3丁目11番地

Director: Yukio Kobayashi. **Hours:** 10–5; closed Mon., New Year season, and when exhibition is being changed. **Adm.:** depends on exhibition. **Route:** This museum, in the downtown section of Tokyo to the south of Tokyo station, is housed in a ferroconcrete former office building. It is a few doors away from the eastern exit of the Kyobashi subway stop (Ginza line) and near the Kyobashi tram stop.

The largest collection of Japanese contemporary art owned by a public institution. In the spring of 1966 it consisted of about 400 Japanese-style paintings, 350 oil paintings, 100 pieces of sculpture, 600 prints, and a few examples of calligraphy. The museum also owns a collection of handicrafts; these, however, are held by the museum's Kyoto branch (No. 123). Purchasing continues.

The museum is now largely an exhibiting organization for the contemporary art of Japan and holds ten loan shows a year, varying from one-man to group exhibitions and representing all media employed by the present-day artist. In November of 1963, for example, there was an exhibition of the ceramics, lacquer, painting, and calligraphy of the late Rosanjin Kitaoji; in the autumn of 1964, a large retrospective show of modern painting, sculpture, ceramics, lacquer, metalwork, textiles, and objects in wood; and four group shows were among the exhibitions held in 1965.

Pieces from the permanent collection are shown only as the nature of the temporary exhibition of the moment requires. Lack of space makes it impossible to comply with requests to show items not on exhibition.

• COMMENTS • The display is well done, with labels in English. Catalogues of varying elaborateness accompany each show; they are in Japanese, but the introductions and the titles of the objects are in English.

Note: A new building, to be erected in the Takebashi section near the Palace Hotel, has been designed and should be completed in 1968. Half the exhibition space will be for the permanent collection, the other half for loan shows.

123. National Museum of Modern Art, Kyoto Branch
(Kokuritsu Kindai Bijutsukan, Kyoto Bunkan), Okazaki Koen, Ukyo-ku, Kyoto. Tel. Kyoto 77-0070.

国立近代美術館　京都分館　京都市右京区岡崎公園

Director: Atsuo Imaizumi. **Hours:** 10–5; closed Mon. and when new exhibitions are being installed. **Adm.:** ¥50, regular exhibitions; ¥100, special exhibitions. **Route:** The museum is in the southwest corner of Okazaki Park (best known as the site of the Heian Shrine), immediately to the left as one enters the park from the street called Jingu-michi. Take tram No. 6 to Higashiyama Niomon and walk east (right) to the park entrance.

A new and handsome exhibition center with two large well-lighted exhibition floors for displays of Japanese and, occasionally, foreign contemporary art and handicrafts. Ten to twelve exhibitions are held during the year, and each is accompanied by a catalogue, generally in Japanese but with English titles and sometimes English text.

• COMMENTS • The displays are handsomely arranged. The museum is well worth visiting for anyone interested in contemporary Japanese art and handicrafts, both for the quality of the exhibitions and for the architecture of the building itself.

Note: This museum is a branch of the National Museum of Modern Art in Tokyo (No. 122); it has no permanent collection, but it houses the handicrafts belonging to the parent museum.

124. National Museum of Western Art (Kokuritsu Seiyo Bijutsukan), Ueno Koen, Taito-ku, Tokyo, Tel. Tokyo 825-5135.

国立西洋美術館　東京都台東区上野公園

Director: Soichi Tominaga. **Hours:** 9:30–5; closed Mon., Dec. 25–Jan. 5, and when exhibition is being changed. **Adm.:** ¥100. **Route:** The museum is just inside Ueno Park, very near Ueno station on either the national railways or the subway. A very complicated structure designed by Le Corbusier and opened in June 1959, it is the second large building on the right of the main road which enters the park.

A collection of 19th- and 20th-century Western art, largely French. The basis of this collection is the large group (over 400 items) of paintings and sculptures collected by the late Mr. Kojiro Matsukata and retained in France during the last war. These were declared French property by the peace treaty but were subsequently given to Japan by the French government.

Most of the important French artists from the early 19th century to the recent past are represented. There are sketches by Delacroix, landscapes, figure pieces, and still lifes by Courbet, water colors by Cézanne, a large group of paintings by Monet, and a smaller group by Pisarro. Degas, Maurice Denis, Fantin-Latour, Forain, Gauguin, Lépine, Gustave Moreau, Marquet, Monticelli, Renoir, and Signac are each represented by one or more works. Painters well known in their day such as Aman-Jean, Jacques-Emile Blanche, Henner, and Carolus-Duran are also included. A large part of the collection is devoted to works by Rodin, including many of his large bronze figures and figure groups, a few of his marbles, and many of his water colors. There is also a considerable group of bronzes by Bourdelle.

The museum has been adding to its collection since its opening. Bronze figures by Maillol and paintings by Léger and Soutine are among the recent acquisitions.

• COMMENTS • The quality of the works varies. The display is well arranged, with the large sculpture shown outside in the museum grounds. The labels are in Japanese and English. There are two special loan shows a year, lasting from one to two months, which usually occupy all the exhibition space. From two-thirds to three-quarters of the permanent collection is on view between the loan shows, and five or six items are changed each time it is reinstalled. There is a well-illustrated booklet in English and French describing the museum and its collection.

125. Neiraku Museum (Neiraku Bijutsukan), 50 Sui-mon-cho, Nara, Nara-ken. Tel. Nara 22-2173.

寧楽美術館　奈良市水門町 50 番地

Director: Junsuke Nakamura. **Hours:** 10–4, Apr., May, Oct., Nov. (Check before going.) **Adm.:** ¥100. **Route:** Take the street leading up-hill from the Kinki Nihon Railway station. Turn left at the main crossing after the prefectural offices, then right. The entrance to the museum, a Japanese house set in a beautiful garden, is a short distance down the road, on the right just as the road bends left.

A very choice collection of about 200 early Chinese bronzes, mostly of the Yin and Chou dynasties, and about 60 mirrors from the period of the Warring States through the T'ang dynasty. There are also Chinese, Japanese, and Korean ceramics, of which about 150 pieces are Chinese (largely of the Sung dynasty), the same number are Japanese, and about 400 are Korean of the Koryo and Yi dynasties.

Nearly every type of bronze vessel known to the Yin dynasty is represented. There are two large *lei,* a variety of *ting* and *li,* a *yen,* and several *chueh.* A number of these pieces are inscribed. There are also two bells of the Chou dynasty, with long inscriptions, and a large *hu* of the Warring States period. A T'ang mirror with a grape-and-seahorse pattern is outstanding, and another with birds and flowers is equally fine. The majority of the mirrors, however, are of the Han dynasty and have the designs typical of that period: human figures, serpentine animal forms, geometric patterns, and bosses.

The Chinese ceramics of the Sung dynasty include Ting bowls, a Ju bowl, a Tz'u-chou bowl with a wave pattern in brown on white, and celadon vases and incense burners. In the Japanese group are a Momoyama Oribe dish, a covered bowl by Kenzan, a *mizusashi* and a dish by Ninsei, and various pieces of Bizen and Satsuma ware. The Korean items include some pieces of the Silla period (both ash-glazed and unglazed), numerous Koryo celadons such as bowls, ewers, and a box (with inlaid and incised designs), and many Yi-dynasty Mishima tea bowls, bowls with monochrome glazes, and vessels in blue-and-white.

• COMMENTS • The quality is excellent, and the installation is charmingly arranged in several rooms of the house. The exhibition changes each spring and autumn, one type of object generally being shown at a time; a small folder in Japanese accompanies each exhibition. Only a small part of the collection is ever on view, and items not on display cannot be seen. The beautiful garden and several teahouses are behind the museum.

126. Nezu Art Museum (Nezu Bijutsukan), 115, 6-chome, Aoyama Minami-cho, Akasaka, Minato-ku, Tokyo. Tel. Tokyo 401-2536.

根津美術館　東京都港区赤坂青山南町 6 丁目 115 番地

Director: Kaichiro Nezu. **Hours:** 9:30–4:30; closed Mon., all of Aug., and Dec. 15–Jan. 15. **Adm.:** ¥50. **Route:** Take Yamate line to Shibuya station; then No. 6 tram and get off at Takagi-cho. Walk back about half a block. A gate in a long blank wall on the right-hand side of the street marks the entrance. Follow a winding driveway, flanked with statues, to the museum building.

A superb collection of Japanese painting, calligraphy, sculpture, ceramics, lacquer, and metalwork, and of Chinese bronzes, painting, sculpture, lacquer and ceramics. There are also some Gandhara sculptures, Korean ceramics, and a small group of very elaborate European clocks.

Among the early Japanese narrative scrolls are an illustrated copy of the *Inga-kyo,* dated 1254 and painted by Keinin and his son Shojumaru and written by Ryosei; a *Juni Innen Engi* and a *Tengu Zoshi,* both Kamakura; a *Yuzu Nembutsu Engi,* dated 1383; and several scrolls of the Muromachi period. *Kakemono* with Buddhist subjects include a Dainichi Nyorai and six framed panels illustrating Zenzai Doji's "Pilgrimage to the Fifty-five Saints," both of the Heian period, and a Sho Kannon, two Aizen Myo-o, the Go Dai Myo-o, a Kongo Satta, and illustrations from the life of the Buddha, to name a few from the Kamakura period. Among the *mandara* of the same period are a Kongo-kai, one picturing the divinities of the Hosso sect, and a Kasuga no Miya.

The best-known painting in the collection is the *Nachi Waterfall,* a work from the late 13th or early 14th century which is based on the concept of *suijaku* (the unity of Shinto and Buddhism) and points to the rise of pure landscape art. There is also a distinguished group of Muromachi landscapes, including one by Shokei, two attributed to Shubun, and *Viewing the Waterfall* by Geiami and dated 1480. The collection also contains several paintings by Buncho, Goshun, Kenzan, and Korin, and an unknown artist has painted three charming scenes from a Kabuki drama.

The screens include one of Korin's masterpieces—the famous pair of sixfold ones with irises on a gold ground—and another pair of sixfold ones of the Muromachi period showing the game of courtly football known as *kemari.* Among the Edo screens are those with designs of kimono on a rack, the cherry blossoms of Yoshino, and the maple leaves of the Tatsuta River, as well as a Bugaku dance by Morikage, wisteria by Okyo, and a landscape by Rosetsu.

Japanese calligraphy is especially well represented. There are fragments of the *Kokinshu* and the *Wakan Roeishu* of the Heian period and a record, dated 1119, of a poetry contest at the home of the *naidaijin* (inner minister). Among the items from the Kamakura period are letters by the priests Myoe and Daito Kokushi and calligraphy by the latter and Shigen Sogen. Pieces of calligraphy by Issan Ichinei and Minki Soshun are dated 1315 and 1330 respectively, while from the 17th century comes a poem scroll by Koetsu on a paper decorated with leaves in gold and silver. Among the sutras are two copies of the *Daihannya-kyo* and the *Kanzeon*

Bosatsu Juki-kyo of the Nara period. A *Kanfugen-kyo* of the Heian period is attributed to Tofu.

The sculptures include a wooden Bosatsu of the Hakuho period, a Jizo and a Fudo of the Heian period, and a Bosatsu by Jokei. Masks for the Noh drama date from the Muromachi and Edo periods.

A very choice group of Japanese ceramics (other than tea-ceremony objects) includes an Oribe square dish and a Yellow Seto bowl (both of the Momoyama period); a jar by Ninsei dated 1688; five circular plates by Kenzan, a square dish by him dated 1711, and two others potted by him and painted by Korin and Soshin respectively; and a charcoal brazier by Mokubei. The lacquer section is equally fine and contains a box for a *kesa* and a sutra box, both of the Heian period, a Kamakura *tebako,* and four Muromachi writing boxes. From the Edo period are a cabinet to hold the volumes of the *Genji Monogatari,* a writing box attributed to Korin, and *inro* by such lacquer artists as Kyuhaku, Seisei, and Zeshin. There are also swords by Rai Kunitoshi, Naga-mitsu, and Unji of the Kamakura period, and some of the Nambokucho period. Sword guards are by Nobuie and Kaneie of the Muromachi period, Mitsuoki and Yasuchika of the Edo period, and Natsuo of the Meiji period. The collection also includes embroidered textiles of the Asuka period, brocades of the Nara period, and a number of Edo-period costumes.

The bronze vessels of the Yin and early Chou dynasties form a group unique for their size and exuberant decoration. Among them are a set of three *ho,* a *tsun,* a fine *yu* with lid and handle, and a *tsun* with two rams' heads. There are also large vessels of the period of the Warring States—notably two basins—and a censer of the Han dynasty. A fine T'ang mirror is inlaid with silver and gold. In the very distinguished group of Chinese Sung and Yuan paintings are two—*Evening Glow over the Fishing Village* and *Bamboo and Sparrows*—attributed to Mu Ch'i, a charming picture of a quail attributed to Li An-chung, a landscape—*The Setting Sun*—by Ma Lin, *Melon and Insects* by Lu Ching-fu, and *Pu Tai and Chiang Mo-ho in Discussion* by Yin T'o-lo. There are also examples of calligraphy of the Yuan dynasty, many of which are dated.

Standing in the entrance to the museum is a large Chinese

white-marble statue of the Buddha (6th century), and in the grounds outside is a T'ang stone shrine. The collection also contains fine small gilt-bronze Buddhist figures dating from the 5th century to the T'ang dynasty and sculptures from the caves of T'ien-lung-shan of the Sui and T'ang dynasties. To be especially noted are a small gilt-bronze stele of two seated Buddhas, dated 489, and a T'ang gilt-bronze plaque with the Buddha, Bodhisattvas, and other attendants in high relief.

From the Han dynasty are pottery houses and other tomb furniture, a painted tomb tile, small lacquer vessels, and a lacquered table dated A.D. 103.

Objects for the tea ceremony form a large and distinguished group. There are tea caddies of the Muromachi and Momoyama periods and the Ming dynasty, many bearing names; a host of tea bowls, which include several by Ninsei, Nonko, and Kuchu, and a splendid group of Korean Ido-type bowls, all named, of the Yi dynasty; Chinese flower vases; Chinese, Japanese, and Korean incense burners and incense containers; and Japanese water jars and iron teakettles.

· COMMENTS · The quality is excellent. The display, arranged in a long rectangular room with a balcony on two sides, is good. The large sculpture, the large Chinese bronzes, and the clocks are always on display. The other exhibits change six or seven times a year. Five to ten percent of the collection is normally on view. There is an illustrated handbook of the collection, in Japanese and English; an illustrated catalogue of the exhibition held at the time of the Olympic games in 1964, also in Japanese and English; and an illustrated booklet on the Chinese bronzes, in Japanese. There is also a wide selection of postcards.

127. Niigata B.S.N. Art Museum (Niigata B.S.N. Bijutsukan), 2 Igaku-cho, Niigata, Niigata-ken. Tel. Niigata 23-5631.

新潟 B.S.N. 美術館　新潟市医学町 2 番地

Director: Etsuo Horiuchi. **Hours:** 10–5:30; closed Mon. and New Year season. **Adm.:** ¥80. **Route:** The gallery is on the ground floor of a new office building which houses the B.S.N., the local broadcasting station. The building, faced with red tile, sits on a small rise of land to the right of the Prefectural Government Office Building and can be reached by the bus to Kencho-mae (about 30 min.).

A collection (the property of the director, who is also the head of the broadcasting station) of contemporary Japanese paintings, both oils and water colors, and a few pieces of contemporary sculpture, displayed in two well-arranged exhibition rooms.

• COMMENTS • The quality of the collection is good, the installation well done. About four to six times a year the collection gives way to loan exhibitions, generally of a contemporary nature. Most of these exhibitions, which are good, are accompanied by catalogues in Japanese.

128. Niihama Municipal Local Museum (Niihama Shiritsu Kyodokan), Oji-machi, Niihama, Ehime-ken. Tel. Niihama 3479.

新居浜市立郷土館　愛媛県新居浜市王子町

Director: Umajiro Inami. **Hours:** 9–5; closed Mon., Sat. p.m., national holidays, and Dec. 28–Jan. 3. **Adm.:** free. **Route:** Take bus from Nishinohama, get off at Yamadaguchi (about 30 min.), and walk straight ahead across a railroad track to the school buildings which are on the left side of the road. The museum occupies several rooms on the upper floor of the building nearest the gate. Ask at the office for the key.

A small collection of Japanese archaeology (consisting largely of pottery of the Yayoi period, Sue ware, stone arrowheads, and chipped and polished stone implements), plus a few local paintings, some calligraphy, and a small group of historical relics.

There are two small black Jomon figurines of excellent quality, a number of good Yayoi vessels, and some equally good Sue pieces. These all come from local excavations, together with a great many pottery fragments.

Among the local historical items (almost all of the Edo period) are a screen showing the local topography, a palanquin, armor, spears, and stirrups. There are also a few ceramics—Arita, Seto, and Karatsu pieces among them—and some charming 19th-century paintings. A metal sutra box and its pottery container date from the Heian period, and there are a number of circular tiles of the Nara period.

• COMMENTS • The overall quality is fair, the display barely adequate. All objects are on view. There is an illustrated booklet in Japanese. This museum is for the archaeologist only.

129. Nikko Tosho-gu Treasure House (Nikko Tosho-gu Homotsukan), Nikkosan, Nikko, Tochigi-ken. Tel. Nikko 4-0114.

日光東照宮宝物館　栃木県日光市日光山

Director: Tadashi Watabe. **Hours:** 8–5, Apr.–Oct.; 8–4, Nov.–Mar. **Adm.:** ¥220 (this includes entrance to the shrine), plus ¥5 for shoe checking. **Route:** Take bus to Nishi Sanjo. Walk uphill and turn right on the first crossroad. The treasure house, a rambling two-story building in the Japanese temple style, is halfway down and on the right-hand side of this tree-lined road leading from the Daiyu-in Mausoleum and the Futa-arasan Shrine to the Tosho-gu.

The collection consists of a miscellaneous group of paintings, lacquer, masks, musical instruments, costumes, arms and armor, and temple furniture, all belonging to the Tosho-gu.

A long Edo scroll depicts the battle of Sekigahara; another shows the Nikko festivals. A triptych of Kannon and birds and flowers is signed Tan'yu. The most interesting paintings and examples of calligraphy, however, are those of the various Tokugawa shoguns, such as Ieyasu, Iemitsu, Tsunayoshi, Yoshimune, and Ieharu. The costumes are mainly those used in the ceremonies of the Tosho-gu. There are also lacquer clothes boxes, palanquins, musical instruments, and a folding chair. The arms include a sword dated 1280, another dated 1469, and a third, made by Yasutsugu, which was presented to the shrine in 1709. A suit of armor belonged to Iemitsu. There are also inkstones, lacquer sets of dishes and trays, sutra boxes, and masks, mostly of the Edo period. Models of the shrine buildings form a separate display.

• COMMENTS • The artistic quality is only fair, but the historical interest is considerable. The display is adequate. Almost all the collection is on view. There is a check list of the contents, in Japanese only.

130. Ninna-ji Treasure House (Ninna-ji Reihokan), Ninna-ji, Omuro Ouchi, Ukyo-ku, Kyoto. Tel. Kyoto 44-0038.

仁和寺霊宝館　京都市右京区御室大内　仁和寺内

Director: Chisho Hanamatsu. **Hours:** 9–4, from 1st to 3rd Sun. in Nov. **Adm.:** ¥60. **Route:** Take bus No. 26, which stops in front of the temple or, from Sanjo Keihan, bus No. 59 to the terminal at Omuro, which is beside the temple. The treasure house, built in the Japanese style, is on the right as one enters the precincts.

A small but interesting collection of Chinese and Japanese painting, Japanese sculpture, documents and books, lacquer, furniture, musical instruments, and textiles, belonging to the temple.

The best-known Chinese painting is a Kujaku Myo-o by Chang Ssu-kung of the Sung dynasty. The Japanese paintings include a portrait of the emperor Uda and a Jizo *mandara* of the Heian period and a portrait of Shotoku Taishi of the Kamakura period. There is a landscape screen by Okyo; another, by Sanraku, pictures the Heiji War. A painting of the Thirty-six Poets is also by Sanraku.

Among the documents are several scrolls of Buddhist teachings in Kobo Daishi's own hand, an inventory of the Jogan-ji dated 873, and a commentary on the *Man'yoshu* dated 1347. There are letters of the emperors Godaigo, Gosaga, and Takakura, and one of the priest Myoe Shonin. There are also medical books of the Heian period.

Figures of Amida Nyorai and two Bosatsu, in wood, are of the early Heian period, while three of the Shi Tenno and an Aizen Myo-o are Kamakura.

A superb lacquer box for manuscripts, a fragment of a *kesa,* and a crystal reliquary (the last a gift of the emperor Uda) date from the Heian era.

• COMMENTS • The quality is excellent, the display adequate. The exhibition changes a little from year to year. There is a brief catalogue. The treasure house is well worth visiting.

131. Nishimura Art Museum (Nishimura Bijutsukan), 297 Yokoyama, Kikko Koen, Iwakuni, Yamaguchi-ken. Tel. Iwakuni 4-0506.

西村美術館　山口県岩国市吉香公園横山 297 番地

Director: Shigenori Nishimura. **Hours:** 8–6. **Adm.:** ¥100. **Route:** Take bus (30 min.) to Kintai-bashi (Kintai Bridge). Walk over the bridge (a charming five-arched construction) and proceed straight ahead through the park as far as the road allows; then turn right, then left, then left again as the road bends. The museum, a new building in more or less traditional style and opened to the public in 1963, is on the right, beside the terminal of the ropeway leading up to the newly built castle.

A large and interesting collection of armor, arms, lacquer, furniture, musical instruments, and costumes, housed on the two upper floors.

There are many complete suits of armor, as well as swords, spears, bows, arrows and arrowheads, quivers for field and ceremonial use, helmets, war fans, saddles and stirrups, and guns, all largely of the Edo period. The notable exceptions are a partial suit of armor of the late Heian period said to have been worn by Taira Shigemori, other partial suits of armor of the Nambokucho and Muromachi periods, a sword made by Moriyoshi in the Nambokucho period, and two swords of the Muromachi period.

The lacquer section contains writing boxes, traveling cases, low tables, and other miscellaneous pieces. Among the costumes are Noh robes, court costumes, *jimbaori,* and firemen's coats. There is also a screen of two hawks attributed to Niten.

• COMMENTS • The quality is excellent; the display is good, with some English labels. There is a descriptive pamphlet in English and an illustrated one in Japanese. The collection is well worth visiting, and the park, with its old samurai houses, is charming.

132. Nyoirin-ji Treasure House (Nyoirin-ji Homotsu-den), Nyoirin-ji, Tono-o, Yoshinoyama, Yoshino, Nara-ken. Tel. Yoshino 3008.

如意輪寺宝物殿　奈良県吉野山塔之尾　如意輪寺内

Director: Teishin Kashima, Chief Priest. **Hours:** 8–5. **Adm.:** ¥50. **Route:** Yoshino is at the end of the Kinki Nihon Railway (1½ hrs.) either from Abenobashi station, Osaka, or from Nara; then by cable car (5 min.) up the mountain. The Nyoirin-ji is about a 10-min. taxi ride or about 50 min. on foot from the cable car. Walk through the village and, some distance beyond, fork left on the narrow dirt road that, after much winding, leads directly to the temple concealed in a grove of tall trees. The treasure house is in two small connecting buildings to the left of the Kondo.

A small collection of painting, calligraphy, sculpture, armor, and swords. It is of especial historical interest for its connection with the Southern Court of the Nambokucho period.

Among the paintings are a *raigo* and one of the Three Thousand Buddhas, both assigned to the Kamakura period; a *Fugen and Monju* said to be by Chodensu; a Yoshino *mandara* of the Muromachi period; and portraits of the emperor Godaigo and his loyal supporter Kusunoki Masatsura by artists of the 19th century. The most important piece of sculpture is a wooden figure of Zao Gongen placed in a wooden painted shrine, both of the Kamakura period. There is also a standing wooden figure of Amida, called Nara and hopefully attributed to the priest Gyogi. The collection includes poems written by the emperor Godaigo, his writing box, and his table, as well as poems written by Hideyoshi at a flower-viewing festival. Also on view are the sword, helmet, saddle, and body armor of Kusunoki Masatsura; the helmet and sword of his father, Kusunoki Masashige; and *kesa* belonging to the temple priests.

• COMMENTS • The quality varies, but the historical interest of the early objects is considerable. The display is crowded into dark rooms, and all objects are normally on view. There is a small leaflet in Japanese describing the collection.

133. Odawara Castle Museum (Odawara-jo Hakubutsukan), Odawara-jo, Saiwai, Odawara, Kanagawa-ken. Tel. Odawara 22-1133.

小田原城博物館　神奈川県小田原市幸　小田原城内

Director: Kenzaburo Ishizuka. **Hours:** 9–5; closed Dec. 29–31. **Adm.:** ¥30. **Route:** At the station exit, turn right and walk straight ahead to the castle moat; turn left and follow the moat to the gate on the south side of the castle precincts. A long flight of steps leads up to the castle.

An interesting local historical collection, opened in 1960 and housed on the second and third floors of the rebuilt castle tower. It contains copies of portraits of various daimyo of the castle, passports for the Hakone barrier, documents of the Hojo family (the first daimyo of the castle), a scroll depicting the armor of the Okubo family (the daimyo in the Edo period), and calligraphy and paintings by members of this family. There are also lacquered toilet sets belonging to the Okubo and swords which once belonged to the Hojo, as well as maps of the castle precincts, guns, armor of the Edo period, and sword furniture. A number of wooden doors, painted by Okamoto Shuki, add color to the exhibition.

The modern industrial products of Odawara are shown on the ground floor.

• COMMENTS • The quality is good, the display is well done, and there are some English labels. Most of the collection—about twenty percent of which belongs to the city, the rest being on loan—is normally on view; changes are occasionally made. There is a pamphlet in English and another in Japanese. The collection is of interest to the general public as well as to the historian.

134. Ohara Art Museum (Ohara Bijutsukan), 312, 1-chome, Shinkawa-cho, Kurashiki, Okayama-ken. Tel. Kurashiki 22-0005.

大原美術館　岡山県倉敷市新川町１丁目312番地

Director: Shin'ichiro Fujita. **Hours:** 9–4; closed Mon., and Dec. 30–Jan. 4. **Adm.:** ¥100. **Route:** Walk straight ahead from the station and turn left just before the International Hotel. Follow this street, which is soon bordered on the left by a canal. The museum, a small Western-style building with a classic façade, stands on the right.

A collection of Western painting and sculpture, almost entirely French and of the second half of the 19th and first half of the 20th century, largely put together by the late Mr. Ohara with the advice of the French artist Aman-Jean. Almost all the better-known French artists of this period are represented, as well as some of the lesser-known ones such as Aman-Jean, Dufresne, and Raffaelli. The chief exceptions to the French Impressionists and those artists loosely grouped under the heading "School of Paris" are an *Annunciation* attributed to El Greco and paintings by Hodler and Segantini. The museum continues to purchase in the contemporary field, and canvases by Marino Marini,

Hans Hartung, and Ben Nicholson have recently been added.

The sculpture is limited to three large pieces by Rodin (which stand in the garden of the museum) and three by Bourdelle.

• COMMENTS • The quality, especially of the paintings, is mixed, but the collection is of particular interest as one of the first of Western art to be made and publicly shown in Japan. The display is adequate, with some English labels. All the collection is normally visible, and the exhibition changes only when new purchases are put on view. There are two illustrated catalogues and a check list, all in Japanese, though the larger of the two catalogues also gives the artists' names in English.

135. Ohara New Art Museum (Ohara Bijutsukan Shinkan), Shinkawa-cho, Kurashiki, Okayama-ken. Tel. Kurashiki 22-5627.

大原美術館新館　岡山県倉敷市新川町

Director: Shin'ichiro Fujita. **Hours:** 9–4; closed Mon. and Dec. 30– Jan. 4. **Adm.:** ￥50. **Route:** Walk straight ahead from the station to the International Hotel (about 15 min.). The new museum, a long one-story building in an interesting mixture of Japanese and Western styles set in a pleasant open area and opened in 1961, is just beyond the hotel, on the left of the street.

A rather small collection of Japanese paintings in the Western manner and some Egyptian and classical antiquities together with Iranian, Turkish, and Hispano-Moresque pottery. The entrance is in the center of the building, with the Japanese paintings and a sculpture by Ossip Zadkine, which stands in a small courtyard, to the left. Among the older artists represented are Aoki, Kishida, Koide, Maeda, Mitsutani, Okada, and Yorozu, while Yasui, Fujita, and Umehara are among those in the slightly younger group.

The collections of antiquities and ceramics are shown in the galleries to the right. In the Egyptian section are a few small figurines of the New Kingdom, many more figures, stone reliefs, and pottery vessels of the late Dynastic period, and a few Coptic textiles and mummy portraits. From the classical world there are a Greek red-figured vase, some

Tanagra figurines, and some fragments of Roman sculpture. The Near Eastern ceramics include Rakka pottery jars and Iranian lusterware of the 13th and 14th centuries, and Kubatcha, Rhodian, and Hispano-Moresque pottery from the 16th to the 18th century.

• COMMENTS • The Japanese paintings are good of their kind; the Egyptian, classical, and Near Eastern sections contain no outstanding pieces. The display is good, with some English labels. There are a check list and two well-illustrated pamphlets on the paintings and the archaeology, all in Japanese. Almost all the collection is on view. The museum is part of that remarkable group of institutions which, standing together in this part of Kurashiki, make this area artistically and scenically unique in Japan.

136. Ohara Pottery Hall (Ohara Tokikan), 312, 1-chome, Shinkawa-cho, Kurashiki, Okayama-ken. Tel. Kurashiki 22-0005.

大原陶器館　岡山県倉敷市新川町 1 丁目 312 番地

Director: Shin'ichiro Fujita. **Hours:** 9–4; closed Mon. and Dec. 30–Jan. 4. **Adm.:** ¥50. **Route:** Enter the grounds of the Ohara Art Museum (No. 134) and follow the path to the right of the museum building which leads to the entrance of the pottery hall, a series of adjoining rooms stretching around the sides of a courtyard and, externally, remodeled from godowns of the Edo period.

A most interesting collection of contemporary pottery, prints, and textiles. The pottery is confined to the work of Hamada, Kawai, and Tomimoto (the "old masters" of the contemporary folk-art movement) and that of their friend, the famous English potter Bernard Leach. The woodblock prints are by Munakata and the textiles by Serizawa. The full range of each artist is shown in one or more rooms.

• COMMENTS • The quality is excellent, as each artist is represented by a selection of his best pieces. The installation is very good, the decoration of each room being well adapted to the work it contains. The labels are in Japanese only, save for the name of the artist. The exhibition does not change. This museum is one of the most interesting in the whole complex in this part of Kurashiki and is well worth visiting.

137. Okayama Art Museum (Okayama Bijutsukan),
78 Uchisange, Okayama, Okayama-ken. Tel. Okayama 23-
1733.

岡山美術館　岡山市内山下 78 番地

Director: Ritsuji Okuma. **Hours:** 9:30–5 (no admission after 4);
closed Mon., day after a national holiday, and New Year season. **Adm.:**
¥100. **Route:** Take tram for Higashiyama and get off at the Uchisange
stop. Walk left to the first main crossing and turn left. The museum, a
handsome new one-story building of brick and concrete built around
an interior courtyard, is on the left, set back from the street.

A very fine collection of Chinese and Japanese paintings
and ceramics, Chinese bronzes and lacquers, and Japanese
swords, armor, calligraphy, lacquer, costumes, and furniture.

There is a charming Chinese scroll, *Ch'ing Ming Festival
at the River,* by Chao Che, dated 1577 and giving a wonderful
picture of Chinese life. The Japanese paintings include a
pair of sixfold screens of horses in their stalls (Momoyama
period), an eightfold landscape screen by Goshun, two
decorative screens of phoenixes and bamboos (Edo period),
a landscape by the *nanga*-school painter Gyokudo, and a
crow by Hokusai.

In the ceramics section are good Chinese T'ang glazed
tomb figurines and fine examples of Sung Ting ware, celadons, Tz'u-chou ware, and a *temmoku* bowl with oil-spot
glaze. There are also Ming blue-and-white and colored
vases, jars, and bowls. The Japanese ceramics include
Momoyama Bizen water containers and good Edo pieces
of Nabeshima and Kakiemon.

The Chinese bronzes are excellent, with several assigned
to the early Chou dynasty. The lacquers are equally notable:
there are two dishes carved with designs of birds and flowers
(assigned to the Yuan dynasty); a number of large circular
Ming food boxes; and one many-tiered rectangular box
decorated with genre scenes inlaid with mother-of-pearl.
Among the Japanese lacquer pieces is a superb set of furniture made for the wedding of a member of the Ikeda family,
the daimyo of Okayama.

The most important Japanese swords are of the Bizen and
related schools. Two, of the late Heian period, are signed
respectively Kanehira and Masatsune. Others, of the Kamakura period, carry the signatures of Yoshifusa, Mitsu-

tada, Nagamitsu, and Sukeyoshi. The earliest suit of armor is of the Nambokucho period; another, less complete, is Muromachi. Two 17th-century suits were worn by members of the Ikeda family.

Among the choice examples of calligraphy are letters of the emperors Gonara, Ogimachi, Goyozei, and Gomizu-no-o and of Hideyoshi, Ieyasu, and Sen no Rikyu. There are also samples of the calligraphy and drawing of Ikkyu and of Hakuin.

The collection further contains many splendid Momoyama and early-Edo Noh robes and several late-Edo *kataginu*.

• COMMENTS • The quality is excellent, as is the installation. About five percent of the collection of some 3,000 pieces is on view at any one time. The exhibition changes every two or three months. There are a pamphlet, a book illustrating some of the outstanding pieces, and a check list of each exhibition, all in Japanese only.

Note: This museum was formerly known as the Hayashibara Art Museum, after the late Ichiro Hayashibara, whose collection forms the basis of the present museum one.

138. Okura Museum (Okura Shukokan), 3 Aoi-cho, Akasaka, Minato-ku, Tokyo. Tel. Tokyo 481-0781.

大倉集古館　東京都港区赤坂葵町 3 番地

Director: Shinkichi Osaki. **Hours:** 10–4; closed Mon., New Year season, and occasionally when exhibition is being changed. **Adm.:** ¥50. **Route:** The museum, a two-story building in Chinese style, stands in the grounds of the Hotel Okura, which is a little to the south of the American Embassy and about equidistant from the Kamiya-cho stop on the Hibiya subway and the Toranomon stop on the Ginza subway. (Both stops are quite far from the museum.)

A large and fine collection of Japanese painting, calligraphy, sculpture, ceramics, masks, swords, lacquer, costumes, and books and of Chinese paintings, sculpture, bronzes, ceramics, lacquer, and books, all originally the private collection of Mr. Kihachiro Okura.

The most important Japanese painting is a scroll, *Zuishin Teiki Emaki* (The Imperial Guard Cavalry), attributed to Fujiwara Nobuzane of the 13th century. Other Kamakura paintings are a *Death of the Buddha,* an Iwashimizu Hachiman *mandara,* and *Shotoku Taishi Expounding a Buddhist Sutra.* Assigned to the Nambokucho period are a Kasuga Deer *mandara,* an Aizen Myo-o, and a Kokuzo Bosatsu. From the Muromachi period are a scroll of the *Yuzu Nembutsu Engi* (Stories of the Origin of Yuzu Nembutsu Buddhism), a bird-and-flower painting by Soyu, and a flower painting by Bompo.

Among the Edo *kakemono* are good ones by Hoitsu, Okyo, Hiroshige, and Tamechika. There are also contemporary paintings by such artists as Taikan Yokoyama (his four paintings comprising *The Mountain* are particularly well known), Kanzan Shimomura, Seison Maeda, Seiho Takeuchi, and Gyokudo Kawai.

The museum has some charming Edo screens. Among them are a pair with designs of fans and waves, another with scenes from the *Genji Monogatari,* a third with a scene of a horse race, and a fourth depicting people enjoying themselves in the country. There is also a pair by Tan'yu (as well as a delightful sketchbook of his) showing men in boats fishing with cormorants and, in addition, a pair by Chinzan of orchids and bamboo, a pair by Okyo picturing geese, and a good screen of birds and flowers by Masanobu.

The Japanese sculpture includes a splendid Heian painted wooden Fugen Bosatsu on an elephant and a Kamakura wooden portrait statue of the priest Horen.

The best-known piece of pottery is a six-sided dish made by Kenzan with a design of Jurojin by Korin, while the best-known piece of lacquer is a superb *tebako* with fan designs (Kamakura period). There are also lacquer writing boxes and a large cabinet from the Edo period and a Korean box, inlaid with mother-of-pearl, of the Koryo period. The swords are of the Heian, Kamakura, and Nambokucho periods, and the most noteworthy piece of calligraphy is a Heian copy of the introduction to the *Kokinshu.* There are a number of Noh masks and a large and superb group of Noh costumes and Noh-play properties, all of the Edo period.

Among the Chinese items are bronze vessels from the Yin dynasty to the period of the Warring States. Weapons and chariot fittings date from the period of the Warring States through the Han dynasty, and mirrors from the T'ang dynasty. Also from the period of the Warring States is a very large and important lacquer bowl from Hui-hsien in Honan Province with decoration similar to that of the "Huai style" bronzes. Chinese sculpture is represented by a Northern Wei standing stone Buddha of a Central Asiatic type with an elaborate *mandorla* and by a seated wooden Kuan Yin of the Sung dynasty. There are good examples of Sung and Ming porcelain, and the few Chinese printed books on display, such as a copy of the encyclopedia known as the *Yu Hai* (Jewel Sea) and a Sung copy of *The Story of San Tsang's Search for Buddhist Sutras,* give a hint of the rich holdings in this field.

In addition, there are a few pieces of Indian medieval sculpture, Siamese sculpture, and numerous Tibetan bronze figures.

· COMMENTS · The quality ranges from good to excellent. The display is well arranged and the labels adequate. About ten percent of the collection is normally on view, with the sculpture, the bronzes, the masks, and the lacquer almost always on display and the paintings and calligraphy changing every two months. There is a large illustrated catalogue of the collection, complete in English and Japanese; a smaller illustrated handbook, in Japanese only; a handbook on the recent paintings, also in Japanese; and a folder in English on the museum.

139. Old Ceramics Hall (Kotokan), Korakuen, Furu-kyo-machi, Okayama, Okayama-ken. Tel. Okayama 72-1147 (Korakuen office).

古陶館　岡山市古京町　後楽園内

Director: Katsunori Munesada. **Hours:** 9–4; closed Mon. **Adm.:** ¥20. **Route:** The museum, a small, unpretentious one-story building, is to the right of the main entrance to the Korakuen, the city's large and very beautiful park. Buses run to the park in 12 min. If the museum should be closed, ask at the main gate for the key.

A small collection of Bizen ware (the Bizen kilns are at Imbe, not far from Okayama) shown in one room of the small building. A very few vases and bowls are called Heian; the greater number of these somber but very handsome vases, jars, and bowls are of the late Muromachi, Momoyama, and Edo periods. Of particular interest is a three-tiered box with openwork designs, surmounted by the figure of a cat and bearing a date of 1621. There are also 17th-century fragments from the kiln. A head in terra cotta is dated Hakuho.

• COMMENTS • The quality is very good, the display adequate. Individual items are occasionally changed. There is no pamphlet, but a few postcards are available. This museum is of great interest to the ceramic specialist.

140. Osaka Castle Tower (Osaka-jo Tenshukaku), Baba-cho, Higashi-ku, Osaka. Tel. Osaka 941-3044.

大阪城天守閣　大阪市東区馬場町

Director: Ryoichi Okamoto. **Hours:** 9–9, Jul.–Aug.; 9–5, Sept.–Jun.; closed Dec. 26–Jan. 1. **Adm.:** ¥40. **Route:** The large precincts of Osaka Castle, on the northern side of which the tower rises, are to the southeast of the Osaka station and east of the main business section. The entrance to the precincts (cars are not admitted) is not far from the Ote-mae tram stop on the Umeda-Abeno line, or it is about 15 min. on foot from the Temmabashi station on the Keihan Electric Railway.

An interesting collection of paintings, calligraphy, metalwork, armor, swords and sword fittings, costumes, and historical documents relating to the history of the castle, its original builder—Hideyoshi—and his court. There is also some local archaeological material, along with models of the castle and its precincts. The collection is shown in the rebuilt (1931) castle tower.

Among the relics of note are a charming screen combining a design of wisteria and poetry by the wife of Hideyoshi, a screen depicting foreigners, a portrait of the tea master Sen no Rikyu, and examples of his calligraphy. Puppets and other objects related to the famous Osaka Bunraku puppet theater are also on view.

• COMMENTS • The quality is good of its kind, and the display is good. About one-third of the collection is normally visible. The collection changes, but only to make way for special loan exhibitions held in the spring and autumn. There is a folder in English describing the castle and giving its history.

141. Osaka Municipal Art Museum (Osaka Shiritsu Bijutsukan), 121 Chausuyama-cho, Tennoji-ku, Osaka. Tel. Osaka 771-4874.

大阪市立美術館　大阪市天王寺区茶臼山町 121 番地

Director: Ryuichi Imamura. **Hours:** 9–5; closed Dec. 29–Jan. 5. **Adm.:** ¥150, including temporary exhibitions. **Route:** The museum, a large Western-style building, is in Tennoji Park, a 5-min. walk from the Abenobashi tram stop or the Tennoji station of the national railways. Walk west, away from the busy crossing, through the park, past the greenhouses, and turn right across the street by the library building. The entrance to the museum building is on the west façade.

A large and very good collection of Japanese, Chinese, and Korean art, housed on two floors of the left wing of the museum. Sculpture, bronzes, ceramics, and lacquer are shown on the ground floor, paintings on the upper floor. Temporary loan shows generally occupy the right wing.

From the Jomon period are stone implements, a good selection of pottery vessels, and fine figurines. The Yayoi period is represented by more fine pottery vessels, *dotaku,* and spearheads. On display from the Kofun era are Sue-ware vessels, a fine *haniwa* horse, beads, *magatama,* bracelets, gilt-bronze horse trappings, and Chinese mirrors unearthed from Japanese tumuli.

A large room is devoted to sculpture, most of which is on loan from temples. Among the items are a Hakuho seated bronze figure, a Fudo and a lovely Sho Kannon of the Heian period, a large late-Heian Kokuzo Bosatsu, and Kamakura figures of Tamonten, Kisshoten, and Jikokuten.

Additional Japanese material includes Nara tiles, a Kamakura Seto jar, Negoro lacquer of the Muromachi period, a brush pot by Kenzan, a teapot by Dohachi, and a good selection of Imari, Iga, Karatsu, Kutani, Nabeshima, and Oribe wares. There are also many *kei, kakebotoke,* and other Buddhist objects on loan from various temples.

In the Chinese section are several Yin bronzes and jars, a few mirrors (Han to T'ang dynasty), some red carved lacquer (one piece of which is called Yuan), Sung celadon, Tz'u-chou and Yueh wares, a Yuan blue-and-white dish, and a group of Ming blue-and-white porcelains.

Korea is represented by pottery vessels of the Silla period, fine Koryo inlaid celadons, and blue-and-white porcelain of the Yi dynasty.

147

The museum is best known for its large collection of Chinese paintings (160 in all) bequeathed by the late Mr. Abe. The most famous one is a small scroll with a portrait of the scholar Fu Sheng; although it has been attributed to Wang Wei, it is generally assigned to an anonymous 9th-century artist. Another famous scroll, depicting the "five planets and the twenty-eight constellations" and attributed to Chan Seng-yu of the 6th century, is probably an 11th-century copy based on a 6th-century design. There is a very interesting landscape, *Distant Peaks and Clouds,* by Mi Yu-jen; a fascinating scroll, *Ming Fei Crossing the Frontier,* by Kung Su-jan; a bold landscape scroll ascribed to Yen Wen-kuei; and a charming small painting of an orchid by Chen Szu-hsiao—all artists of the Sung dynasty. Among the Yuan artists are Ni Tsan, with a broad landscape showing a pavilion by a stream, and Chai Chen, with a tall mountain landscape.

Much of the strength and interest of the Abe collection lies in its Ming and Ch'ing paintings. The former, to name but a few, include works by Ch'iu Ying, Chao Tso, Ch'en Tao-fu, Huang Tao-chou, Tung Ch'i-ch'ang, Shen Chou, T'ang Yin, Wen Chia, and Yang Wen-ts'ung. The Ch'ing dynasty is equally well represented, with characteristic works by Ch'ien Tu, Kao Ch'i-p'ei, Kao Feng-han, Lang Shih-ning (the Jesuit, Father Castiglione), Pa Ta Shan Jen, Wang Shih-ning, Wu Li, and Yun Shou-p'ing, among many others.

The calligraphy includes an inscription for the new year in a cursive hand by Mi Fei and a scroll of Li Po's poems copied by Su Shih.

· COMMENTS · The quality is excellent and the display adequate, with a few English labels. The exhibition changes five or six times a year, and about ten percent of the collection is on view at any one time. There is a small pamphlet in Japanese about the museum and its activities as well as an illustrated catalogue, also in Japanese but with an English list of plates, of the Abe collection.

142. Osaka Municipal Museum (Osaka Shiritsu Haku-butsukan), Osaka Castle precincts, Baba-cho, Higashi-ku, Osaka. Tel. Osaka 941-7177.

大阪市立博物館　大阪市東区馬場町　大阪城内

Director: Shoei Mishina. **Hours:** 9–5. **Adm.:** ¥100. **Route:** The Osaka Castle precincts are to the southeast of the Osaka station and east of the main business section. The entrance to the precincts (cars are not allowed) is not far from the Ote-mae tram stop on the Umeda-Abeno line, or it is about 15 min. on foot from the Temmabashi station on the Keihan Electric Railway. The museum, a large Western-style building opened in 1960, is on the right of the road leading from the entrance to the tower.

A group of interesting objects relating to the history and culture of Osaka and a collection of Japanese archaeology and folk arts. The galleries to the left of the entrance on the first floor and most of those on the second floor generally contain the permanent collection. Loan shows are held on the third floor.

The archaeological collection includes Jomon and Ya-yoi pottery; *dotaku* and stone and metal arrowheads of the Yayoi period; a few Kofun-period *haniwa* and some Sue ware; and tiles of the Asuka and Nara periods. Models of tombs and dwellings are an interesting feature of the display.

Among the items in the fine-arts section are a pair of sixfold screens showing the Shitenno-ji and the Sumiyoshi Shrine, another depicting the harpooning of a whale, and a third showing the Gion quarter of Kyoto. There is also a scroll giving a bird's-eye view of Osaka. A large number of prints round out this section.

The collection also contains puppets, masks, spinning and weaving tools, and even the accounting and measuring equipment of an old-fashioned store. The historical section includes maps, documents, and records of the Osaka region.

• COMMENTS • The quality is good. The display, particularly from an educational point of view, is excellent. Thirty percent of the permanent collection is normally on view, and most of the archaeological exhibition never changes. The collections are gradually being increased. Illustrated catalogues of temporary exhibitions and illustrated annual reports are available, but in Japanese only.

143. Otaru City Museum (Otaru-shi Hakubutsukan), 15, 3-chome, Temiya-cho, Otaru, Hokkaido. Tel. Otaru 2-1258.

小樽市博物館　小樽市手宮町 3 丁目 15 番地

Director: Isao Matsui. **Hours:** 9–4:30, Apr.–Sept.; 9–4, Oct.–Mar.; closed Mon. and national holidays. **Adm.:** ¥20. **Route:** Take Chuo bus for Temiya-cho; get off at Hakubutsukan-mae. Turn to the right for 1 block, crossing a railroad track, and then left for 2 blocks. The museum, a large dark-gray cut-stone Victorian-style building, is on the left side of the street.

A general museum with exhibits of natural history, geology, and marine transportation on the ground floor and archaeology, armor, ceramics, and Ainu material on the upper floor. The archaeological collection has many arrowheads, stone implements, and pieces of pottery from the middle and late Jomon periods, plus examples of Kofun Sue and Haji ware. There are also photographs of rock carvings in the nearby Temiya cave and a cross section of a shell mound. The Ainu material includes garments with the characteristic Ainu decoration, necklaces, wooden and bark utensils, lacquer vessels made for the Ainu by the Japanese, snowshoes, swords, arrows, fish traps, decorated libation wands, ceremonial headbands, and *inau*. There are also models of Ainu houses and of the sacred area to the east of the house where groups of *inau,* called *nusa,* are set up.

There is a very interesting display of swordsmiths' tools in the armor section. A selection of the pottery and porcelain of Hokkaido and a group of local historical documents are also on view. Beyond the main exhibition room is a small gallery where a special loan show is held once a year. Paintings by local artists are sometimes shown here.

• COMMENTS • The quality is fair, the display adequate. The main exhibition is changed about every other year, generally to make room for new archaeological material as the museum continues to excavate on the Shakotan Peninsula, to the west of Otaru; normally, about one-third of the total collection is on view. There is an illustrated folder in Japanese. The museum is worth visiting if one is in the neighborhood.

Note: The building has some historical interest as the site of the meeting of the Russo-Japanese convention for border demarcation following the Russo-Japanese war.

144. Oyamazumi-jinja Treasure House (Oyamazu-mi-jinja Kokuhokan), Oyamazumi-jinja, Miyaura, Omi-shima, Ehime-ken. Tel. Omishima 32.

大山祇神社国宝館　愛媛県大三島宮浦　大山祇神社内

Director: Chief Priest. **Hours:** 8–5, Apr.–Sept.; 9–4, Oct.–Mar. **Adm.:** ¥140. **Route:** The shrine is at the port of Miyaura on the island of Omishima in the Inland Sea. Take boat from Onomichi, Mihara, or Takehara on Honshu or from Imabari on Shikoku. On reaching boat landing, walk straight ahead along the main street of the town to the entrance, marked by a *torii,* of the shrine precincts (about 10 min.). The treasure house is up a flight of steps to the right of the main building.

An extraordinarily fine collection of Japanese arms, armor, and documents, plus some other material, housed in a new ferroconcrete building designed in the traditional godown style and in an adjoining older wooden building. This collection, one of the greatest of its kind, is remarkable for the number and condition of its early suits of armor and for its swords. It boasts the earliest known armor of the historical period: a number of fragments from the early 10th century. There are also several Heian suits (two of which have matching helmets), more of the Kamakura, a large number of the Nambokucho, and rather fewer of the Muromachi and Momoyama periods. Among the suits with historical associations are the armor of Minamoto Yoshitsune and Minamoto Yoritomo. A large group of helmets dates from the Kamakura and Nambokucho periods.

The swords, usually shown in the older building, are mostly from the Heian, Kamakura, and Nambokucho periods. One was dedicated to the shrine by Minamoto Yoritomo, another by the emperor Gomurakami, and a third by Taira Shigemori. Bows and arrows are shown along with the swords.

Among the other objects in the collection are a Chinese T'ang mirror said to have been given to the shrine by the empress Saimei, a necklace of *magatama,* a remarkable group of about a hundred small mirrors ranging from the Nara to the Edo period, a Kamakura *karabitsu,* two bronze water vessels presented by Taira Shigemori, a Namboku-cho box for armor, a copy of the *Hokke-kyo* given by the emperor Takakura, a pair of wooden dogs of the Heian period, and a wooden towel rack of the Kamakura period. Rare items are a helmet, a bow, and some arrows of Mongolian type from the Yuan dynasty. A topographical paintting of the shrine precincts dates from the Muromachi period. Of the six portable shrines usually on view, three date from the Nambokucho period. The large group of documents include directives of the emperor Godaigo and of Ashikaga Takauji.

• COMMENTS • The quality is excellent. The display in the new building is very good, fair in the older one; there are a few English labels. Changes are made in the exhibition four times a year. There is a good illustrated booklet on the shrine and the collection. No one interested in arms and armor, or indeed in Japanese art, should miss this treasure house.

145. Rinno-ji Jokodo Treasure House (Rinno-ji Jokodo Homotsuden), Nikkosan, Nikko, Tochigi-ken. Tel. Nikko 4-0531.

輪王寺常行堂宝物殿　栃木県日光市日光山

Director: Eikai Sugawara. **Hours:** 8–5, Apr.–Oct.; 8–4, Nov.–Mar. **Adm.:** ¥60. **Route:** Take bus or tram to the Nishi Sanjo stop and walk up the hill. The treasure house is in a large red-painted detached temple building, the Jokodo, which belongs to the Rinno-ji and is opposite the *torii* of the Futa-arasan Shrine.

An interesting group of paintings, sculpture, metalwork, lacquer, masks, armor, swords and sword fittings, temple furniture, sutras, historical documents, and printed books.

Among the paintings are Edo scrolls of the history of Ieyasu and the Tosho-gu and of the founding of the temples at Nikko. A Yellow Fudo is assigned to the Kamakura period, as well as a painting of the three tutelary deities of the Nikko temples. From the Muromachi period is a group portrait of patriarchs of the Tendai sect. The metalwork includes a large mirror of the Kamakura period, a Nambokucho copper bowl, heads from priests' staffs of the Kamakura and Muromachi periods, and gongs and cymbals of the latter period. The collection also has a number of Noh masks, a Momoyama bookshelf, and lacquer sutra boxes of the Muromachi and Edo periods.

A copy of the *Hannyashin-gyo* is assigned to the Nara period, while another copy of this sutra and copies of the *Hokke-kyo* and the *Kanfugen-kyo* are of the Kamakura period. The books include Ming copies of the Chinese novels *Hsi Yu Chi* and *Chin P'ing Mei*. Printing blocks for the *Hokke-kyo* and the Ryokai *mandara* are also on view. In the large documents section are, to name but a few pieces, a certificate of a degree given to a Tendai priest in 1294, a prayer written by Ieyasu, an order of Iemitsu, a record of a dialogue between Dengyo Daishi and a Chinese priest, a scroll depicting the funeral services of the eleventh shogun, Ienari (1787–1837), and poem cards by the Muromachi emperors Gotsuchimikado and Gokashiwabara.

• COMMENTS • The quality is good. The display, given the difficulty of converting a temple building into a museum, is quite good; there are some English labels. Changes are made occasionally in the exhibition, but a number of the best things are not usually on view. There is a booklet in Japanese.

146. Ryokan Memorial Collection (Ryokan Kinenkan), Izumozaki-machi, Niigata-ken. Tel. Izumozaki 370.

良寛記念館　新潟県出雲崎町

Director: Shizuo Sato. **Hours:** 9–4; closed Tues. **Adm.:** ¥50. **Route:** Take Echigo line of Japanese National Railways from Niigata or Kashiwazaki and get off at Izumozaki; then take bus that runs from the station to Izumozaki-machi and get off at Ryokan Kinenkan-mae (15 min.). Walk up the road to the left for 300 yards. The museum, a very handsome one-story building in the contemporary Japanese manner, stands at the top of the cliff, with a superb view over the coast and the sea, and above Izumozaki-machi, where Ryokan was born.

An interesting collection of the calligraphy and writings of the priest Ryokan (1758–1831), and some of his personal possessions as well as portraits of him, charmingly shown in a building designed by Yoshiro Taniguchi and opened in 1964.

Among the writings are some of Ryokan's poems, beautifully mounted, his copy of the *Hannyashin-gyo,* a section of the *Hokke-kyo* with his annotations, and other samples of his calligraphy. Portraits of him are by such diverse artists as

Kokei (who depicts him at the Entsu-ji), Gyokudo Kawai, Hoshun Yamaguchi, and Yukihiko Yasuda. Among his possessions are a *nyoi* and a *shakujo*.

• COMMENTS • The quality is very good, and the display is excellent. Part of the exhibit changes two or three times a year; about thirty percent of the collection is on view at any one time. There is a small illustrated pamphlet on the local sites connected with Ryokan, which includes the museum. There are also postcards of some of the objects. The charm of the building and its setting, as well as the quality of the material, make this museum well worth visiting.

147. Sado Museum (Sado Hakubutsukan), Aza Yahata, Sawada-machi, Sado-gun, Niigata-ken. Tel. Kawaharada 2447.

佐渡博物館　新潟県佐渡郡佐和田町字八幡

Director: Kanzaemon Kikuchi. **Hours:** 8–5, Apr.–Oct.; 9–4, Nov.–Mar.; closed Dec. 29–Jan. 5. **Adm.:** ¥50. **Route:** The museum is on the opposite side of the island from Ryotsu, on the road between Kawaharada and Mano and next door to the Kokusai Sado Kanko Hotel. Take Minami-sen (Southern line) bus from bus terminal near boat landing at Ryotsu and get off at Yahatakan-mae. The museum, a two-story building of contemporary design, is near the bus stop.

An interesting collection of local archaeology and handicrafts. On the ground floor are contemporary Sado Island ceramics from Aikawa, contemporary metalwork from Sawane, and small stone votive figures, mostly of Jizo and of a type still made today, from a local temple. Also on view is a wooden figure of Daikokuten, a good example of folk sculpture. A portrait of the emperor Juntoku, exiled to Sado in 1221, and a fragment of Nichiren's writing recall the period when these famous people lived in exile on the island.

On the upper floor are Bunraku puppets, Noh masks, a few Noh costumes, and masks for temple dances. There is also a display of miners' lamps and ladders and scrolls illustrating the gold-mining industry on Sado.

As Sado is rich in archaeology, there is an extensive archaeological section containing some Jomon pottery vessels, a pottery figurine, stone implements, considerable

Yayoi pottery, a Kofun sword and metal rings, arrowheads, Sue-ware vessels, and a great number of tubular beads, many of the last in various stages of completion. Maps, charts, and photographs of the sites amplify the display. There are also circular tiles from the Tempyo site of the nearby Kokubun-ji.

Behind the museum are reconstructions of a Yayoi dwelling and godown, a garden containing specimens of local rocks, and an Edo farmhouse, completely furnished, which was moved to and re-erected on its present site.

• COMMENTS • The quality is good, and so is the display. About forty percent of the collection is on view, and no changes are made in the exhibits. There is a booklet in Japanese. Visitors to Sado should not miss this museum.

148. Saijo Municipal Local Museum (Saijo Shiritsu Kyodo Hakubutsukan), Akeyashiki, Saijo, Ehime-ken. Tel. Saijo 3199.

西条市立郷土博物館　愛媛県西条市あけやしき

Director: Shin'ichi Tokunaga. **Hours:** 9–5; closed Mon., last day of month, national holidays, and New Year season. **Adm.:** ¥20. **Route:** Take bus from bus station, to left of railway station, for Minato; get off at Saijo Koko-mae. The museum, a small frame building, is near the bus stop, on the right side of the street and on the edge of the canal.

A small local collection of archaeology, arms and armor, ceramics, painting, and calligraphy. The paintings include one of monkeys by Unkei and an early-Edo screen illustrating the topography of the region. There is an abundance of calligraphy by local masters. Among the ceramics are a few pieces of Sue ware, some Nara tiles, a good Oribe covered dish with a design of a Dutch ship, a Takatori bowl, a Bizen sakè bottle, an Old Seto water container, and a Tamba vase. Inkstones and some mirrors (one of the latter is Chinese of the T'ang dynasty) are also on view. In the historical section are several suits of armor, helmets, spears, guns, and a cannon, as well as a palanquin, coins, and paper money, all of the Edo period.

Natural history occupies half the exhibition space.

• COMMENTS • The quality is only fair, the display just adequate. Half the paintings and calligraphy are shown at any one time; all the other material is always on view. Changes in the display are made occasionally. There is a pamphlet in Japanese. The museum is worth seeing only if one happens to be in the neighborhood.

149. Saito Ho-onkai Museum (Saito Ho-onkai Hakubutsukan), 3 Taishoji Uramon-dori, Sendai, Miyagi-ken. Tel. Sendai 22-4777.

斎藤報恩会博物館　仙台市大聖寺裏門通3番地

Director: Yonosuke Saito. **Hours:** 9–4; closed Mon., Jul. 25, and national holidays. **Adm.:** ¥20. **Route:** Take the tram for Tohoku Daigaku Byoin (Tohoku University Hospital) and get off at the Reija Senta-mae stop. The museum is in the left, or northeast, section of a large E-shaped ferroconcrete building, a short distance beyond the tram stop, on the left and set well back from the street. (As it is not easy to find, it is better to go by taxi, which takes 5 min.)

A small archaeological collection, sandwiched in between natural-history exhibitions. It consists of Jomon pottery, chipped and polished stone tools, and bone implements; fragments of Yayoi ware; and some very large burial jars dating from the end of the Kofun period to the Heian period. Two suits of armor from the Edo period are also on display.

• COMMENTS • The quality is fair, the display poor. Fifty percent of the collection is normally on view, but in the spring of 1966 the collection was being catalogued, and more items were to be exhibited when the work was done. The exhibition as it then stood was of minor interest, save for the large burial jars.

150. Saito Municipal Museum (Saito Shiritsu Hakubutsukan), Tsuma, Saito, Miyazaki-ken. Tel. Saito 635.

西都市立博物館　宮崎県西都市妻

Director: Chairman, Saito Board of Education. **Hours:** 8:30–5; closed Mon., national holidays, and New Year season. **Adm.:** free. **Route:** Take bus from Miyazaki station to Saito (50 min.); then a local bus to the museum stop, Hakubutsukan-mae. (From Miyazaki by taxi it takes about 30 min.) The museum, a low L-shaped wooden building, is on the edge of town.

The collection consists of objects from the Saitobaru tomb group, largely of the Yayoi and Kofun periods, crowded together in a rather ramshackle building. It includes chipped and polished implements of stone, Yayoi pottery vessels, bronze mirrors and harness fittings, and iron swords and pieces of iron armor. The last are very interesting, but they and the swords are crumbling to bits, since no care is taken of them. There are also models of the Saitobaru tomb sites.

• COMMENTS • Given the fame of the site and the quality of the objects found there, this is a disappointing museum; but most of the important pieces have been taken away and are to be seen elsewhere—for example, in the Tokyo National Museum (No. 184) or the Goto Museum (No. 28). The display is poor. There is no change in the exhibition, and there are no pamphlets or folders. As it now exists, only the most ardent scholar of Japanese archaeology would be interested in this collection.

151. Sakitama Archaeological Hall (Sakitama Koko-kan), Sakitama-jinja, Sakitama, Gyoda, Saitama-ken. Tel. Gyoda 56-1111 (Gyoda City Office).

前玉考古館　埼玉県行田市前玉　前玉神社内

Director: Under Gyoda Board of Education. **Hours:** 9–4; closed Mon. and national holidays. **Adm.:** ¥20. **Route:** Take Takasaki line from Ueno, Tokyo, to Fukiage (1½ hrs.); then a taxi to the shrine (15 min.). Or continue on the train to Kumagaya (1½ hrs. by express from Ueno), change to the branch line for Gyoda (10 min.), and take bus to Sengen-jinja (15 min.), as the shrine is called locally. The museum, a one-room building, is to the left of the entrance to the precincts.

A small collection of local archaeology, consisting of a very few fragments of Jomon pottery, a few more Yayoi frag-ments, a number of *haniwa,* fragmentary Sue-ware vessels, and pieces of Kofun armor, swords, and a mirror. Among the *haniwa* are several figures, two horses, and a quantity of heads. Chipped stone implements are also on view.

• COMMENTS • The quality is fair, the display barely ade-quate and unchanging. Given the extraordinary number of tumuli (9) in the immediate vicinity, it is a pity this museum has so little to show; all the best pieces have been removed to the Tokyo National Museum (No. 184). There is a small pamphlet in Japanese. Only the most enthusiastic specialist would be tempted by the present contents of this museum.

152. Sannomiya Local Museum (Sannomiya Kyodo Hakubutsukan), Sannomiya-san, Isehara-machi, Kanagawa-ken. Tel. Isehara 95-3237.

三ノ宮郷土博物館　神奈川県伊勢原町三ノ宮山

Director: Sanji Nagai, Chief Priest. **Hours:** Open on request. **Adm.:** ¥30. **Route:** Isehara is on the Odakyu line, between Shinjuku station, Tokyo, and Odawara. Take bus from Isehara station for Tsurumaki Onsen; get off at Godo and ask for the Sannomiya-san, which lies about ½ mile to the north in a clump of trees on a low hill, well to the right of a large Western-style building. (By taxi, from the station to the shrine, the trip takes about 15 min.)

A small collection of Japanese archaeology, excavated locally, housed in a wooden building to the right of the main building of the small shrine. The body of the collection is from the Kofun period and includes handsome *magatama,* swords, sword pommels, rings, mirrors, Sue-ware vessels, Haji-ware dishes, and fragments of *haniwa* figures. There are also fragments of Jomon pottery, a few pieces of Yayoi ware, some Nara tiles, a sutra box, and an Old Seto jar.

• COMMENTS • The quality of the Kofun material is good. No attempt is made at display, and the labels, in Japanese only, are very scant. All the material is present, either in cases or in boxes. Excavations continue. There is no pamphlet. A specialist in the Kofun period alone would be interested in this museum.

153. Sanuki Folk Art Museum (Sanuki Mingeikan) Ritsurin Koen, Ritsurin-cho, Takamatsu, Kagawa-ken. Tel. Takamatsu 3-6806.

讃岐民芸館　香川県高松市栗林町　栗林公園内

Director: Kunibo Wada. **Hours:** 9–4:30; closed last Thurs. of every month and Dec. 28–31. **Adm.:** ¥20. **Route:** Take bus to Ritsurin Koen and get off at Koen-mae. The museum is one of a group of new buildings to the right, just after entering the park by the east gate.

A large and varied group of Japanese handicrafts housed in a charmingly designed new museum (opened in November 1965) and installed with a certain modern folk flavor. Among the objects are many kinds of household items, such as lamps, some fine chests and cabinets, wooden dishes, lacquer bowls, baskets, and a special collection of locks. The ceramics form a particularly distinguished group, with handsome sakè bottles and big sturdy Tamba jars; there is also a large group of brightly decorated oil bottles. Gunpowder canisters, money boxes, carpenters' tools, fans, dragon masks, and toys are also included.

• COMMENTS • The quality is very good and the display well done. There is a pamphlet in Japanese. About 400 of the 2,700 items owned by the museum are on view at any one time, but the exhibition changes twice a year. The museum building encloses two handsome courtyards and is a pleasure to visit.

Note: The Takamatsu Municipal Museum (just inside the east gate of Ritsurin Park; open 9–4, closed Mondays and the New Year season; admission depending on the exhibition) serves as an exhibiting center for local schools and cultural organizations.

154. Seicho-ji Tomioka Tessai Gallery (Seicho-ji Tomioka Tessai Sakuhin Chinretsujo), Seicho-ji, Yoneya Kiyoshi, Takarazuka, Hyogo-ken. Tel. Takarazuka 6-2260.

清澄寺富岡鉄斎作品陳列場　兵庫県宝塚市米谷(字)清
清澄寺内

Director: Bishop Sakamoto. **Route:** Take Hankyu line from Umeda station, Osaka, either to Takarazuka or to Kyosukojin (the popular name for the Seicho-ji), which is one stop before Takarazuka. A bus runs from either station to the temple on the 28th and 29th of every month for the temple festival. Otherwise, take a taxi (10 min.).

This temple houses a collection of more than a thousand paintings and examples of calligraphy by Tessai Tomioka (1836–1924), all the property of Bishop Sakamoto.

The collection contains the best examples of Tessai's work. A new exhibition hall is being built and is scheduled to open in 1967; in the meantime, the collection is not on view to the public. However, those wishing to see the paintings may be able to do so on previous written application.

155. Seisonkaku (Seisonkaku), 37, 1-chome, Dewa-machi, Kenroku Koen, Kanazawa, Ishikawa-ken. Tel. Kanazawa 61-7874.

成巽閣　石川県金沢市兼六公園出羽町 1 丁目 37 番地

Director: Kan'ichi Yoshitake. **Hours:** 8:30–4:30; closed Jan. 1. **Adm.:** ¥80. **Route:** The museum is in the southwest part of Kenroku Park. Take the tram to Dewa-machi Kokuritsu Byoin-mae, the stop by the National Hospital on Dewa-machi. The park entrance is a 2-min. walk from this stop. Keep the Ishikawa Prefectural Art Museum (No. 54) on the left, and follow the wall of the Seisonkaku compound to the entrance to the museum.

A very large Japanese-style building erected in 1863 by Maeda Nariyasu, the former daimyo of the region, as a retreat for his mother. It now contains a large collection belonging to the Maeda family. On display, in cases, in various tokonoma, and on the walls, are good paintings of the Kano school, portraits of members of the Maeda family, and examples of calligraphy. A narrative scroll in color, assigned to the Kamakura period, and a long scroll in black and white by the emperor Gokogon are occasionally shown. The sliding screens are well painted, and the metal fittings are charming. The collection also includes some costumes and costume accessories, armor, lacquer, porcelain, pottery, and furniture.

• COMMENTS • The decorative arts and the majority of the paintings are all of fairly recent date, but together with the house and the garden they give a picture of the possessions of a daimyo and his family set in their own surroundings which is unrivaled in Japan. The display is good, but the labels are in Japanese only. Normally, about one-fourth of the collection is on view, and the exhibition changes with the seasons. There is a pamphlet in Japanese. Taken as a whole, the house and its possessions are worth visiting, and the park is one of the most beautiful in Japan.

156. Sendai Municipal Museum (Sendai-shi Hakubutsukan), Sannomaruato, Kawauchi, Sendai, Miyagi-ken. Tel. Sendai 25-2557.

仙台市博物館　仙台市川内三の丸跡

Director: Daisaku Tozawa. **Hours:** 9–4; closed Mon., day after a national holiday, and Dec. 28–Jan. 4. **Adm.:** ¥30 (¥80 for special exhibitions). **Route:** Take city bus to Oimawari Jutaku stop; then cross the Hirose River and turn left, opposite the Sports Palace. The museum, a new two-story building in the Western manner, is set well back from the street. (It can also be reached in about 5 min. by taxi.)

A collection of objects, all of the Edo period and formerly the possessions of the Date family, the well-known daimyo of Sendai. Among the items are portraits of members of the family, paintings by the third daimyo, tea-ceremony objects, lacquer, musical instruments, clothing, saddles and stirrups, bows and arrows, swords, and seals. There are also many *shikishi* and other examples of calligraphy and a very large number of family documents.

• COMMENTS • The quality is good, as is the display. Special loan shows are held in the spring and autumn of each year, at which time the permanent collection is not on view. Objects from the Goto Museum (No. 28) were shown in the autumn of 1964 and possessions of the Maeda family in the spring of 1966. Illustrated catalogues usually accompany the special exhibitions. The museum is well worth visiting, both for its permanent collection and for the temporary exhibitions.

157. Seto Ceramics Exhibition Hall (Seto Tojiki Chinretsukan), Kurasho-cho, Seto, Aichi-ken. Tel. Seto 4191.

瀬戸陶磁器陳列館　愛知県瀬戸市蔵所町

Director: Juzo Kato. **Hours:** 8:30–5; closed Mon., national holidays, and New Year season. **Adm.:** ¥10. **Route:** Take Seto line of the Nagoya Railway from Horikawa station, Nagoya, to Seto. From the station, proceed straight ahead to the street bordering the river, turn left (upstream) on this street, and then right over the fourth bridge. The museum is on two floors of a new building called the Ceramic Center, just across the river.

An interesting collection of old and new ceramics of the region. The more recent wares are shown on the ground floor and include much blue-and-white of the Meiji period and many porcelains designed for the Western market. There is also a model of an old kiln.

On the upper floor are fragments of green-glazed Heian ware, medium-sized jars with a darker glaze of the Kamakura and Muromachi periods, black-glazed jars of the

Momoyama period, Edo tea caddies, a Shino dog, Oribe dishes, and many Seto dishes and bottles.

• COMMENTS • The quality of the olderwares is good, as is the general display. The exhibition does not change. Part of the collection is the property of the Ceramic Center; the remainder is on loan. This museum is of interest to the ceramic specialist, particularly for its Heian, Kamakura, and Muromachi pieces.

158.   Shibayama Haniwa Museum (Shibayama Haniwa Hakubutsukan), 298 Shibayama, Shibayama-machi, Chiba-ken. Tel. Shibayama 0004.

芝山はにわ博物館　千葉県芝山町芝山 293 番地

Director: Tokue Hamana. **Hours:** Open on request. **Adm.:** ¥40.
Route: Take Keisei line train from Ueno station, Tokyo, to Narita (1½ hrs.). From Narita, a bus runs 5 times a day to the village of Shibayama (about 1 hr.); or the trip can be made in about ½ hr. by taxi. The museum, consisting of two separate ferroconcrete buildings, lies in the precincts of the Nioson-ji. Inquire at the temple office for someone to open them and then climb the flight of steps to the right of the Kondo, bear right at the top, keep the pagoda on the left, and cross an open space a short distance beyond the pagoda to the museum buildings.

An extraordinarily interesting collection of *haniwa* figures and related archaeological material. There is also a small collection of local folk art.

The archaeological material, which is housed in the new building to the left, comes from two adjoining tumuli, Tonozuka and Himezuka, in the vicinity of the temple. They are dated from A.D. 400 to 450. Tonozuka, the larger tumulus, has yielded many pottery heads of men, women, and animals, as well as a small house and cylinders surmounted by quivers and fans. Inside the tomb were found a sword, a large *magatama,* metal bells, and other metal objects. Many of the *haniwa* from Himezuka are quite complete: curious figures with tall hats, beards, and long, curling locks. The tomb interior also yielded a sword, horse trappings, *magatama,* some pieces of Sue ware, and a variety of small metal objects. Large photographs of the sites complete the display.

The folk art, which occupies the building on the right, consists of local costumes and costume accessories.

• COMMENTS • The quality of the archaeological material is excellent and makes Shibayama well worth a visit. The display is good, with a few labels in English. The most important pieces, except for a few still to be repaired, are on view. Excavations are continuing. There is a good illustrated pamphlet, in Japanese only, describing the collection and the sites.

159. Shido-ji Treasure House (Shido-ji Homotsukan), Shido-ji, Shido-machi, Kagawa-ken. Tel. Shido 28.

志度寺宝物館　香川県志度町　志度寺内

Director: Techo Sogo, Chief Priest. **Hours:** Open on request. **Adm.:** ¥20. **Route:** Turn right on the main highway, then left on the first paved road. The temple is about 400 yards down this road, on the right, a little before the road turns sharply to the right (about 15 min. on foot). The treasure house is in front of the Kondo, on the edge of a recently restored 16th-century garden.

A small but very interesting collection of Japanese painting and calligraphy, with a few pieces of sculpture. The collection is best known for its six large *kakemono* of the Nambokucho period illustrating the history of the temple, with their accompanying scrolls of text. (Four of these are in the treasure house; two are in the Tokyo National Museum.) There is also a hand scroll on the same theme attributed to Tosa Mitsuoki, a charming painting of a man with a monkey signed Tan'yu, and a large Chinese painting (called Sung) of men playing *wei ch'i* in a landscape. Two Buddhist paintings of Aizen and Jizo carry labels of Kobo Daishi and Eshin Sozu, while a painting of a Zen priest is attributed to Sesshu. A painting of a demon is by Gennai.

Among the pieces of calligraphy are a record in Minamoto Yoshitsune's hand of a gift he made to the temple, a sample of the writing of the poet Fujiwara Teika, and another of the Zen priest Muso Kokushi. A copy of the *Ninnokyo* is said to be by Michizane. The sculpture includes a seated Dainichi Nyorai of the Heian period. There is also a small pottery *hibachi* by Dohachi.

• COMMENTS • The quality of the calligraphy and of the paintings illustrating the history of the temple is excellent. The display is barely adequate. About half of the 60 objects owned by the temple are normally on view. Despite its lack of proper installation and some overly optimistic labels, the treasure house is worth visiting.

160. Shimane Prefectural Museum (Shimane Kenritsu Hakubutsukan), 1 Tono-machi, Matsue, Shimane-ken. Tel. Matsue 2-0117.

島根県立博物館　島根県松江市殿町1番地

Director: Saburo Tezeni. **Hours:** 9–5; closed Mon., national holidays, and New Year season. **Adm.:** ¥30 (¥150 for special exhibitions). **Route:** The museum, a handsome new building in the International style, lies near the castle precincts. Take bus to Kita Matsue and get off at Hakubutsukan-mae, the stop in front of the museum (10 min.).

In November 1965 this museum, only recently opened, had no collection of its own. It houses, however, some archaeological material from local excavations or on loan from local temples and shrines, as well as some Buddhist objects lent by various temples, including three large *kakebotoke*, several smaller plaques, and a mirror, all of the Heian period, a small Kannon of the Tempyo period, and some small sutra boxes and *waniguchi* of the Muromachi period.

The most important material in the museum is a fine collection of 157 ancient musical instruments for the performance of Gagaku, the music of the court. These were the property of a branch of the Tokugawa family and are now on a long-term loan.

There is also a small group of local ceramics, including tea bowls of Hirose and Rakuzan, or Izumo, ware.

· COMMENTS · The quality and the display are good; there are some English labels. The collection, however, is apt to be put aside to make room for temporary loan exhibitions, usually of a local character, of which there are two each spring and autumn. The museum is of interest primarily to the student of Japanese music.

161. Shimane University Archaeological Collection (Shimane Daigaku Bunrigakubu Rekishigaku Kenkyushitsu-nai Shiryoshitsu), Shimane Daigaku, Matsue, Shimane-ken. Tel. Matsue 21-7100.

島根大学文理学部歴史学研究室内資料室
島根県松江市　島根大学内

Director: Kiyoshi Yamamoto. **Hours:** Open on request. **Adm.:** free.
Route: The university lies on the outskirts of Matsue. Take bus marked
Daigaku, which stops at the entrance to the university grounds (20 min.).
The collection is in a room at the rear of the upper floor of the main
building; since it is difficult to find, ask at the information office for
a guide.

A small collection of Japanese archaeology, excavated locally. It contains some fragments of Jomon pottery and one
small Jomon pot, several pieces of Yayoi ware, and considerable material of the Kofun period. In the last group are
small and large Sue-ware vessels, some of which are glazed,
Haji-ware vessels, iron swords, a lacquer comb, a mirror,
tubular beads, blue glass beads, *magatama,* and a stone for
polishing the *magatama.*

• COMMENTS • Little attempt has been made to display
the objects, but they can be adequately seen; there are
few labels, and those in Japanese only. The best pieces are
normally on view. The collection is of interest only to the
specialist.

162. Shizuoka Archaeological Museum (Shizuoka
Kokokan), 410 Takamatsu-cho, Shizuoka, Shizuoka-ken.
Tel. Shizuoka 85-0476.

静岡考古館　静岡市高松町 410 番地

Director: Masahiro Mochizuki. **Hours:** 9–4; closed Mon., day following a national holiday, and New Year season. **Adm.:** ¥20. **Route:** The
museum, a small Western-style one-story building, lies on the outskirts of Shizuoka. Take the bus to Toroiseki (30 min.). From the bus
stop, turn left and walk for 4 blocks. The museum and the archaeological
site occupy the next block to the right of the road.

A fascinating collection of objects from the adjoining Toro
site, a large dwelling area of the middle to late Yayoi period.
There is a considerable amount of pottery, but the large
number of wooden items makes the collection unique. There
are wooden farming tools (plows, spades, rakes, and hoes),
kitchen implements (mortars and pestles, mallets and ladles,
cups and bowls, and spoons), drills for making fire, and the
large rectangular boards with rounded ends used by the

inhabitants of the area for walking in the rice fields. Low stools have also been preserved, as well as fragments of looms and dugout canoes.

In addition to the Yayoi pottery vessels, decorated with scratches and comb marking, there have been found some Sue-ware pieces and a vessel with ash glaze. The exhibition also includes a *dotaku* and such stone objects as axes, knives, weights, arrowheads, and *magatama*. Carbonized grains of rice, other seeds, and nuts are shown, usually in the jars in which they were found.

On the adjoining site are the foundations of many oval-shaped dwellings, each surrounded by a small moat, and rectangular godowns. Three houses and one godown have been reconstructed.

• COMMENTS • The quality is good to excellent (particularly the wooden objects), and the display is good. Ten percent of the some 2,000 objects is on view. There is a good illustrated pamphlet, in Japanese, on the site and the collection. Both the museum and the site are most important for the picture they give of Yayoi culture.

163. Shoso-in Treasure House (Shoso-in), Todai-ji, Nara, Nara-ken. Tel. Nara 22-2705.

正倉院　奈良市　東大寺内

Director: Hiroshi Doi. **Hours:** Items from the Shoso-in are exhibited at the Nara National Museum (No. 119) for a short period late in Oct. and early in Nov. Check the dates before going. **Adm.:** ¥50. **Route:** The treasure house, an 8th-century building and originally the godown of the Todai-ji, stands in a walled enclosure to the north of the Daibutsuden (Hall of the Great Buddha). A large rectangular building, made of logs and set high on stilts, it is now empty, as two new fireproof godowns to house the collection were put up a few years ago in the enclosure. Admission to the enclosure, but not to the godowns, may be obtained through one's embassy during the autumn period when the items from the Shoso-in are on view at the Nara National Museum.

The Shoso-in was used as the repository for the personal belongings of the emperor Shomu, which were dedicated to the temple by his widow in 756, as well as for a great variety of objects used in the inauguration ceremony for the Daibutsu, which took place in 752. This collection now forms the oldest surviving museum in the world. Many of the objects are of exceptional beauty and finesse, and all are remarkably well preserved. Among the items are manuscripts, sutras, screens, paintings, pottery vessels, glass objects, lacquer, gilt-copper vessels, textiles, felt rugs, masks, mirrors, jewels, silverware, writing materials, musical instruments, clothing, armor, weapons, carpenters' tools, and Buddhist banners and objects used in Buddhist ceremonies.

The best-known paintings are a set of screen panels representing court ladies standing under flowering trees. Another painting, in ink on hemp, shows a Bodhisattva sitting on a cloud. Further pictorial designs are found on the plectrum guards of the *biwa:* painted, or of wood inlaid with mother-of-pearl, they show figures and animals in a landscape. The textiles form an extraordinarily varied and large group. There are fabrics dyed in batik (wax resist) with designs of animals, birds, and trees; gauzes with abstract patterns; and brocades and twills with roundels enclosing heraldic figures and hunting scenes of a Near Eastern flavor. There are also felt rugs with floral patterns.

One bronze mirror has a typical Chinese T'ang design of animals, birds, and grapevines; another has a flower design of inlaid mother-of-pearl; and a third has delicate birds and flowers of gold and silver inlaid in lacquer. Enormous silver bowls are engraved with hunting scenes of Sassanian inspiration. The numerous pottery bowls are glazed in several colors, splashed on in spots. Ivory is used for foot rules, on which designs of animals and flowers have been carved and stained; it is also used, together with deerhorn, to inlay with enchanting genre scenes the edges of a gaming table. The masks, 164 in all, were made for the Gigaku dances; their varied expressions show the power and humor of the Japanese wood carvers. Among the many lacquered objects are an octagonal mirror box decorated with birds and foliage in lacquer, gold, and silver over a leather ground, and a *kin* of lacquered wood decorated with figures of musicians and fairies on a ground carpeted with flowers and trees in gold and silver embedded in the lacquer.

Items such as coats, trousers, leggings, and socks, a costume for the Gigaku, sashes, slippers, needles, knives, pillows, armrests, low tables, boxes, gaming tables and dice, and medicines give a very vivid picture of the court life in 8th-century Japan.

Some objects in the Shoso-in were probably imported from China; others, such as the textiles and rugs, contain patterns and techniques associated with Sassanian Persia and Central Asia. The provenance of many of these items is still being debated.

· COMMENTS · The quality is superb. The exhibitions in the Nara National Museum are well arranged, with very full labels in Japanese but minimal in English, and an illustrated catalogue, with English titles, for each exhibition, published by the museum. There is a handsome illustrated book *Treasures of the Shoso-in,* published by the Asahi Shimbun Publishing Company, Tokyo, 1966, as well as a short illustrated leaflet on the building and its contents, in English, published by the Imperial Household Agency. Anyone interested in Oriental art should see as much of this collection as possible.

164. Soma Gyofu Memorial Collection (Soma Gyofu Kinenkan), 52 Omachi, Itoigawa, Niigata-ken. Tel. Itoigawa 603.

相馬御風記念館　新潟県糸魚川市大町 52 番地

Director: Chairman of Board of Education. **Hours:** 8:30–5; closed Sun. **Adm.:** free. **Route:** Walk down the main street leading away from the station. The museum, a Japanese-style house separated from the street by a wall and a small garden, is on the left, about 70 yards after the street turns to the right.

The personal possessions and collections of the writer Gyofu Soma, shown in the godown at the rear of his former house. The personal possessions consist of his letters, manuscripts, illustrated poem cards, inkstones, and brushes. The collections vary from a number of Noh masks and masks for temple festivals, puppets, and tea bowls to a group of archaeological items including small pottery figurines and a few pieces of Yayoi pottery and polished stone tools. There is also a selection of folk arts made up of pilgrims' hats; straw snowshoes, boots, and gloves; *geta* for walking on sand; and a miscellany of odds and ends.

As Soma was a great admirer of the calligrapher and poet, the priest Ryokan, he collected many of his letters and a few portraits of him. Soma's study, which is on the upper floor of the house, is also shown, and his published works are collected in a room on the ground floor.

• COMMENTS • The quality of the Soma objects varies from fair to poor; that of the Ryokan material is good. Little attempt is made at display. About half the objects are normally on view; a few pieces are occasionally changed. There is an illustrated pamphlet in Japanese describing the house and the collection; a complete catalogue, also in Japanese, lists all the objects and the literary material. Artistically, the Ryokan material has some interest for the specialist; otherwise, the collection is of interest only to the literary pilgrim.

165. Sugino Gakuen Costume Museum (Sugino Gakuen Isho Hakubutsukan), 223, 4-chome, Kamiosaki, Shinagawa-ku, Tokyo. Tel. Tokyo 449-8151.

杉野学園衣装博物館　東京都品川区上大崎４丁目 223 番地

Director: Shigeichi Sugino. **Hours:** 9–5; closed Sun., and Dec. 29–Jan. 4. **Adm.:** ¥30. **Route:** Take Yamate line from Tokyo Central Station to Meguro, then a taxi, since the museum, a five-story Western-style building faced with pilasters, is hard to find. It is on the same street, but on the opposite side, as the Gajoen Kanko Hotel; taxi drivers will probably not know the museum, but they will know the hotel.

A collection of Western and Eastern costumes displayed in three medium-sized galleries on as many floors. There are Western dresses from the 1890's to the 1920's, some few 18th-century European garments, reproductions of earlier European clothing, a few European peasant costumes, Chinese and Southeast Asian clothing, very fine Ainu and Taiwanese garments, and a good selection of Edo kimono and Noh costumes. There are also Japanese court uniforms in the Western style, a Japanese garment worn by the emperor Meiji, Japanese court dress of the Edo period, and Western-style dresses made for Japanese women in the late 19th century.

The *Nara Emaki,* a hand scroll of the Edo period, is shown to illustrate various types of Edo clothing. Sample books of Japanese materials complete the exhibition.

• COMMENTS • The quality is fair to good. The display is adequate, and there are a few labels in French. All the collection is always on view. The museum was opened in 1957 as an adjunct to the neighboring Sugino Junior College for Dressmaking. It is unique in Japan, but its interest for Westerners is limited.

166. Sumitomo Collection (Sen'oku Hakkokan), 25 Shimo Miyanomae-cho, Shikagatani, Sakyo-ku, Kyoto. Tel. Kyoto 77-2095.

泉屋博古館　京都市左京区鹿ケ谷下宮前町 25 番地

Director: Shozo Hotta. **Hours:** 10–4, from 4th Sun. in Oct. for 2 weeks, in good weather only. **Adm.:** ¥100. **Route:** The museum, a two-story Western-style building, is to the left of the entrance to the Sumitomo family property in the eastern section of the city. It is advisable to take a taxi.

A very large and superb collection of Chinese bronze vesles, Chinese and Japanese mirrors, and a few Chinese bronze Buddhist figures, all the property of the head of the Sumitomo family.

The majority of the bronzes are of the Yin and early Chou dynasties; a few are of the middle Chou; and quite a number date from the Warring States period and the Han dynasty. The best-known bronze vessel is a very elaborate Yin-dynasty *yu* in the form of an animal holding a child. Almost as well known and of the same period is a huge drum with human faces on the sides. An armrest, also of the Yin period, is unique. The collection is also noted for its large number of Yin *lei,* for its numerous bells of all periods, and for its Han and T'ang mirrors.

Among the gilt-bronze Buddhist figures is one of Maitreya dated 498. A special item is a T'ang miniature bronze coffin and stand, around which are placed four figures.

In the much smaller Japanese section are a large *dotaku* and a spearhead of the Yayoi period, and several Kofun mirrors.

• COMMENTS • The quality and the variety of the more than 500 pieces make this one of the great Oriental bronze collections of the world. The display is good, with some labels in English. Anyone with even the slightest interest in Chinese art should see this collection.

167. Suntory Art Gallery (Suntory Bijutsukan), Palace Hotel Annex, 9th floor, 10, 1-chome, Marunouchi, Chiyoda-ku, Tokyo. Tel. Tokyo 211-6936.

サントリー美術館　東京都千代田区丸の内1丁目10番地
パレスホテルビル9階

Director: Keizo Saji. **Hours:** 10–5; closed Mon., New Year season, and for short period when exhibition is being changed. **Adm.:** ¥100. **Route:** To reach the Palace Hotel, walk straight ahead from the main entrance of Tokyo station for 3 long blocks, then turn right. The hotel occupies the second block to the right; the entrance to the annex is around the corner from the hotel entrance.

The fine permanent collection of this gallery consists of Japanese lacquer, ceramics, glass, iron teakettles, costumes, masks, paintings, and prints, with the lacquer predominating. The main activity of the gallery, however, is to hold a constant series of loan exhibitions, for which the permanent collection generally forms a basis.

The Kamakura lacquer objects include a *tebako,* an incense caddy, a red tray, and a red bowl on a high foot. From the Muromachi period are a mirror box, a writing box, a writing table, a box for stationery, a hot-water jug, and several bowls. Two small *sumiaka,* writing boxes, a rice container, a drum-shaped wine barrel, and a pillow containing an incense burner date from the Momoyama period. The Edo period is represented by a bookcase for the volumes of the *Genji Monogatari,* a drum body, and lunch boxes in tiers—among other pieces. The lacquered costume accessories include combs and hair ornaments.

In the ceramic group are a few Jomon bowls, a yellow-glazed Seto wine ewer, an Oribe dish and cover, and a Shigaraki flower vase (these three of the Momoyama period) and, from the Edo period, a good selection of Kakiemon dishes and bowls, Imari bowls, a Banko saké bottle, and an Iga jar. The glass section contains Satsuma cut-glass bowls and a brush pot and a Nagasaki blue glass wine ewer, all of the Edo period. There are also Edo Noh masks and costumes and Edo kimono. An Ashiya iron teakettle and a Temmoyo teakettle date from the Muromachi period.

Among the paintings are a pair of Momoyama *namban* sixfold screens, some large figures of dancers which were originally panels of an Edo-period sixfold screen, a pair of twofold screens of autumn flowers by Korin, scenes from

171

the *Ise Monogatari* by Sotatsu, and an album of landscapes by Taiga. The prints include examples by most of the important 18th- and 19th-century artists of the *ukiyo-e* school.

• COMMENTS • The quality of both the permanent collection and the loan exhibitions is very high, and the installation is very well done, with complete labels in English. The loan shows, which generally last from six weeks to two months and are primarily concerned with the decorative arts, are accompanied by handsome illustrated catalogues in Japanese with check lists in English. The more important exhibitions are held in the spring and autumn, and the character of any loan show determines the items on view from the permanent collection.

A small library and reading room adjoin the gallery and provide a fine view over the Imperial Palace gardens. Both gallery and reading room offer, in the center of Tokyo, a haven of beauty and tranquility that should not be missed.

168. Suwa Municipal Art Museum (Suwa-shi Bijutsu-kan), Nakahama-machi, Suwa, Nagano-ken. Tel. Suwa 1217.

諏訪市美術館　長野県諏訪市中浜町

Director: Yukio Oguchi. **Hours:** 9–5:30; closed Mon., national holidays, and Dec. 28–Jan. 3. **Adm.:** ¥50. **Route:** The museum is on the shore of Lake Suwa, beside the Katakura Kaikan. On leaving Kamisuwa station on Chuo line, turn left and proceed along the main street, then fork left under the railway and take the second street to the left. The museum is on the right, beyond the second hotel (10 min.).

A collection of local archaeology and contemporary Japanese paintings, sculpture, and handicrafts, displayed in a two-story building of part Western, part Japanese style. The archaeology is usually shown on the ground floor, to the right of the entrance. There are good pottery vessels, a few figurines, and an enormous number of stone arrowheads of the middle Jomon period. From the Kofun period are Sue-ware and Haji-ware vessels, *magatama,* rings, cylindrical beads, pieces of armor, and horse bits.

The contemporary arts normally occupy the rest of the ground floor and the upper floor. The exhibition usually contains most of the 30-odd pieces owned by the museum, the remainder being loans. The large majority of the paintings and sculpture are by Japanese artists working in the Western manner.

• COMMENTS • The quality of the archaeology is good, that of the contemporary arts fair. The installation is perfectly adequate. Eighty percent of the archaeology is generally on view, but the cases may be pushed aside at any time to make room for a special show. The contemporary section changes two or three times a year, and one or more special exhibitions are held during the year. There is a pamphlet on the archaeological material and a check list of the contemporary material which also lists the special exhibitions held during the past ten years. The museum is of interest to the specialist in either of the two fields represented.

169. Tajimi Municipal Old Ceramics Exhibition Hall (Tajimi-shi Kotoki Chinretsukan), c/o Chamber of Commerce, Shin-machi, Tajimi, Gifu-ken. Tel. Tajimi 22-0165/6.

多治見市古陶器陳列館　岐阜県多治見市新町

Director: Shoroku Kato, President of the Chamber of Commerce.
Hours: 9–4:30; closed Mon., national holidays, and New Year season.
Adm.: ¥20. **Route:** Cross over the river and turn immediately left upstream. The Chamber of Commerce Building, a Western-style office structure, is a short distance upstream on the right (about 20 min. on foot).

A small but interesting group of ceramics, all from kiln sites in the neighborhood of Tajimi, housed in two rooms to the left of the entrance hall. This area was part of the old Mino Province, where kilns have been active since the end of the 16th century. The collection consists largely of Oribe ware, including a group of charming small dishes, with some good Shino dishes and tea bowls and a little Seto. There are also a good many fragments. No dates are given, but the majority of the pieces are probably of the Edo period. In the same building is a display room for contemporary local wares.

• COMMENTS • The quality is good, but almost all the items belong to private collectors, the city owning only a few. The display is well arranged. The exhibition changes occasionally. There is a small illustrated pamphlet in Japanese. The museum is of interest only to the specialist in ceramics.

170. Takaoka City Art Museum (Takaoka-shi Bijutsu-kan), Kojo Koen, Sadazuka-cho, Takaoka, Toyama-ken. Tel. Takaoka 3-2032.

高岡市美術館　富山県高岡市定塚町　古城公園内

Director: Taketoshi Jozuka. **Hours:** 9–5; closed Mon., Dec. 27–Jan. 5, and when special exhibitions are being installed. **Adm.:** free when the permanent collection is on view; varying charges for special exhibitions. **Route:** The museum, a largish Western-style ferroconcrete building, is on the edge of Kojo Park, in the old castle grounds. The No. 1 bus goes to the park.

The permanent collection consists of a small group of contemporary paintings in both the Western and the Japanese manner, and sculptures, metalwork, lacquer, textiles, and ceramics by local artists and artisans. It is, however, seldom on view, for the museum is primarily an exhibiting gallery, holding each year a series of loan shows from April 1 to December 27. In November 1964, for example, a very good loan exhibition of Kutani ware occupied all the galleries.

· COMMENTS · The collection is adequate, as is the display. Some of the loan exhibitions are accompanied by good catalogues in Japanese.

171. Takayama Local Museum (Takayama Kyodo Hakubutsukan), 75 Kami Ichino-machi, Takayama, Gifu-ken. Tel. Takayama 2-1205.

高山郷土博物館　岐阜県高山市上一之町 75 番地

Director: Miki Kobayashi. **Hours:** 8:30–5, Apr.–Oct.; 8:30–4:30, Nov.–Mar.; closed Mon. and national holidays. **Adm.:** ¥30. **Route:** The bus from the station stops in front of the museum, a pleasant Japanese-style building.

An interesting and very extensive collection of local folk arts, plus local archaeological and historical material.

On the ground floor are the exhibits illustrating the local life of the recent past. These include a variety of articles for household use (storage jars, wooden bowls, straw baskets, mirror stands, standing and traveling lamps, weights and measures, money boxes, flint-and-steel sets for making fire, spinning wheels, and a loom). A large section is devoted to clothing, which includes farmers' clogs, straw hats and coats, felt coats and snowhoes, as well as firemen's coats and workmen's jackets. There is also a selection of farm tools including the special plows for rice fields, fire-fighting equipment, and the entire furnishings of an old-fashioned shop. One room is devoted to the extremely interesting sculpture in wood by the 17th-century priest-sculptor Enku.

The upper floor contains the archaeology and the local crafts. All the archaeological items come from the Hida area, the nearby region of the Japanese Alps, and include largely fragmentary Jomon pottery and stone tools of all five stages; Yayoi pottery; and relics of the Kofun period such as Sue ware, fragments of armor, a few *magatama* and other ornaments, a mirror, and a sword. In the crafts section are examples of trays and other items of the local Shunkei lacquer, a transparent yellowish-brown lacquer which allows the grain of the wood to be seen. There is also a good display of the products of the local kilns, with such names as Ito, Genjuro, Yamada, and Sampukuji; the oil dishes and those with horse-eye designs are very good. The work of local sculptors and swordsmiths, as well as portraits of the local daimyo and other worthies, coins, firearms, topographical views, and local records are also shown on this floor.

• COMMENTS • The quality is good, the display adequate. Ten percent of the collection is normally on view, and the exhibition is occasionally changed. There is a descriptive pamphlet in Japanese. The museum is worth visiting, especially for the sculpture of Enku, the folk arts, and the local products.

172. Tea Cult Museum (Chado Bijutsukan), Oaza Okano-machi, Takayanagi, Kariwa-gun, Niigata-ken. Tel. Takayanagi 100.

茶道美術館　新潟県刈羽郡高柳町大字岡野町

Director: K. Murayama, owner. **Hours:** closed. **Route:** The museum is on the edge of the small village of Takayanagi, in a beautiful valley about 12 miles south of Kashiwazaki. Take the bus from Kashiwazaki to Okano-machi and get off at Teikanen-mae (1 hr.). Cross the road and climb up the winding stone steps to a second road, on the other side of which lies the entrance to the museum.

This museum, which has a fine collection of objects pertaining to the tea ceremony, has been closed since 1962. It is hoped that it will be reopened sometime in the future. The garden may be visited.

· COMMENTS · The beauty of the garden and of the unspoiled village repay one for the long trip.

173.   Tekisui Art Museum (Tekisui Bijutsukan), 60 Yama-ashiya-cho, Ashiya, Hyogo-ken. Tel. Ashiya 2-2228.

滴翠美術館　兵庫県芦屋市山芦屋町 60 番地

Director: Mrs. Chika Yamaguchi, owner. **Hours:** 10–4:30; closed Mon. and when exhibitions are being changed. **Adm.:** ¥100. **Route:** Take Hankyu line from either Osaka or Kobe to Ashiyagawa. On leaving the station, turn left on the street that runs at right angles to the railroad; then take the second street to the left (by the post office), then the first large street leading uphill to the right. The entrance to the museum, a large private house set well back from the street, is on the right, about 100 yards past the first crossroad (10 min.).

An interesting group of Chinese and Japanese objects, installed on the upper floor of one wing of the house. The museum was opened in 1964 and draws for its exhibitions on the collections of the members of the Yamaguchi family, adding at times a few items borrowed from the outside.

Among the Chinese items that have been shown are stone bas-reliefs of the Han dynasty, an excellent group of Sung and Yuan ceramic grave pillows, and paintings from the Yuan to the Ch'ing dynasty. Many of the grave pillows have charming bird, animal, or flower designs in black on white or green. There is a fine small landscape assigned to the Yuan dynasty, a good landscape scroll by Hsu Chih of the Ming dynasty, another by Wang Chao of the 17th century, and many paintings of the Ch'ing dynasty by such artists as Lo Mu, Lo Liang-feng, Mei Ch'ing, and Kao Feng-han.

Japanese objects that have been exhibited include a large group of Otsu paintings, Seto oil dishes, Old Imari ware, a remarkable group of dolls and ceramic figurines, a collection of battledores and shuttlecocks, and other toys and games.

Korean ceramics and paintings of the Yi dynasty have also been on display.

• COMMENTS • The quality is generally good. The installation is well done. About four exhibitions are held each year, with an illustrated pamphlet to accompany each one. There is also a leaflet on the museum. All the publications are in Japanese only. The museum is worth visiting.

174. Tenri Gallery (Tenri Gallery), Tokyo Tenrikyokan (9th floor), 19, 1-chome, Nishiki-cho, Kanda, Chiyoda-ku, Tokyo. Tel. Tokyo 292-0501.

天理ギャラリー　東京都千代田区神田錦町１丁目19番地
東京天理教館９階

Director: Akio Koizumi. **Hours:** 9–4, Mon.–Fri.; 9–3, Sat.; closed Sun., national holidays, Dec. 30–Jan. 4, and for a week or 10 days when exhibition is being changed. **Adm.:** free. **Route:** The museum is on the 9th floor of the Tokyo Tenrikyokan, which serves as the Tokyo headquarters of the Tenri sect. It is at the Mitoshiro-cho stop on the bus line to Arakawa Dotei, near the Y.M.C.A. building.

This gallery, which was opened in 1962, has no permanent collection of its own but stages four exhibitions a year, drawing the material from the collections of the Tenri Museum (No. 175) in Tenri. In the past few years, the gallery has held exhibitions of "Arts and Crafts of Ancient Greece," "Clay Burial Figures of Ancient China," "Ancient Pottery Roof Tiles of the Far East," "Ancient Persian Art," and "Chinese Tomb Reliefs of the Han Dynasty."

• COMMENTS • The exhibitions are very well installed, and there are some English labels. An illustrated catalogue, in Japanese but usually with English subtitles, accompanies each exhibition. The gallery is well worth visiting.

175. Tenri Museum (Tenri Sankokan), 1 Furu, Tenri, Nara-ken. Tel. Tenri 2-1511.

天理参考館　奈良県天理市布留１番地

Director: Kiyo-o Fukuhara. **Hours:** 9–4; closed Sun. and Dec. 27–Jan. 5. **Adm.:** free. **Route:** The museum is located on the upper floors of the northeast corner of the large complex of new buildings to the east of Tenri Temple. It is reached in about 15 min. on foot, going east from the Tenri station on the Kintetsu Electric Railway or from the main bus stop on the local bus line from Nara.

An extensive and excellent collection of Japanese and Korean pre-Buddhist antiquities; Chinese art up to the T'ang dynasty; Near Eastern, Egyptian, and classical antiquities; medieval Iranian pottery; pre-Columbian antiquities; and ethnological material from North and South America, the South Pacific, the Asiatic mainland, India and Ceylon, the Near East, and Central Africa. The collections, belonging to the Tenri sect organization, are constantly being enlarged, but there is little Buddhist or Christian art.

The early Japanese and Chinese material and the Near Eastern and classical collections are shown on the fourth floor, which is usually closed but can be opened on request. The other collections are on the second and third floors.

The Japanese archaeological collection is very good. It includes prehistoric stone weapons and tools and utensils of bone and shell; Jomon pottery; Yayoi pottery and good *dotaku;* and fine *haniwa* figures, a coffin, Sue-ware vessels, swords, mirrors, and jewels of the Kofun period. There are also roof tiles of the Asuka and Nara periods and an equally extensive collection of roof tiles from the Chinese colony of Lo-lang in Korea and the Korean kingdoms of Koguryo, Paekche, and Silla. The early Chinese section is noted for its variety and quality. There is a good selection of neolithic pottery, followed by Yin and Chou bronze vessels, jades, and pottery. There are also lacquer vessels, pottery, tomb figurines, and mirrors of the Warring States period, and, from the Han dynasty, mirrors, tomb figures (including many models of houses, barns, and wellheads), roof tiles, and pottery tomb pillars and slabs. A large group of tomb figures dates from the Six Dynasties, while the T'ang dynasty is represented by superb tomb figures, many brilliantly glazed, and rare silver vessels, mirrors, and glass.

The collections from the Near East, Egypt, Greece, and Rome are smaller in extent but nonetheless give a good account of these civilizations. There are clay vessels and figurines from the ancient Iranian sites of Nahavand and

Gilan; bronzes from Luristan; Parthian and Sassanian bronzes and glass objects; and a large group of 9th- to 14th-century Iranian pottery. The Egyptian items include a mummy case, bas-reliefs, and figurines. From ancient Greece there is a full range of pottery; there are also Tanagra figurines, gold jewelry, glass, and Cypriote pottery. The Etruscans are represented by their pottery, and the Romans by a variety of small sculptures.

The pre-Columbian items include Mexican stone and pottery figures, Mexican pottery vessels, and Peruvian pottery, textiles, stone tools, and shrunken heads. The American Indian collection contains totem poles from the Northwest Coast, beadwork from the Plains, and basketry and pottery from the Southwest. Hunting masks and a kayak represent the Eskimo. The large collections from the South Pacific include wooden masks, shields, weapons, stone tools, canoes, furniture, textiles, drums, and carved wooden figures. The African section has wooden masks and figures, drums, and weapons, largely from Central Africa.

There are Thai masks, Javanese shadow-play figures, puppets, masks, wooden shields, krises, and textiles, and Sumatra, Borneo, the Celebes, the Philippines, and the aboriginal tribes of South Taiwan are represented by clothing, carvings, and other wooden objects. India is represented by musical instruments, textiles, and bronze figures of Hindu deities; Ceylon, by its wooden masks. The Central Asian group includes religious objects, costumes, and costume accessories, largely from Nepal and Tibet. From the Near East are carpets and costumes.

Chinese life in the 19th century is illustrated by a large collection of costumes and costume accessories and household utensils. From Korea come furniture, costumes, and musical instruments; and from Japan, puppets, games, *ema,* and other folk arts. The civilization of the Ainu is shown by clothing, jewelry, libation wands, weapons of the hunt, and household items.

• COMMENTS • The ethnological collections are rare for Japan, and the excellent archaeological collections are essential for the study of the early Japanese and Chinese cultures. The display is clear, though at times somewhat crowded, and there are a few English labels. There is no regular exhibition schedule, but the installation is occasionally changed, and about ten percent of the collection is normally visible. There is a large illustrated handbook, in Japanese only, and a smaller one, in English, to the ethnological collections. An idea of the other collections may be obtained from the illustrated catalogues, in Japanese but usually with English subtitles, issued for the exhibitions of material from the museum held in the Tenri Gallery, Tokyo (No. 174). There is also a brief pamphlet in Japanese and English and a small illustrated booklet in Japanese for the entire collection.

176. Tibetan Collection at the Kotoku-ji (Zoshukan), Kotoku-ji, Taba-cho, Hanamaki, Iwate-ken. Tel. Hanamaki 4614.

蔵収館　岩手県花巻市たば町　光徳寺内

Director: Gizo Kamakura. **Hours:** Open on request. **Adm.:** free. **Route:** Any bus from the station stops at Kami-cho, which is less than 100 yards from the temple. (By taxi, 10 min.) Ask locally for directions. The collection is housed in a small concrete building to the left of the entrance to the temple precincts.

A small collection of Tibetan objects, collected by Mr. Tokan Tada, a noted Tibetan scholar, consisting of priests' robes, hats, prayer wheels, *vajra,* religious books with carved wood covers, six paintings, and some bronze statuettes. Among the last is a figure of Gautama. The paintings depict the deified reforming monk Tsong-kha-pa and other Lamaist deities.

　• COMMENTS • The quality and the display are fair; the infrequent labels are in Japanese only. There are a small pamphlet and a folder in Japanese. All of the collection is normally visible. It has no important display items and is of interest only to specialists in the Tibetan field.

177. Togari-ishi Archaeological Hall (Togari-ishi Kokan), Minamioshio, Toyohira, Chino, Nagano-ken. Tel. Chino 2101.

尖石考古館　長野県茅野市豊平南大塩

Director: Fusakazu Miyasaka. **Hours:** 9–5; normally closed Mon., but can, in fact, be opened any time on request. **Adm.:** ¥20. **Route:**

The museum is about 6 miles northeast of the center of Chino. Take a bus to the village of Minamioshio (45 min.), then walk on for a short distance uphill. The museum, a small, fairly new ferroconcrete building with a façade in the shape of a parabolic curve, stands to the left of the road. (As the bus runs infrequently, it is far easier to take a taxi from Chino, a trip of about 20 min., though half the distance is over rough country roads.)

A collection of Jomon stone and pottery objects, largely from the nearby site of Togari-ishi. One of the great Jomon sites of Nagano Prefecture, it has yielded thousands of items. Among these are some very interesting small figurines; large, elaborately decorated jars; and a number of ornaments, including some circular earrings. A group of early-Jomon pointed vases and late-Jomon vessels is also shown. There are, in addition, some paleolithic stone tools from Shibukawa and photographs and maps of the sites to round out the exhibition.

The actual site of Togari-ishi, near Toyohira village and some distance beyond the museum, is on a plateau on the west slope of Mount Tatsugatake and has been made into an archaeological park with some reconstructed houses.

• COMMENTS • The quality is excellent; the display (which almost never changes) is adequate. About five percent of the collection is on view, but this includes the best display pieces. There is an illustrated pamphlet in Japanese which also contains a map showing the location of the sites and the roads from Chino to the museum. Although the museum is admittedly of interest chiefly to the specialist, the quality of the Jomon pieces should attract anyone interested in a fine archaeological collection.

178. Tohoku University Archaeological Collection
(Tohoku Daigaku Kokoshiryoshitsu), Tohoku Daigaku, Katahiro-cho, Sendai, Miyagi-ken. Tel. Sendai 23-5111.

東北大学考古資料室　仙台市片広町　東北大学内

Director: Professor Nobuo Ito. **Assistant Director:** Professor Hayashi.
Hours: Open on request. **Adm.:** free. **Route:** Take tram for Tohoku Daigaku Byoin (Tohoku University Hospital). Get off at Tohoku University stop; go through the gates and continue ahead on the main road. The collection is housed in a small red brick building that stands by itself near the far end of this road, on the right and in front of a large new building.

A large and interesting study collection of Japanese archaeology, chiefly of the Jomon period, from excavations in the Tohoku area and on Hokkaido. All five stages are represented, with the display chronologically arranged. Pottery vessels predominate; there are few large figures, but there is a considerable group of small fetishes. The collection also contains some *haniwa* figurines, mostly fragmentary, and a unique suit of Ainu armor.

• COMMENTS • The quality is good; the installation is crowded but adequate. About ten percent of the collection is normally visible; special exhibitions of the material are arranged for conferences. The university continues to excavate. The collection is primarily for the use of university students or other specialists.

Note: There is a project to move the university to another part of the city and to build, on the new site, a museum for the proper display of the archaeological material.

179. To-ji Treasure House (To-ji Homotsuden), To-ji, Kujo-dori, Nishi Kujo-machi, Minami-ku, Kyoto. Tel. Kyoto 69-3325/6.

東寺宝物殿　京都市南区西九条町九条通　東寺内

Director: Chokaku Kimura, Chief Priest. **Hours:** 9–4; the Kodo is open every day; objects from the treasure house may be shown in one of the temple buildings for several days beginning June 15, the date of the temple festival; the treasure house may be open in the autumn and at one or two other unspecified dates during the year. **Adm.:** ¥50 for Kodo; ¥150 for Kodo and treasure house. **Route:** The temple, southwest of Kyoto station, can be reached by bus No. 9. Get off at To-ji-mae. The treasure house, of ferroconcrete in the godown style, is at the end to the right of the paved walk leading from the street. The Kodo is in the temple precincts, on the left.

The new treasure house, opened in October 1965, holds many of the famous statues, paintings, sutras, and other objects owned by the temple. The objects are sometimes shown on the two upper floors of the building.

Among the large pieces of sculpture are a Jizo of the Heian period, a Bishamonten standing on three small figures (called Chinese of the T'ang dynasty), a seated figure of Hachiman, another of Monju Bosatsu seated on a chair, and a seated female deity, all of the Heian period.

There is a remarkable group of paintings, including the famous large portraits of seven patriarchs of the Shingon sect. Of these, five are by the Chinese artist Li Chen and were brought back from China in 806 by Kobo Daishi; two were painted after his return to Japan. A set of ten seated Juniten was painted by the monk Kakunin to replace those lost in a fire at the temple in 1127. Another set of the same deities, shown standing, is mounted on a screen and was painted by Takuma Shoga in 1191. A Juichimen Kannon and a *Doshi-kyo mandara* are of the Kamakura period.

The manuscripts include a *Fushincho* in Kobo Daishi's own hand, and his *Seirai Mokuroku* (Memorandum on the Presentation of the List of Newly Imported Sutras) in the hand of Dengyo Daishi. Documents include a record of the To-ji's treasures of the Kamakura period as well as Kamakura-period accounts of seven temples in the Kyoto and Nara areas. There is also a bill of sale for some land, dated 752.

From the Heian period there are a lacquer armrest and a beautiful black-lacquer *kesa* box with a design of birds and waves. There are also a series of Heian gilt-bronze alms bowls and a small stupa, while a *vajra,* a bell, and a tray, all of gilt bronze, are of the T'ang dynasty.

· COMMENTS · The quality is superb, and the installation is good, though the cases are old-fashioned and cumbersome. There is an illustrated catalogue for the treasure house and the Kodo.

The **Kodo,** the second building on the right from the entrance to the temple precincts, has been arranged for the display of the other important pieces of sculpture for which the temple is famous. The best known are the Go Nyorai, the Go Bosatsu, the Go Dai Myo-o, two of the Shi Tenno, a Bonten, and a Taishakuten. The statues are arranged according to the precepts of the *Ninno-gokoku-kyo mandara*. Even though the Go Nyorai and one of the Go Bosatsu are later copies, the group still gives an amazing impression of Heian sculpture.

· COMMENTS · The quality is excellent, the installation is impressive, and some of the labels are in English. There is a pamphlet in Japanese and English. The Kodo should be seen by all who are interested in Japanese sculpture.

Note: The proper name of the To-ji is Kyo-o-gokoku-ji.

180. Tokiwayama Collection (Tokiwayama Bunko), 1993 Fueta, Kamakura, Kanagawa-ken. Tel. Kamakura 1828.

常盤山文庫　鎌倉市笛田 1993 番地

Director: Tsusai Sugawara. **Hours:** 10–4, Sun. and national holidays; 1–4, Sat.; closed Aug. and Dec. 1–Feb. 28. **Adm.:** free. **Route:** Take bus for Fujisawa and get off at Uchikoshi, the first stop after the tunnel. Take the dirt road to the left that leads downhill, across another dirt road, and then uphill. The museum is housed in a group of large farmhouses on the left side of this road; the entrance is up a flight of stone steps, past stone lanterns, and through a gate.

A superb collection of Chinese and Japanese painting and calligraphy, plus a few pieces of Chinese and Japanese sculpture and some Japanese handicrafts.

The calligraphy is famous, with very fine examples from the Chinese Sung and Yuan dynasties and from the Japanese Heian, Kamakura, and Nambokucho periods. Among the Chinese items are specimens (to name but a few) of the calligraphy of Wu-chun Shih-fan, Chun-hai Yuan-chao,Tui-keng Te-ning, and Shih Liang-chung of the Sung dynasty, and of Yueh-chien Wen-ming, Ku-lin Ch'ing-mao, and Yun-wai Yun-hsiu of the Yuan dynasty. From the Heian period are fragments of anthologies such as the *Kokinshu*, the *Man'yoshu*, the *Iseshu*, and the *Wakan Roeishu*, some of which are attributed to such calligraphers as Gyosei, Kinto, Sadanobu, Sari, and Tofu. A piece of calligraphy by Shigen Sogen is dated 1279, and there are also a prayer written by Ashikaga Takauji and some fine pieces by Issan Ichinei. Many well-known priests of the Kamakura period are represented, including Daito Kokushi, with a letter.

The Chinese Sung paintings include a fine *kakemono* of a landscape and an album painting of white jasmine. From the Yuan dynasty are figures of Shih Te, Bodhidharma, and a Lohan.

Among the early Japanese items are a remarkable Heian painting of the Thousand Buddhas, a Fudo Myo-o of the

184

Nambokucho period, and a Kujaku Myo-o, a Shaka triad, a Rakan, and scenes from the *Ise Monogatari* painted over a sutra written in Sanskrit—all of the Kamakura period. The Muromachi period is represented by a white-robed Kannon by Shuho, a figure of Toshimi by Sesshu, *Snowy Landscape* by Shutoku, *Birds* by Sesson, *Flower Basket* and *Eight Views of the Hsiao and the Hsiang* by Unkei, and several charming unsigned landscapes. A screen depicting a shooting contest on horseback, *Inu Ou Mono,* is from the Momoyama period, while from the Edo period come a figure of Fukurokuju by Shokado, *Swallows* by Tan'yu, *Kannon and a White Heron* by Naonobu, a sixfold landscape screen by Chokuan II, and *Eight Views of Lake Biwa* (Omi Hakkei) by Yusetsu. From the contemporary period are seventeen screens painted by Tessai.

The sculpture includes a tall early-Heian Juichimen Kannon, a very delicate standing Amida Nyorai of the later Heian period, and an equally delicate T'ang-dynasty Chinese stone figure of a Bodhisattva in high relief.

The tea-ceremony objects include bamboo spoons once used by the tea master Sen no Rikyu, Shino tea bowls of the Momoyama period, and a tea bowl by Ninsei. A lacquer writing box from the Muromachi period is particularly handsome.

• COMMENTS • The quality is excellent, and the display is charmingly done in an informal way. Of the 2,000 items in the collection about 50 are shown at any one time; the sculpture is always on view, and the other pieces are changed each month. A pamphlet in Japanese, but with a brief English foreword, describes the collection in some detail. A very good idea of the collection may be obtained from an illustrated catalogue in Japanese issued in the autumn of 1964 for an exhibition of the collection held at the Matsuzakaya Department Store in Tokyo.

Note: Permission to visit the collection when it is closed during the winter may be granted on request made in writing in advance.

181. Tokoname Ceramic Research Center (Tokoname Togei Kenkyujo), 45 Hikake, Tokoname, Aichi-ken. Tel. Tokoname 5-3970.

常滑陶芸研究所　愛知県常滑市樋掛 45 番地

Director: Gasuka Ina, President of the Center; Yoshiharu Sawada, Curator and Member of the Commission. **Hours:** 9–5; closed during New Year season. **Adm.:** free. **Route:** From Nagoya, take the Meitetsu Railway to Tokoname (50 min.), then a bus to Hikake. The building, a contemporary ferroconcrete structure with lavender mosaic decoration, stands on a low bluff overlooking the city.

A small but most interesting collection of early Tokoname ware, shown in the exhibition room to the left of the entrance hall. There are a number of jars, partially glazed in light green, and some small unglazed jars, bowls, and fragments, all of the Heian period. From the Kamakura period are huge pots, and one of the main features of the collection: a tile with the face of a demon. A few jars and other vessels of the Edo period, together with samples of the present-day products of the center, complete the display. The early pieces were all found locally, Tokoname having been the site of one of the "six old kilns" of Japanese ceramic history. It is still an important ceramic center.

Ceramics made now at the research center are displayed and sold in a room to the right of the entrance hall. Behind the main building, in separate quarters, are ceramic workshops and kilns.

• COMMENTS • The quality is very good, and the display is well arranged in lighted wall and floor cases. Fifty percent of the collection is normally on view. Changes are occasionally made in the exhibition, but there is no regular schedule. There is an illustrated pamphlet in Japanese. The center, for both its collection and its contemporary work in ceramics, is of great interest to any student of Japanese pottery.

Note: The Tokoname Ceramic Hall (Tokoname Tojikan), 30, 1-chome, Yashikida, Tokoname), which is sometimes listed as a museum, is an exhibition hall for the contemporary ceramic products of Tokoname. It also shows a few of the early ceramic pieces that belong to the research center.

182. Tokugawa Art Museum (Tokugawa Bijutsukan), 27, 2-chome, Tokugawa-cho, Higashi-ku, Nagoya, Aichiken. Tel. Nagoya 941-6626.

徳川美術館　名古屋市東区徳川町 2 丁目 27 番地

Director: Goroku Kamagawa. **Hours:** 9–4; closed for New Year season and when exhibition is being changed. **Adm.:** ¥100 (¥150 for special exhibitions). **Route:** Take No. 16 bus for Chayagasaka; get off at the Shindeki stop (20 min.), walk left for 1 block, then turn right. The museum, a ferroconcrete building, is the second on the left and set back from the road. (Do not be deceived by distances as shown on maps of Nagoya; they are enormous.)

A superb and very large collection of nearly all forms of Japanese art, except sculpture, as well as a number of Chinese paintings and ceramics.

The best-known Heian paintings in the collection are 43 segments of the *Genji Monogatari Emaki,* attributed to Fujiwara Takayoshi; they are exhibited about once every ten years. Kamakura scrolls include *Monogatari Emaki* (an unidentified story) in 12 segments; *Saigyo Monogatari Emaki* (Biography of the Priest Saigyo), 1 segment, attributed to Fujiwara Tsunetaka; *Tenno Sekkan Ei Zukan* (Portraits of Emperors, Regents, and Advisers to Emperors), 1 segment; *Yareko Tonto Ekotoba* (A Fable of Rebirth in Paradise), 1 segment; and *Haizumi Monogatari* (The Story of a Buddhist Nun). From the first half of the 17th century is a charming folding screen, *Honda Heihachiro Esugata* (The Exchange of Letters Between Two Shy Lovers). Other screens of this and the Momoyama period depict the gay plebeian life of the age, and an interesting scroll of the early Edo period illustrates the Kabuki theater. The black-and-white paintings include *kakemono* of Kanzan and Jittoku by Shokei and a Daruma by Niten.

The Chinese paintings are assigned to the Sung and Yuan periods. Among them are a dragon, a tiger, and a landscape attributed to Mu Ch'i and figure paintings inscribed by Ch'an Buddhist priests.

The examples of calligraphy range from the writings of a Chinese Ch'an Buddhist priest of the Sung dynasty to family heirlooms such as a letter by Ieyasu and writings by Hidetada (the second Tokugawa shogun), Mitsumoto (the second daimyo of Owari province), and Chiyo-hime (eldest daughter of Iemitsu, the third Tokugawa shogun).

Among the rare ceramic pieces are a Chinese Sung celadon incense burner, Japanese tea bowls of the Muromachi period, and an incense burner by Chojiro. The Noh robes and masks, a large and handsome group, are among the finest in Japan. The collection also has two swords of the Kamakura period, as well as armor worn by Ieyasu and many of his personal possessions. In addition to these, the museum owns one of the most remarkable sets of lacquer furniture in Japan. Consisting of some 60 pieces, it was made as part of the dowry of Chiyo-hime on her marriage to Mitsumoto. The set is called "Hatsune," for many of the pieces have excerpts from that chapter of the *Genji Monogatari* worked into the design.

• COMMENTS • The quality is excellent. The installation is only fair, and the building itself poorly kept. There are a a large and expensive illustrated catalogue in Japanese and an illustrated booklet in Japanese and English. The exhibition changes on an average of once a month, with about one percent of the collection on view at any one time.

Note: For all requests to see objects not on view, apply to the Tokyo office of the museum: Tokugawa Reimeikai Foundation, 42, 4-chome, Mejiro-cho, Toshima-ku, Tokyo. (Tel. Tokyo 971-1022.)

183. Tokushima Prefectural Museum (Tokushima Kenritsu Hakubutsukan), Nishiyama-machi, Tokushima, Tokushima-ken. Tel. Tokushima 2-9011/2.

徳島県立博物館　徳島市西山町

Director: Taketoshi Hinode. **Hours:** 9:30–4:30; closed Mon., national holidays, 3rd Thurs. of every month, and Dec. 28–Jan. 4. **Adm.:** ¥20. **Route:** The museum is in the same new building as the station of the ropeway leading up to Tokushima Koen. Take the bus to Ropeway-mae, or walk (10 min.) to the end of the broad street leading away from the railway station.

The museum, which occupies the third, fourth, and fifth floors of the building, contains a small but good collection of Japanese archaeology and a small group of contemporary painting and sculpture by local artists working in the Western manner. The collection also contains some coins, puppet heads, sword furniture, and a seated Jizo of the Muromachi period.

In the archaeological section are *sekibo* probably dating from the end of the Jomon period, Yayoi *dotaku* of varying sizes, and Kofun swords, spearheads, an iron helmet, fragmentary mirrors, good *magatama,* tubular beads, several large *haniwa* figures, and a good selection of Sue pottery.

• COMMENTS • The quality of the archaeological material is good, and those interested in Yayoi and Kofun objects will find a visit worth while. The display is well done and unchanging.

184. Tokyo National Museum (Tokyo Kokuritsu Hakubutsukan), Ueno Koen, Taito-ku, Tokyo. Tel. Tokyo 822-1111.

東京国立博物館　東京都台東区上野公園

Director: Nagatake Asano. **Hours:** 9–4:30, Mar.–Oct.; 9–4, Nov.–Feb.; 9–5, national holidays; closed Mon. (except during special loan exhibitions), Dec. 26–Jan. 2, and sometimes when special exhibitions are being installed or removed. **Adm.:** ¥50. **Route:** The museum stands in ample grounds in Ueno Park. It is about a 5-min. walk from the Ueno stop (near which there is a map of the park) on either the Ginza or the Hibiya subway line. (It is about 20 min. by taxi from the center of Tokyo.)

The museum is the largest in Japan and has the finest and most extensive collection of Japanese art and archaeology in the world. It also has excellent collections of Chinese and Korean art and archaeology, sculpture from Gandhara and nearby regions, a few archaeological specimens from Europe and America, and ethnological items from Hokkaido, Taiwan, Korea, and the South Pacific islands.

The art collections and a selected group of Japanese archaeological items are shown in the main building, opposite the entrance gate; the main Japanese archaeological collections and the early Buddhist objects are generally housed in the Hyokeikan, a somewhat smaller building to the left of the entrance. Two teahouses and two dwelling houses of the Edo period and a Kamakura godown are to be seen in the garden to the right of and behind the main building, and an Edo gateway has been placed to the left of the main gate in the wall enclosing the museum grounds.

To give even a partial list of the contents of the museum would tax the limits of this guide and the reader's patience. There is only space in which to list the various types of objects and to mention a few by name.

The Japanese archaeological section is both very large (over 36,000 items) and very comprehensive. It includes Jomon pottery vessels of all stages, rare Jomon masks, and very unusual Jomon figurines of people and animals; Yayoi pottery, Yayoi *dotaku* noted for their size and number, and several Yayoi bronze mirrors; and Kofun metalwork including mirrors, helmets, horse trappings, swords, sword pommels, and a saddle cover, as well as *haniwa* of human figures, armor, animals, boats, and houses.

The best-known Buddhist paintings are probably the Heian ones of Fugen Bosatsu and of the Sixteen Rakan. There are also sutras and many fine examples of calligraphy of the Heian period. The museum owns many narrative scrolls, mostly of the Kamakura period, illustrating biographies of priests, legends of shrines and temples, accounts of civil wars, records of poetry contests, and ghostly tales. Superb paintings by Sesshu, Sesson, and Gakuo are highlights of the Muromachi *suiboku* painting, and *kakemono* and screens cover every school of the Momoyama and Edo periods. The large print collection includes almost every famous name in the field from Moronobu and the Kaigetsudo to Hiroshige and Hokusai.

The Buddhist sculpture is largely on long-term loan from various temples, but the museum does own an Asuka Amida triad in bronze, a Nara Nikko Bosatsu in dry lacquer, a Heian Fudo Myo-o, and a Kamakura seated figure of Minamoto Yoritomo. Buddhist ritual objects date from the Asuka, Nara, and Heian periods, and there is a fine series of mirrors from the Nara to the Edo period and of Muromachi iron teakettles.

The whole range of Japanese pottery, from the Nara period to the present and of Japanese porcelain of the Edo period is amply shown by examples from every well-known kiln. Noh and Kyogen masks and Noh costumes of the Momoyama and Edo periods are fully represented, as are various types of kimono, and the history of arms and armor is well illustrated. The very large lacquer collection includes a Heian *tebako* with a design of wheels in a stream, a writing box by Koetsu, another by Korin, and a standing shelf of the 17th century.

Among the Chinese sculptures are a Bodhisattva standing against a *mandorla* (Northern Ch'i dynasty) and a T'ang seated Bodhisattva from T'ien-lung-shan. A large painting, assigned to the 8th century, of figures under a tree comes from Turfan in Central Asia. Sung painting is well represented by a charming picture of an angler attributed to Ma

Yuan and two paintings by Liang K'ai, one of the sixth patriarch of the Zen sect and the other of a snowy landscape. Excellent Chinese ceramics date from the neolithic period and from the Han to the Ch'ing dynasty.

• COMMENTS • The quality is superb. It is regrettable that the installation is not commensurate with the importance of the museum or the quality of the collections. There are sporadic labels in English. Five to ten percent of the collection is apt to be on view at any one time; scholars may see objects not on display by making application in writing. In principle, the exhibitions, except for the sculpture which is almost always on view, change every month, the schedule being made up for about ten months in advance. The best objects are usually on view in the spring and autumn. Temporary loan shows are also apt to be held in the spring and autumn, and some of the gallery space for the permanent collection may be taken to accommodate them.

An idea of the contents of the museum can be had from the volume *One Hundred Masterpieces from the Collection of the Tokyo National Museum,* which is in Japanese but with English subtitles. An excellent notion of the extent of the Japanese holdings can be had from the catalogue of the exhibition held at the time of the 1964 Olympics, in which about a third of the objects came from the museum's own collections. Illustrated catalogues in Japanese and English, such as those devoted to the Chinese ceramics and the Japanese prints, are most instructive on special aspects of the collections.

Note: A new building to the right of the entrance is under construction and should open in 1968. The Gallery of Horyu-ji Treasures (No. 26), to the left of the entrance, houses the objects from the Horyu-ji lent by the Imperial Household.

185. Tokyo University Archaeological Collection
(Tokyo Daigaku Reppinshitsu), Tokyo Daigaku, 1 Motofuji-cho, Bunkyo-ku, Tokyo. Tel. Tokyo 812-2111, ext. 2349.

東京大学列品室　東京都文京区本富士町１番地　東京大学内

Director: Professor Tsuguo Mikami. **Hours:** open on request made by telephone or in writing. **Adm.:** free. **Route:** Take bus from Tokyo Central Station for Arakawa Dotei; get off at Todai Seimon-mae, the front gate of the university campus. The museum is in the second building on the right of the broad walk leading away from the gate. Enter by the main door, go to the 2nd floor, and turn right. The collection is in the corner room.

A very large collection of Chinese and Japanese archaeology, with smaller sections devoted to the New World, the Near East, and Southeast Asia.

In the Chinese section are neolithic pottery; oracle bones; Yin pottery; Yin and Chou jades; Han to T'ang tomb figurines; Han tomb tiles, mirrors, and swords; T'ang ceramics; and small pieces of Buddhist sculpture. The Japanese group contains Jomon and Yayoi pottery from known sites (including some Yayoi pieces from the nearby type site), a *dotaku,* good *haniwa,* and some Sue ware of the Kofun period. (One of the *haniwa* figures, that of an apparently laughing man, is well known.)

Siamese bronzes, Khmer stone heads, and American Indian and pre-Columbian pottery round out the collection.

• COMMENTS • The quality is good, but no attempt is made at display, and there are almost no labels. About eighty percent of the items are normally on view. Although the collection lacks large showpieces, it offers good study material for the archaeologist.

Note: In the corridor on the third floor of the Department of Anthropology Building (the large old brick building to the right of the Aka-mon entrance to the campus) are many cases containing a very large number of Jomon pottery vessels of all periods, an equally large number of Yayoi pottery vessels, some fine *dotaku,* huge *haniwa* houses and horses, and a big group of *haniwa* heads. Weapons, masks, and other objects from the South Seas are displayed on the staircase. The Japanese archaeological material is excellent, but again there is no attempt at display, and the labels are very scant. There is a plan to combine the material from both buildings and show it all together in a new building nearby.

186. Tokyo University of Arts Exhibition Hall (Tokyo Geijutsu Daigaku Chinretsukan), Ueno Koen, Taito-ku, Tokyo. Tel. Tokyo 828–6111.

東京芸術大学陳列館　東京都台東区上野公園

Director: The director is always a professor of the university; incumbent

changes every two years. **Hours:** 10–4; closed Sat. and Sun., mid-Dec.–
Mar., and mid-Jul.–Aug. **Adm.:** free. **Route:** The exhibition hall, an
old two-story brick building, is in the grounds of the Tokyo University
of Arts, 2 blocks to the west and on the opposite side of the street from
the Tokyo National Museum (No. 184). Turn sharp left as you enter
the university grounds.

A rather small but varied and excellent collection of Chinese
and Japanese art. The earliest Japanese painting is a section of the *Inga-kyo* of the Nara period. From the Heian
period is a painted wooden panel from the five-story pagoda
of the Daigo-ji, Kyoto, and a copy of the *Konkomyo-kyo*. The
best-known Kamakura painting is an *emakimono,* the *Ono no
Yukimi Goro Emaki* (Story of an Imperial Visit to Ono for
Snow Viewing). Other Kamakura items are a Kongokai
mandara, a Miroku, and a copy of a chapter of the *Hokke-
kyo* written in Sanskrit. A pair of paintings, *Bamboo and
Hibiscus,* attributed to Sesson, a landscape by Shosen, and
a landscape by Kantei, to name a few, are of the Muromachi period; from the 16th century are paintings by
the first Doan and Motohide. The Edo period has a large
representation, with works by Chinzan, Gyokudo, Kagei,
Shunsho, and Taiga, among others, while from the Meiji
period come works by Gaho and Hogai. The university also
owns paintings (mostly oils) and handicrafts by Japanese
artists of the late 19th and the 20th century.

Among the pieces of Japanese sculpture are two excellent
bronze Buddhist figures of the Nara period and a seated
Dainichi Nyorai of the Kamakura period. A Bishamonten
by Higo Hokkyo Jokei, dated 1224, is an excellent example
of late-Kamakura sculpture.

The collection also contains embroidered textiles from
the Horyu-ji, fine mirrors (note particularly a Heian mirror
engraved with the figure of Zao Gongen, and another dated
1007), and sword fittings and lacquer of the Momoyama
and Edo periods.

Chinese metalwork includes early vessels, mirrors, and
harness fittings. A Han bronze tube with inlaid design in
other metals is especially fine. There are also good examples
of Han lacquer from Lo-lang, and a painting of a Lohan
is assigned to the Sung dynasty. Chinese ceramics are represented by Yin pottery, a good series of Han and T'ang
grave figurines, and Sung grave pillows. Interesting bronze

193

Buddhist figures include a much-bejeweled figure of a Bodhisattva of the Sui dynasty and a fine Northern Wei Buddha, while fragments of stone sculpture date from the 6th century to the T'ang dynasty.

• COMMENTS • The quality is excellent, the display adequate. It is difficult to say what the visitor may find on view, since the hall is used for five or six small exhibitions a year, chosen to illustrate certain phases of the university's curriculum. Normally, in the autumn, about ten percent of the permanent collection is shown, with the sculpture, bronzes, ceramics, and lacquer on the ground floor and the painting upstairs. However, there are exceptions, and it would be wise to check before going.

Behind the exhibition hall is a second building, on the ground floor of which is a small collection of Japanese sculpture, in wood and bronze, of the recent past.

187. Tottori Folk Art Museum (Tottori Mingei Bijutsu-kan), 124 Kawara-cho, Tottori, Tottori-ken. Tel. Tottori 5203.

鳥取民芸美術館　鳥取市瓦町 124 番地

Director: Shoya Yoshida. **Hours:** 9–4; closed for New Year season. **Adm.:** ¥60. **Route:** From the station, take the right fork and then the first main street to the left. The museum, a tall Japanese-style building, is about 50 yards down this street, on the left.

A very interesting collection of folk art, housed on two floors of the museum building. It is the property of Mr. Yoshida and specializes in ceramics and furniture. There are Chinese ceramics of the T'ang, Sung, and Ming dynasties, a good selection of Japanese folk pottery, and a few Korean and European pieces. There are also Japanese lacquer vessels, Chinese and Japanese textiles, and an excellent selection of Japanese wooden chests and Chinese and Korean cupboards.

• COMMENTS • The quality is good, and the display, particularly that on the second floor, is arranged with great taste. A very small percentage of the more than 5,000 objects in the collection are on view at any one time, but some changes are made in the installation every two or three months. There is a pamphlet in Japanese. The museum is well worth visiting.

Note: A small octagonal building that stands to the right of the museum houses a large collection of small stone Buddhist figures, all from the Tottori region, originally marking the graves of children.

188. Toyama Municipal Local Museum (Toyama Shiritsu Kyodo Hakubutsukan), Sogawa, Toyama, To-yama-ken. Tel. Toyama 2-7911.

富山市立郷土博物館　富山市総曲輪

Director: Akira Egiri. **Hours:** 9–4:30; closed Mon. **Adm.:** ¥20.
Route: The museum is in a newly built tower on the castle grounds, to the left of the entrance. The castle compound is on the right side of the broad avenue leading south from the station, just beyond the municipal buildings and about 500 yards from the station.

A small collection of Japanese paintings, ceramics, lacquer, prints, armor, folk art, and archaeology, plus a certain amount of historical material and some natural history. The exhibition space on the ground floor is divided among the fine arts, natural history, and archaeology. Objects of historical interest are shown on the upper floor.

The archaeological material, which is sometimes removed from exhibition to make way for a loan show, consists largely of Jomon, Yayoi, and Kofun pottery. In the fine-arts section are a painting in the manner of Hoitsu, additional paintings by local artists, Imari and blue-and-white porcelain, and a few pieces of lacquer. The historical section includes armor, a model of a farmhouse, oil lamps and dishes, late-19th-century prints, and local historical documents.

• COMMENTS • The quality is fair; the installation is very good, but the scanty labels are in Japanese only. The exhibition on the ground floor changes about once a month and is often amplified by borrowing. About one-third of the collection is usually on view. There is an illustrated folder in Japanese. The museum is worth visiting if one happens to be in the neighborhood.

189. Tsurugaoka Hachiman-gu Treasure House (Tsurugaoka Hachiman-gu Homotsuden), Tsurugaoka Ha-chiman-gu, Yukinoshita, Kamakura, Kanagawa-ken. Tel. Kamakura 2-0315.

鶴ケ岡八幡宮宝物殿　鎌倉市雪の下　鶴ケ岡八幡宮内

Director: Minoru Okada. **Hours:** 8–5, Apr.–Oct.; 9–4, Nov.–Mar.; closed Sept. 13, Dec. 13, and Dec. 28–Jan. 1. **Adm.:** ¥20. **Route:** The shrine precincts are reached in 10 min. on foot from the Kamakura station (Yokosuka line) by turning left down the main street, crossing a busy intersection, and passing under a *torii*. The shrine buildings are in the rear of the compound, beyond the Kanagawa Prefectural Museum of Modern Art (No. 69), and are approached by a long flight of steps. The treasure house is to the left of the main shrine buildings.

An interesting miscellaneous collection of arms and armor, costumes, masks, sculptures, and other items belonging to the shrine.

One of the most important pieces is a Kamakura writing box, decorated with chrysanthemums growing along a bamboo fence. From the same period are some very fine swords and a statue of Sumiyoshi Myojin. There is also a Muromachi portrait, in wood, of Minamoto Yoriyoshi (the great warrior who founded the shrine in 1063) and a statue of Benzaiten. A wooden measure belonging to the emperor Gosanjo is dated 1070 and a *kakebotoke*, 1444. The armor, saddles, bows, and arrows on show are of the Muromachi and Edo periods, as are the Bugaku masks and the fine embroidered and brocaded kimono and ladies' court costumes.

The collection also contains Chinese celadon vases dedicated to Hideyoshi, Meiji lacquer dedicated to the emperor Meiji, a Korean bronze bell, neolithic stone tools, examples of Haji ware, Kamakura roof tiles, and examples of Kamakura-bori of the Muromachi period. Western-style paintings of the shrine and of Enoshima complete the display.

• COMMENTS • The quality goes from fair to excellent. The display is adequate, with some scanty labels in English. Few changes are made in the exhibition, save for the swords and armor; the best of the former are exhibited at the New Year season, and certain possessions of Minamoto Yoritomo are placed on view in April at the time of his festival.

190.　Tsuyama History Hall (Tsuyama Kyodokan), 26 Minami Shinza, Tsuyama, Okayama-ken. Tel. Tsuyama 4567.

津山郷土館　岡山県津山市南新座 26 番地

Director: Teruo Kunimasa. **Hours:** 9–4; closed Mon., national holidays, and Dec. 28–Jan. 4. **Adm.:** free. **Route:** The museum, a two-story godown-type building on the left of a small entrance court, is in the center of the city. As there is no bus and as the museum is hard to find, it is best to take a taxi (about 5 min.).

A small collection of local archaeological objects and a considerable number of historical documents, samples of calligraphy, and books. The archaeological material, shown on the upper floor, comes largely from the site of a nearby Yayoi-period dwelling and consists of pottery vessels, stone implements, a plain *dotaku,* and some metal tools. There are also *magatama,* iron swords, and some Sue ware (particularly notable is an elaborate vessel with a very high pierced foot) of the Kofun period. Also on the upper floor is a small selection of local pottery.

The books, documents and letters, examples of local calligraphy, and some figures of local deities are shown on the ground floor.

In an open shed, to the right of the museum building, is a group of large pottery coffins from Kofun tumuli of the region.

• COMMENTS • The quality is fair, the installation adequate. The display of local pottery changes three or four times a year; otherwise, the exhibit remains the same. There is no pamphlet, but a few postcards are available. Save for the coffins, the collection is more interesting for its historical than for its archaeological material.

Note: The Yayoi-period dwelling site on which the building has been reconstructed is a short distance outside the city, on the side away from the railway. The museum supplies a map showing its location, as well as the site of the nearby Kofun tumuli.

191. Ueda Municipal Museum (Ueda Shiritsu Hakubutsukan), Ueda Koen, Shinsan-machi, Ueda, Nagano-ken. Tel. Ueda 1274.

上田市立博物館　長野県上田市新参町　上田公園内

Director: Yoshishige Hiramatsu. **Hours:** 9–4; closed Mon. **Adm.:** ¥50. **Route:** Take bus to Ueda Koen, which is in the upper part of the city. The museum is housed in three small towers, part of the remains of Ueda Castle.

The south tower contains relics of the Sanada family (the local daimyo), and a small collection of folk art; the north tower, natural history and Jomon and Yayoi pottery; and the west tower, further souvenirs of the Sanada and other feudal families consisting of arms, armor, costumes, and banners.

• COMMENTS • The quality is fair, the display poor. All the collection is normally on view. Excavations continue in the neighborhood, and newly discovered material is added to the permanent collections. As of the autumn of 1963, the collections were of only minor interest.

Note: A new exhibition hall stands in the park grounds, in front and to the right of the castle. It is used for temporary shows, most of which have to do with local history.

192. Uesugi Shrine Treasure House (Uesugi-jinja Keishoden), Uesugi-jinja, Minami Horibata-machi, Yone-zawa, Yamagata-ken. Tel. Yonezawa 3-3190.

上杉神社稽照殿　山形県米沢市南堀端町　上杉神社内

Director: Yoshifumi Daijoji, Chief Priest. **Hours:** 9–4; if shut, it can be opened on request. **Adm.:** ¥50. **Route:** Take Shirabu Takayu line bus, and get off at Jinja-mae. The treasure house is to the right of the main shrine building, set in a large wooded area.

A very interesting collection, shown in one large room, of paintings, books, documents, costumes, textiles, armor, swords, and spears, largely the personal property of Kenshin (1530–78) and Yozan (1751–1822), members of the Uesugi family and local daimyo.

Among the paintings are a Bishamonten and a Ryokai *mandara* of the Heian period, a Kamakura Amida triad, and a pair of sixfold screens by Kano Eitoku showing scenes in and around Kyoto. The books include a copy of the Chinese historian Ssu-ma Chien's *Shih Chi* (Historical Record) and a copy of the *History of the Han Dynasty* printed in the Sung dynasty, while the documents include a copy of the *Hannyashin-gyo* written by the emperor Gonara, Kobo Daishi's *Shogei Shichi-in Shiki* of the early Heian period, imperial orders of the emperor Gonara, and petitions, lesson books, and other examples of Kenshin's writing.

The collection is noted for its fine 16th-century costumes —*kosode, dobuku, jimbaori,* and *hakama*—all the property of Kenshin. There is also a *kesa* belonging to him, for he regarded himself as a priest, and an *eboshi.* An odd item is a European velvet mantle. The several suits of armor were also the property of Kenshin and Yozan.

The swords, all by Kamakura swordsmiths, form a notable group; two are attributed to Tomomitsu and Motoshige respectively, a third is signed Sukemune, a fourth Nagamitsu, and a fifth Kunimune. There are also spears, spearheads, arrows, war fans, helmets, and a group of matchlocks, all used by the Uesugi family retainers.

Two items that are unusual for such a collection are a Sung-dynasty celadon vase and a small reliquary of the Hakuho period.

• COMMENTS • The quality is excellent; the display adequate, with a few English labels. About five percent of the 1,000 objects in the collection are normally on view. The exhibition changes two or three times a year, and there is a small folder for each show. There is also a leaflet, with one illustration, listing the most important items. The treasure house is well worth visiting.

193. Ukiyo-e Library (Ukiyo-e Bunko), 93 Nikaido, Kamakura, Kanagawa-ken. Tel. Kamakura 2-7676.

浮世絵文庫　鎌倉市二階堂93番地

Director: Kinosuke Hirose, owner. **Hours:** 9–4, Sat., Sun., and national holidays; closed Jul.–Aug. and Dec. 1 to 1st Sat. in Mar. **Adm.:** ¥50. **Route:** Take bus for Daitonomiya to the end of the line near the Kamakura-gu; then walk back along this street for a very short distance. The museum, a new building designed by the architect-owner in the contemporary Japanese style, is on the left, set back from the street.

A collection of about 5,000 prints, plus some books, of which about 70 to 100 prints are shown at any one time in the one-room gallery. The collection includes works by well-known printmakers from the early primitives to Hiroshige and Hokusai in the 19th century. The exhibition is changed every month.

• COMMENTS • The gallery itself is well designed, but the

installation is somewhat hampered by the fact that many of the prints must be seen through two layers of glass, that of the framed print and that of the vitrine.

194. Wakayama Prefectural Art Museum (Wakayama Kenritsu Bijutsukan), Wakayama-jo, Ichiban-cho, Wakayama, Wakayama-ken. Tel. Wakayama 23-2467.

和歌山県立美術館　和歌山市一番丁　和歌山城内

Director: Hideo Nakatani. **Hours:** 9–5; closed Tues. during large exhibitions, Sun. during smaller ones; also closed Dec. 28–Jan. 5 and when exhibition is being changed. **Adm.:** depends on exhibition. **Route:** The museum is within the castle precincts. Trams from both the Higashiya Wakayama station of the national railways and the Wakayama station of the Nankai line stop at the entrance to the grounds (Koenmae). Cross the footbridge over the moat and turn right under the castle walls. The museum, a new building, is on the right beyond a playing field.

This new museum, with good exhibition rooms on three floors, is now used for temporary exhibitions, since the permanent collection consists of only a few Japanese paintings by local artists. The museum usually stages four shows a year and at other times lends its galleries to local organizations.

The museum's own exhibitions are of excellent quality. In the past they have shown Japanese painting in the Japanese manner from the Meiji era to the present, Japanese painting and sculpture in the Western manner, the paintings and writings of Nankai, ceramics from Wakayama Prefecture, and paintings by Rosetsu and by the contemporary artist Masakatsu Hidaka.

• COMMENTS • The displays are well arranged. Illustrated catalogues accompany each of the major exhibitions, and there is also a small illustrated pamphlet on the museum, all in Japanese. The museum is worth visiting for its own exhibitions.

195. Waseda University Tsubouchi Memorial Theater Museum (Waseda Daigaku Tsubouchi-hakase Kinen Engeki Hakubutsukan), Waseda Daigaku, 1-chome, To-

tsuka-cho, Shinjuku-ku, Tokyo. Tel. Tokyo 341-4144; 341-2141.

早稲田大学坪内博士記念演劇博物館　東京都新宿区戸塚町
１丁目　早稲田大学内

Director: Kohei Ijima. **Hours:** 9–4, weekdays; 9–2, Sat.; closed Sun., national holidays, 2nd Mon. of every month, Oct. 21, Aug. 1–Sept. 2, and Dec. 29–Jan. 7. **Adm.:** free. **Route:** Take Yamate line to Takatano-baba, then bus to Waseda Seimon-mae, the stop directly in front of the university's main gate. The museum, a version of an English Tudor building, is at the right-hand end of the second crosswalk from the main entrance to the university grounds. (The university can also be reached from the Waseda stop on the new Tozai subway line.)

The only collection in Japan devoted exclusively to the arts of the Oriental and Occidental theaters. It is housed in a building modeled after the Fortune Theater, while the porch represents the stage of an Elizabethan theater. The museum is dedicated to the memory of Shoyo Tsubouchi, the translator of Shakespeare and the leading figure in the Japanese theater world from the 1880's until his death in 1935.

In a large room on the third floor are housed the parts of the exhibition most interesting to the Westerner: Gigaku, Bugaku, and Noh masks; Bunraku puppets; Noh and Kabuki costumes; musical instruments and other theatrical accoutrements; and models of stages. Here and elsewhere in the museum are also shown, in rotation, some of the 50,000 theatrical prints which the museum owns. The right-hand wing of this floor contains Chinese and Javanese shadow-play puppets, Chinese theatrical costumes, musical instruments, and masks. There are also mementos of the Shinsei Shimpa theater (the theater that served as a bridge between the classical Kabuki and the modern theater movement of the Meiji era) and of the Shingeki (the modern Japanese theater).

On the second floor are materials relating to the European and American theater: prints, photographs, stage and costume designs, manuscripts, texts, and directors' notes. A room on the first floor is devoted to the cinema, showing cameras, projectors, and stills from well-known films. A large theatrical library and a reading room are also on this floor.

• COMMENTS • The quality is fair to good. The display is fair. There is a small handbook in English, published in 1953, and a more recent one in Japanese.

196. Yahata Municipal Art Museum (Yahata Shiritsu Bijutsukan), 4-chome, Hon-machi, Yahata, Fukuoka-ken. Tel. Yahata 67-5414.

八幡市立美術館　福岡県八幡市本町 4 丁目

Director: Yoshihisa Inoue. **Hours:** 9–5; closed Dec. 28–Jan. 2 and when exhibition is being changed. **Adm.:** ¥100. **Route:** Walk south on the main street leading away from the station for about 5 min. The museum, a brick and glass building in the International style, is on the left side of the street, just beyond the traffic circle.

This newly built museum is, to date, primarily an exhibition hall, though it does own a small collection of contemporary Japanese oil paintings, drawings, and sculpture, as well as some reproductions. It arranges two loan shows a year, usually of contemporary art, and items from the museum's collection may be included if they fit in with the nature of the show. At other times, it lends its two spacious galleries to outside organizations.

• COMMENTS • The display is well done, and a catalogue accompanies the museum's own shows. There is also an illustrated pamphlet on the museum and its activities. All the publications are in Japanese.

197. Yamaguchi Prefectural Museum (Yamaguchi Kenritsu Hakubutsukan), Torigoe, Kamiunorei, Yamaguchi, Yamaguchi-ken. Tel. Yamaguchi 294.

山口県立博物館　山口市上宇野令鳥越

Director: Hanomi Usugi. **Hours:** 9–4:30, Mar.–Nov.; 9–4, Dec.–Feb.; closed Mon., national holidays, and New Year season. **Adm.:** ¥30. **Route:** Take bus to Kencho-mae (the prefectural office) and walk south, or downhill, for about 100 yards. The museum, a large frame building, is on the right.

This museum, though largely devoted to science and natural history, does possess a collection of Japanese archaeology. However, only a few stone tools and Kofun *magatama* and tubular beads and decorative stone pieces are on display, the remainder being in storage pending the construction of a new building scheduled to begin in 1966.

There is also a special collection devoted to the Meiji Restoration and to the leaders in it from Yamaguchi Prefecture. It includes portraits of these men, historical prints, illustrated books, calligraphy, and other documents.

• COMMENTS • The display is adequate. There is an illustrated folder on the museum in Japanese.

198. Yamato Bunkakan (Yamato Bunkakan), 969 Sugawara-cho, Nara, Nara-ken. Tel. Nara 45-0544.

大和文華館　奈良市菅原町 969 番地

Director: Yukio Yashiro. **Hours:** 10–5 (no admission after 4); closed Mon. and when new exhibition is being installed. **Adm.:** ¥50. **Route:** The museum, a very handsome building designed by Professor Isoya Yoshida, is within walking distance of the Gakuen-mae station on the Kinki Nihon Railway line from Nara to Osaka. From the south side of the station, cross the main road and take the street leading southeast and downhill, and then the first road to the right. The entrance to the museum grounds is on the left, with the building at the top of a hill in a setting of great natural beauty.

A superb collection of Japanese and Chinese art assembled by the director since the Pacific War. The museum was opened in 1960, and both the building and its contents are the gift of the late Mr. Torao Oita, president of the Kinki Nihon Railway.

From the Heian period there are two famous illustrated scrolls (both 12th century): the *Nezame Monogatari* (Tale of Nezame) and the *Ichiji Rendai Hokke-kyo* (an illuminated copy of the Lotus Sutra with a lotus-flower pedestal under each character). There are also rare Buddhist iconographic paintings from the same period. The Kamakura period is represented by two *mandara,* of which one—the Kasagi *mandara*—is of especial interest since it is thought to show the Kasagi Temple and its colossal stone relief of Miroku, now vanished. There are also a portrait of the poetess Kodai Kimi, a scroll of the *Ise Monogatari,* and fine illustrations of the " Ukifune " chapter of the *Genji Monogatari.*

An early painting in the Zen manner—*Bamboo and Sparrow*, by the priest-painter Kao—and a picture of the Buddhist deity Yuima Koji by Bunsei, with the date of 1457 in its long inscription, are from the 15th century. From the 16th century are a superb pair of sixfold screens attributed to Shubun and, by Sesson, a painting of Ryodohin and his dragons and a fine pair of flower-and-bird screens. A portrait of a lady, in color, dates from the Momoyama period. The most striking screens in the collection, dating from the first half of the 17th century, are those formerly in the Matsuura family collection: a pair depicting the diversions of a group of young women, painted in strong colors on a gold ground. There is also a painting of a woman playing a stringed instrument, done in the Western manner by Nobukata. From the Edo period comes a portrait of a beauty by Choshun, while Korin is represented by a portrait (the only one known to be by him) of Nakamura Kuranosuke, a box with a design of fans, a tray with a wave pattern, and another with a painting of Mount Fuji. There is also a tray of paulownia wood painted by Kenzan with a design of a bamboo basket, a charming poem card by Koetsu, and, by Sotatsu, a painting of Kanzan, another of one of the Thirty-six Poets, and one of cherry blossoms. Two scenes from the *Ise Monogatari* are attributed to Sotatsu.

Chinese paintings include works attributed to the Sung artists Ma Yuan, represented by *Bamboos and Swallows;* Chao Ta-nien, by *River Scenery and Autumn Mist;* and Mao I, by *Cats and Dogs Playing.* There is also a fine pair of scrolls by Li Ti.

Among the pieces of calligraphy are a 12th-century manuscript of the *Iseshu,* a fragment of the *Man'yoshu* of the same period, writings by Chinese and Japanese priests of the 12th to the 14th century, and a sample of Koetsu's writing on a ground strewn with leaves.

Japanese sculpture is represented by a few early Buddhist figures and a rare one of a Shinto deity. Mirrors, a *kei,* and sword fittings show the quality of 12th- and 13th-century metalwork. An *apsara,* embroidered on a hanging, comes from the Horyu-ji and is of the Asuka period.

The ceramics include several *haniwa* figures which are quite complete and show the original painting. From the Nara period is a bowl glazed in two colors, while among the late pieces are a Karatsu bowl, an Old Kutani bottle, and Old Imari jars, all of the 17th century. There is a famous tea bowl called "Yugao" (Evening Glory) by Ken-zan, and he and Korin combined their talents on a square incense burner. An incense box in the shape of a duck is the work of Ninsei. Chinese ceramics are represented by very good tomb figures from the Han to the T'ang dynasty and by Sung red and black Ting bowls, a Northern Sung cel-adon vase, and Tz'u chou vases, ewers, and a pillow, also of the Sung period. A Yueh vase is of particular interest, for there is a date of 1080 in an inscription under the glaze. From the Ming dynasty are good examples of blue-and-white and overglaze-enamel wares.

Chinese metalwork includes a silver-plated T'ang mirror and gold filigree ornaments of the Six Dynasties.

· COMMENTS · The quality is excellent, and the dis-play, arranged in a large room with an interior court, is equally fine. The labels are in both Japanese and English. There are about 850 items in the collection, and additions are being made each year. The exhibition changes from four to six times a year, with the best paintings shown in the autumn and about ten percent of the collection on view at any time. There is usually a loan show in the spring. The publications include the *Selected Catalogue,* which il-lustrates masterpieces in the collection, *Yamato Bunka* (a quarterly), occasional catalogues for special exhibitions, and a folder describing the museum.

No one should miss this museum; the quality of the objects, the architecture of the building, and the beauty of the site form an unforgettable combination.

199. Yamato Historical Museum (Yamato Rekishi-kan), Unebi-machi, Kashiwara-shi, Nara-ken. Tel. Kashi-wara 478.

大和歴史館　奈良県橿原市畝傍町

Director: Yoshiharu Otani. **Hours:** 9–4:30; closed Mon. p.m., Tues., national holidays, and Dec. 26–Jan. 6. **Adm.:** ¥20. **Route:** Kashiwara is reached by the Kinki Nihon Electric Railway from either Nara or Osaka (45 min.). The museum, a large frame building, is a 10-min. walk down the broad street leading away from the station, on the right-hand side.

A very interesting collection of Japanese archaeology excavated from sites in the district. From the Jomon-period sites of Kashiwara and Okawa are vessels and shards with impressed cord patterns, ornaments, bone needles, and horn implements. The Yayoi period is represented by a good series of typical pottery vessels, stone implements, wooden farm tools, and *dotaku,* coming, in part, from the two Yayoi sites of Tokoiseki and Kumagawa. Excavations of the tumuli of the Kofun period have produced swords, mirrors, short body armor, *magatama,* fine stone and gold ornaments, horse trappings, a good group of Sue-ware vessels, a large pottery coffin (from Utahime-machi), stone and Sue-ware mortuary urns, and *haniwa* figures. Among the last are small models of houses and quivers. A large wooden well-head and an equally large wooden tube are unusual items.

The museum also has a good selection of circular and crescent-shaped roof tiles of the Asuka and Nara periods. Models of the tombs and photographs of the sites accompany the exhibitions.

• COMMENTS • The quality is very good, the display adequate. The best pieces are normally on view; changes are occasionally made as the excavations continue and new pieces are added. There is a good illustrated booklet on the collection, in Japanese. The museum is well worth a visit, particularly for the specialist in Japanese archaeology.

200. Yashima-dera Treasure House (Yashima-dera Homotsukan), Yashima Yamaue, Takamatsu, Kagawa-ken. Yashima 4-9418.

屋島寺宝物館　香川県高松市屋島山上

Director: Ryuzui Nakai, Chief Priest. **Hours:** 8–5. **Adm.:** ¥30. **Route:** The temple is on top of a mountain, some distance from the center of Takamatsu. Take the Kotohira Dentetsu to Yashima, then a bus from the station to the cable car, and the cable car to the top of the mountain. Then walk to the temple, keeping to the left when the road forks. The treasure house is to the left of the Kondo. The entire trip takes almost 1 hour.

A small collection of Japanese paintings, calligraphy, ceramics, and other objects belonging to the temple. The paintings include two scrolls ascribed to Tosa Mitsunobu (one of the battle at Yashima between the Taira and the

Minamoto, the other of the garden of the Yashima-dera), a Daruma and a Kannon bravely labeled Sesshu, a Kannon signed Tan'yu, a screen labeled Tosa Mitsuoki, and a pair of paintings by a Kano artist. There is also a portrait of the priest Ganjin and a *Yashima Monogatari*. The calligraphy includes writings by the emperors Gokomatsu and Goyozei.

Among the other objects are a white banner of the Genji, a sutra cover presented by the cloistered emperor Goshirakawa, relics said to have been presented by Ganjin, a sword that belonged to Tokugawa Ieyasu, and the alms book of the temple, dated 1610.

• COMMENTS • The quality is fair, the display barely adequate. About half the collection is normally on view, and the exhibition never changes. There is an illustrated pamphlet in Japanese. If one is visiting the temple, with its beautiful garden and its marvelous site, one might as well include the treasure house, for, although on artistic grounds it is hardly worth the trip, the material is of historical interest.

201. Yokosuka City Museum (Yokosuka-shi Hakubutuskan), Kurihama, Yokosuka, Kanagawa-ken. Tel. Uraga 780.

横須賀市博物館　横須賀市久里浜

Director: Yata Haneda. **Hours:** 9–4:30; closed Mon., national holidays, Feb. 15, and Dec. 29–Jan. 3. **Adm.:** free. **Route:** Take train to Kurihama, two stations beyond Yokosuka. The Keihin Kyuko Beach bus passes the museum, which is about 300 yards down the road from the station towards the town and at the far end of a large pink building, in a modified Japanese style, that lies to the left of the road.

A collection of local archaeological finds, material dealing with Commodore Perry's landing at Kurihama Beach in 1853 (the museum was founded one hundred years after this event), and much natural history, all housed in one end of the building.

The archaeological material, displayed on the ground floor, consists of Jomon pottery of the early, middle, and late periods; stone and bone implements, *haniwa,* and iron swords from the Kofun period; and Yayoi pottery, beads, and ornaments, all from local sites on the Miura Peninsula.

Maps and photographs of the sites accompany the objects.

On the upper floor are prints, paintings, and documents relating to Commodore Perry's landing at the nearby beach.

• COMMENTS • The quality of the collections is good; the display, especially that of the archaeological material, is well done. Thirty percent of the collection is normally on view, and the archaeological exhibit is occasionally changed. There is a small illustrated folder, in Japanese with some English, and the museum publishes a regular archaeological report, in Japanese only.

202. Yonezawa Local Museum (Yonezawa Kyodo Hakubutsukan), Minami Horibata-cho, Yonezawa, Yamagata-ken. Tel. Yonezawa 3-0161.

米沢郷土博物館　山形県米沢市南堀端町

Director: Hiroshi Oka. **Hours:** 9–4; closed Mon., national holidays, and New Year season. **Adm.:** free. **Route:** The museum is in a ferro-concrete building to the left of the Uesugi Shrine precincts and across a small stream. Take Shirabu Takayu line bus to Jinja-mae.

A rather large collection (about 1,500 objects) of local folk arts and historical documents, a small part of which is displayed on the upper floor of the building that houses the city library.

The collection is noted for its group of wooden toys representing animals and birds, known as *Sasano-bori ningyo,* after the village of Sasano in Yamagata Prefecture, where they are made. It is also noted for its examples of the local Narushima ware.

• COMMENTS • The quality is good of its kind, the display as well done as the quarters allow. The collection is taken off display whenever a temporary loan exhibition occupies the premises.

203. Yoshimizu-jinja Collection (Yoshimizu-jinja Sho-in), Yoshimizu-jinja, Yoshinoyama, Yoshino, Nara-ken. Tel. Yoshino 3024.

吉水神社書院　奈良県吉野町吉野山　吉水神社内

Director: Ryuhei Nakazawa. **Hours:** 8–4:30 in winter, 8–5 in summer. **Adm.:** ¥50. **Route:** Yoshino is at the end of the Kinki Nihon Railway (about 1½ hrs.) either from Abenobashi station, Osaka, or from Nara; then by cable car (5 min.) up the mountain; then by bus to Naka-machi. Proceed on foot a short way and turn left under a stone *torii*. The shrine is at the end of this path.

An interesting collection of paintings, calligraphy, documents, arms and armor, metalwork, lacquer, musical instruments, and a few ceramics, housed in a building that was once the residence of the emperor Godaigo. Many of the objects were associated with him, for his court (the Southern Court) was at Yoshino from the time he fled Kyoto in 1337 until his death in 1339. In addition to samples of his writing, objects which belonged to him include a Ryokai *mandara,* two tea caddies, musical instruments, and a musical score.

There are also examples of the calligraphy of the emperors Gofukakusa, Gokomatsu, Gomizuno-o, Higashiyama, and Reigen, as well as a piece by Ikkyu. Two groups of poems, one charmingly written by the mother of the emperor Antoku, the other at a flower-viewing party held at Yoshino by Hideyoshi, are also on view.

A suit of armor, a saddle and stirrups, and a sword were the property of Minamoto Yoshitsune. Other objects in the collection include a fine *dotaku,* an early square *tsuba,* a Heian sutra box, a lacquer stand assigned to the Nambokucho period, a long lacquer box of the Muromachi period, and Noh masks of the Muromachi and Momoyama periods.

Among the paintings are a set of three scrolls—a Kannon between birds and flowers—and some screens by Eitoku and Sansetsu.

• COMMENTS • The quality is good, the installation very well arranged in a delightful building. There are no changes in the exhibits. There is a check list, in Japanese, of the objects, and a few postcards are available. The collection is well worth visiting, both for itself and for its setting.

Note: Many of the important possessions of the shrine are held by the national museums in Nara and Tokyo.

204. Yukiguni Folk Society Research Institute (Yukiguni Minzoku Kenkyujo), Akita College of Economics, 12, 1-chome, Ibarajima, Akita, Akita-ken. Tel. Akita 2-6627/8/9.

雪国民俗研究所　秋田市茨島 1 丁目 12 番地
　　　　　　　　秋田経済大学内

Director: Gyoju Odate. **Hours:** Open on request. **Adm.:** free. **Route:** Take bus for Araya and get off at Daigaku-mae, the college stop (20 min.). The college grounds are on the left side of the road, and the collection is housed on the ground floor of the building to the left of the entrance.

A large collection of regional folk arts, consisting of cotton and straw garments, a few wooden chests, some tobacco pipes, a large number of lamps, braziers, and cooking and other household utensils. The examples of the local pottery, the Naraoka ware, are good, and a special feature of the collection are the masks used for the Bangaku, a local folk dance.

Farming tools and machinery, fishing equipment including boats, and spinning wheels and looms are shown in a shed to the right of the entrance to the college grounds.

• COMMENTS • The collection, good of its kind, is of interest chiefly to specialists in folk arts. The display is adequate, the scanty labels in Japanese only. Bulletins of the society, in Japanese, illustrate and describe the collections.

205. Zenko-ji Jodo Sect Treasure House (Zenko-ji Daihongan Homotsukan), Zenko-ji, Motoyoshi-cho, Nagano, Nagano-ken. Tel. Nagano 2-1360.

善光寺大本願宝物館　長野市元善町　善光寺内

Director: Chief Priest. **Hours:** 6–4 in summer, 7–4 in winter; **Adm.:** ¥10. **Route:** The Zenko-ji is at the upper end of the main shopping street of Nagano. This treasure house is on the left, just before the first gate of the temple precincts.

A small group of paintings, calligraphy, documents, sculpture, lacquer, and costumes, all the property of the temple. There is an early-19th-century statue of a priest, and most of the lacquer is of fairly recent date. The costumes, consisting of ladies' dresses and parasols of the early 20th century, are the relics of an imperial visit to the temple.

• COMMENTS • The quality is fair, the display adequate. The treasure house, set in a charming garden, is of only minor interest.

206. Zenko-ji Tendai Sect Treasure House (Zenko-ji Daikanjin Homotsukan), Zenko-ji, Motoyoshi-cho, Nagano, Nagano-ken. Tel. Nagano 2-2460.

善光寺大勧進宝物館　長野市元善町　善光寺内

Director: Chief Priest. **Hours:** 6–4 in summer, 7–4 in winter. **Adm.:** ¥20. **Route:** The Zenko-ji is at the upper end of the main shopping street of Nagano. This treasure house is on the left, before the second or main gate of the temple.

A collection of Japanese painting, calligraphy, documents, sculpture, lacquer, metalwork, and musical instruments. There are also several wooden shrines and palanquins.

The paintings include several of the Kano and Tosa schools ascribed to such artists as Tsunenobu, Mitsuyoshi, and Matabei, as well as some Chinese paintings of the Ch'ing dynasty. The few pieces of sculpture, the lacquer, and the musical instruments are all of the Edo period.

• COMMENTS • The quality is fair to good, as is the installation. All objects are normally on display, and the exhibition never changes. The treasure house is set in a charming garden and is worth seeing if one is in the neighborhood.

207. Zentsu-ji Treasure House (Zentsu-ji Homotsukan), Zentsu-ji, Zentsuji, Kagawa-ken. Tel. Zentsuji 111.

善通寺宝物館　香川県善通寺市　善通寺内

Director: Yuei Kametani. **Hours:** 9–5. **Adm.:** ¥50. **Route:** The town of Zentsuji is most easily reached by bus from Kotohira or Takamatsu. Get off at Akamon-mae, turn left if coming from Kotohira, right if from Takamatsu, and walk through the red gate at the end of the street. Continue through the temple compound and along a broad stone path to the Kondo. Tickets must be obtained here for the treasure house, which is behind and to the left of the Kondo. (Resist the attempt made to lead one to the treasure house by way of a dark underground passage by asking to be taken there direct.)

A collection of Japanese painting, calligraphy, sculpture,

ceramics, and metalwork, as well as several Chinese paintings, shown in one long corridor and a small two-story building. The earliest object is a fine *dotaku*. The best-known statue is a Nara-period figure of Jizo. There are other statues piously said to be by Kobo Daishi, who was born in Zentsuji. The paintings include a Daruma attributed to Kano Motonobu and a portrait attributed to Tosa Mitsunobu. The documents include letters by the emperor Gomizuno-o, Hideyoshi, Ieyasu, and the Zen priests Ikkyu and Takuan. One piece of calligraphy is said to be by Kobo Daishi. There is a copy of the *Hokke-kyo* written by the emperor Kameyama, and another copy of the same sutra has a figure of a Buddha beside each character. There is also a handsome pottery *hibachi* by Gennai on view.

· COMMENTS · The quality runs from fair to good, but the display is barely adequate. A pamphlet on the temple illustrates a few of the objects in the treasure house. Half the collection is normally on view, and changes in the exhibits are infrequent. The treasure house is worth visiting if one is in the neighborhood.

208. Zuigan-ji Museum (Zuigan-ji Hakubutsukan), Zuigan-ji, Matsushima-machi, Matsushima, Miyagi-ken. Tel. Matsushima 21.

瑞巌寺博物館　宮城県松島市松島町　瑞巌寺内

Director: Ryuho Kato, Chief Priest. **Hours:** 7–6 in summer, 7–4:30 in winter. **Adm.:** ¥50. **Route:** Turn left on the main road and continue past the Park Hotel to the boat landings (5 min.). The entrance to the temple is opposite the landings, on the left side of the road.

The museum, if one can call it that, consists merely of two wall cases standing in the right-hand corridor of the Kondo, which lies at the rear of the temple complex. Among the contents are Korean and *temmoku* tea bowls, a few Noh masks, some calligraphy, a pair of cut-glass candlesticks given by Pope Paul V to Hasekura Tsunenaga (a retainer of Date Masamune) when he visited Rome in 1615 as Masamune's ambassador, a metal bell said to have come from the Ching Shan Temple in China, and a very damaged statue of Bishamonten.

· COMMENTS · The contents of the cases hardly merit a

visit, but the temple itself and its Kano-school screens are very fine indeed. There is an illustrated pamphlet in Japanese describing the temple.

Glossary

Ainu: a Caucasic people originally spread over the whole Japanese archipelago, in historic times confined to northeast Honshu, now surviving in small numbers on Hokkaido. ⌐Satta.

Aizen Myo-o: a manifestation of Dainichi Nyorai or of Kongo

Amida: Buddha Amida, the Lord of Infinite Light; the most widely worshiped of all the Buddhas.

Amida triad: the Buddha Amida between two Bosatsu.

Antoku: child emperor; reigned 1180–83; drowned at the battle of Dannoura in 1185, when the Taira were defeated by the Minamoto.

Anyang: region in northern Honan Province and site of the capital of the Yin dynasty from about the middle of the second millennium B.C. Excavations there have revealed oracle bones, bronzes, jades, and stone sculpture.

apsara: Buddhist angel.

Ashikaga Takauji (1305–58): first of the Ashikaga shoguns, who ruled Japan during the Muromachi period.

Basho (1644–94): the most distinguished *haiku* poet of his age. As a hobby, he painted pictures in the *suiboku* style.

Benzaiten: female deity of speech and learning. Depicted as a beautiful woman, she bestows ability, wisdom, and good fortune.

bijutsukan: art museum.

Bishamonten: one of the Shi Tenno, also called Tamonten. He holds a pagoda in his left hand, a spear in his right, and guards the north. ⌐a fretted neck.

biwa: stringed musical instrument with a pear-shaped body and

Bodhidharma (in Japanese, Daruma): Indian monk who came to China in 520 and founded the Ch'an (Zen) sect of Buddhism.

Bodhisattva (in Japanese, Bosatsu): Buddhist deity who has renounced Buddhahood in order to work for the salvation of all beings.

Bompo (1344–c. 1420): priest and painter, generally of flowers.

Bonten: Japanese name for Brahma.

Book of History: Second of the Five Confucian Classics, it consists of short speeches and reports attributed to rulers and ministers from the earliest times down to the early Chou period.

Book of Rites: The *Li Chi,* the most famous of the texts comprising the Fourth Confucian Classic; a compilation of texts dating from the middle Chou to the early Han period and dealing largely with rites and rituals.

Bosatsu: Japanese name for Bodhisattva.

Brahma: Indian deity, the supreme god of the Brahmans; worshiped in Japan as Bonten, guardian of the Buddhist Law and Protector of the World.

Bugaku: ancient court dance of a semi-religious nature in which masks covering only the face were worn. See also Gigaku.

Buncho (1764–1840): prolific painter of the *nanga* school.

bunjinga: see *nanga.*

bunka: culture.

Bunraku: the puppet theater, with its home in Osaka, in which very large puppets handled by three men are used.   ⌈school.

Bunsei (mid-15th century): painter of the Muromachi *suiboku*

Buson (1716–83): distinguished painter of the *nanga* school.

Ch'an: the meditative sect of Buddhism, introduced in the 13th century from China into Japan, where it was called Zen.

Chang Ssu-kung: Said to have lived in the Sung dynasty, he was a Chinese painter of Buddhist subjects; better known in Japan than in China.   ⌈during the early 11th century.

Chao Ch'ang: Chinese painter noted for his flower pieces; worked

Chao Ta-nien: painter of the Sung dynasty; relative and friend of Emperor Hui Tsung; also called Chao Ling-jan.

chia: ancient Chinese bronze round tripod vessel, with a handle on the side and two capped columns rising from the rim; used for heating wine.

chien: ancient Chinese bronze water mirror, in the shape of a large basin with two or more ring handles.

Chikuden (1777–1835): generally considered the greatest *nanga-*school painter of his time.

Chinzan (1801–54): painter of the *nanga* school.

cho: town street; same as *machi.*   ⌈also known as Mincho.

Chodensu (1352–1431): distinguished Muromachi *suiboku* painter;

Chojiro (1515–92): first great potter of Raku ware.

Chokuan II: painter working in the mid-17th century; son of Chokuan I, who founded the Soga school, an outgrowth of the

chome: subdivision of a city area.   ⌊Muromachi *suiboku* school.

Chosei (1010–91): sculptor.

Choshun (1682–1752): painter of the *ukiyo-e* school; specialized in female figures.

chueh: ancient Chinese bronze vessel of tripod shape with a handle
   and an open spout on the sides and capped columns rising from
   the rim; used for heating wine.

daigaku: university.
Daikokuten: one of the Seven Gods of Good Luck.
daimyo: feudal lord of a province.   ⌈Buddhism.
Dainichi Nyorai: the Supreme and Eternal Buddha in Esoteric
Daito Kokushi (14th century): prominent priest, founder and
   first abbot of the Daitoku-ji, Kyoto, the most active center of
Daruma: Japanese for Bodhidharma.   ⌊the Zen sect in Japan.
Dasoku (second half of 15th century): painter of the Muromachi
   suiboku school.
Date Masamune: daimyo of Sendai in the early Edo period.
Dengyo Daishi (767–822): honorary title of Saicho, the Buddhist
   priest who studied in China and then founded the Tendai
   sect in a monastery on Mount Hiei, above Kyoto.
Doan (d. 1571): feudal lord and painter of the *suiboku* school.
dobuku: coat worn over the *kosode.*
Dohachi (1783–1855): Kyoto potter of wares for the tea ceremony
   and of porcelain decorated in the manner of the Korin school.
Donyu (1599–1656): third in the line of Raku potters and generally considered the greatest; popularly known as Nonko.
Dosojin: guardian deity of travelers.
dotaku: bronze bell-shaped object of the Yayoi period.

eboshi: court hat made of lacquered black gauze.
Edo: early name of Tokyo; also name of the historical period
   from 1615 to 1868.
Eigen Honin (1107–51): priest of the Ninna-ji at Kyoto.
E Inga-kyo: illustrated Sutra of Cause and Effect (picture scroll).
Eiraku Hozen (1795–1854): potter known for his use of the over-
   glaze-enamel technique.
Eitoku: see under Kano.
ema: votive painting.
emaki: see *emakimono.*
emakimono or *emaki:* horizontal scroll painting; picture scroll.
Emma: a king of hell.
Enku (d. 1695): sculptor of Buddhist and Shinto deities. His
   figures are left in the rough, and the chisel marks are visible.
   He worked in the prefectures of Gifu and Aichi.
Enno Gyoja (d. 701): Although never ordained as a priest, he

lived an austere, solitary life and is regarded as the pioneer of the Buddhist mountaineer priests.

Eshin Sozu (942–1017): painter and priest of the Tendai sect.

Fudo: see Fudo Myo-o.

Fudo Myo-o: chief of the Godai Myo-o and a manifestation of Dainichi Nyorai. Represented with a fierce aspect, he holds a sword and a rope and has flames behind him.

Fugen Bosatsu: Japanese for Samantabhadra.

Fujin: god of wind.

Fujiwara: family of painters of the Yamato-e school. Prominent members: Nobuzane (1176–c. 1268), Takasuke (14th cen.), Takayoshi (mid-12th cen.), Tsunetaka (second half of 12th

Fujiwara clan: ruling family of the Heian period.   ⌊cen.).

Fujiwara Teika (1162–1241): poet and critic who defined the classic canons of Japanese verse; responsible for the formation of

Fujiwara Toshinari (1114–1204): poet.   ⌊Japanese literary taste.

Fukukensaku Kannon: "Kannon with the Never Empty Net."

Fukurokuju: one of the Seven Gods of Good Luck.

Fushimi: emperor; reigned 1288–98.

futaoki: tile on which to rest the dipper during the tea ceremony.

Gagaku: music of the court.

Gaho (1835–1908): painter in the Japanese style.

Gaki Zoshi: Scroll of Hungry Ghosts (picture scroll).

Gakuo (early 16th century): Zen priest and painter of the Muromachi *suiboku* school.

Gandhara: region comprising part of northwest India, Pakistan, and Afghanistan; seat of a school of Roman-Buddhist art of the 2nd to the 6th century.   ⌈in 753, reorganized the Ritsu sect.

Ganjin: Chinese priest who, though blind when he reached Japan

Ganku (1749–1838): independent painter, member of no school.

Gantai (1782–1865): painter, pupil of his father Ganku.

Gautama: see Sakyamuni.

Geiami (1431–85): painter of the Muromachi *suiboku* school.

geijutsu: fine arts.

Genji Monogatari: The Tale of Genji, written in the first decade of the 11th century by Lady Murasaki. The greatest novel in Japanese literature, it mirrors the court life and aesthetic preoccupations of the Heian aristocracy.

Gennai (1723–79): painter of the *yoga* (foreign) school. His real name was Hiraga Kokurin; Gennai was his name as a priest.

Gessen (1721–1809): painter and priest; once a pupil of Okyo.
geta: wooden clogs.   ⌜worn. See also Bugaku.
Gigaku: ancient dance in which masks covering the head were
go: five.   ⌜precepts of a *mandara.*
Go Bosatsu: group of five Bosatsu arranged according to the
Godaigo: emperor; reigned 1318–39.
Godai Myo-o: the Five Great Kings, guardians of the Buddhist
   faith. They have fierce and terrifying forms. Fudo is the most
   important.
Go Dairiki Bosatsu: the Five Powerful Bodhisattvas.
Gofukakusa: emperor; reigned 1246–59.
Gohanazono: emperor; reigned 1429–64.
Gokashiwabara: emperor; reigned 1500–26.
Gokogon: emperor of the Northern Court; reigned 1353–71.
Gokomatsu: emperor; reigned 1392–1412; also emperor of the
   Northern Court, 1382–92.
Gomizuno-o: emperor; reigned 1611–29.
Gomurakami: emperor; reigned 1339–68.
Gonara: emperor; reigned 1526–57.
Go Nyorai: the Five Buddhas, sometimes called the Five Buddhas
   of Wisdom. According to the Kongokai *mandara* they are Dai-
   nichi, Ashuku, Hosho, Amida, and Fuku Joju.
Gosaga: emperor; reigned 1242–46.
Gosanjo: emperor; reigned 1068–72.   ⌜Murakami in 951.
Gosen Wakashu: 20 volumes of poetry, compiled under Emperor
Goshirakawa: emperor; reigned 1155–58.
Goshun (1752–1811): painter; founder of the Shijo school, an
   offshoot of the Maruyama school founded by Okyo.
Gotoba: emperor; reigned 1183–98.
Gotsuchimikado: emperor; reigned 1465–1500.
Gouda: emperor; reigned 1274–87.
Goyozei: emperor; reigned 1586–1611.
Gozanze Myo-o: one of the Godai Myo-o.
-gu: suffix usually meaning "(Shinto) shrine."
Gundari Myo-o: one of the Godai Myo-o.
-gyo: see *-kyo.*   ⌜living near Kyoto.
Gyogi (667–730): priest at the Yakushi-ji, Nara; later, a hermit
Gyokudo (1745–1821): painter of the *nanga* school.

Hachi Dai Doji: the Eight Messengers of Fudo Myo-o.
Hachiman: Shinto deity, the god of war.
haiku: verse form of 17 syllables arranged in pattern of 5–7–5.

Haji: plain, unglazed, porous red pottery of the Kofun period.

hakama: loose trousers.

Hakone Gongen Engi: Legends of the Hakone Shrine (picture scroll).

hakubutsukan: museum. ⌈style.

Hakuin (1685–1768): Zen priest and painter in a rough, satirical

Hamada, Shoji (1894–): well-known contemporary potter.

haniwa: pottery cylinders—sometimes surmounted by such objects
   as a human figure, an animal, a house, or a quiver—placed
   around the tumuli of the Kofun period.

Han Shan (in Japanese, Kanzan): one of two (the other is Shih
   Te) Chinese comic sages and practitioners of Ch'an Buddhism
   who lived in a Chinese monastery in the 7th century. They are
   regarded as incarnations of Bodhisattvas. ⌈794 to 1185.

Heian: early name of Kyoto; also name of the period lasting from

Heiji Monogatari: the story of the Heiji insurrection in 1159, which
   began the struggle between the Taira and the Minamoto
   families. ⌈(picture scroll).

Heike Kindachi Soshi: Anecdotes of a Nobleman of the Heike Family

hibachi: ceramic, metal, or wood brazier in which charcoal is
   burned to warm a room.

Hideyoshi (Toyotomi Hideyoshi; 1536–98): military dictator.
   Born a peasant, he served Oda Nobunaga and in 1582 became

Higashiyama: emperor; reigned 1687–1709. ⌊ruler of Japan.

Higo Hokkyo Jokei: sculptor of the late 12th to early 13th century. ⌈maker of the *ukiyo-e* school.

Hiroshige (1797–1858): well-known landscape painter and print-

ho: ancient Chinese bronze kettle with closed spout, handle,
   cover, and three or four legs; used for holding wine.

Hoen (1804–67): painter of the Shijo school.

Hogai: see under Kano.

Hoitsu (1761–1828): distinguished painter of the school of Korin.

Hojo: the ruling family during the Kamakura period.

Hojo Soun (1432–1519): daimyo of the region now largely contained in Shizuoka Prefecture.

Hojo Tokimune (1251–84): member of the Hojo family; regent in
   Kamakura from 1268 until his death.

Hokke-kyo: the Lotus Sutra. ⌈ukiyo-e school.

Hokusai (1760–1849): well-known painter and printmaker of the

homotsuden: treasure house.

homotsukan: treasure hall.

Honen Shonin (1133–1212): founder of the Jodo (Pure Land or
   Amida's Paradise) sect of Buddhism.

Hosso: Buddhist sect introduced from China about 650; it claims that the only reality is consciousness.

Hossoshu Hiji Ekotoba: The Story of the Founder of the Hosso Sect of
Hotei: Japanese name for Pu Tai. ⌊ *Buddhism* (picture scroll).

hu: ancient Chinese bronze wine jar or ewer with a wide body that narrows toward the shoulder and a foot rim.

Huai style: style of decoration appearing on Chinese bronzes of the Warring States period; so named by the Swedish archaeologist B. Karlgren after bronzes found in the Huai River valley that runs through the provinces of Anhwei and Kiangsu.

Hui Tsung: Sung-dynasty emperor (ruled 1101–25), painter, and collector; established an imperial painting academy.

Ichiji Kinrin: the supreme title of Buddha in Esoteric Buddhism.

Ieharu: tenth Tokugawa shogun; ruled from 1760 to 1786.

Iemitsu: third Tokugawa shogun; ruled from 1623 to 1651.

Ieyasu (1542–1616): a member of the Tokugawa family, prominent in the armies of Nobunaga; became master of Japan after Hideyoshi's death; founder and greatest member of the Tokugawa shogunate.

Ikkyu (1394–1481): Zen priest known for his learning, his poetry, and his unconventional behavior; was once chief abbot of the Daitoku-ji in Kyoto.

inau: shaved wooden sticks used in Ainu religious ceremonies.

Inga-kyo: see *E Inga-kyo.*   ⌈waist by men in the Edo period.

inro: small box for holding drugs, pills, or ointment, carried at the

Ise Monogatari: Tales of Ise, a collection of verse, mainly by the nobleman and poet Ariwara no Narihira (823–80), each verse being preceded by a prose section indicating the occasion of its composition.

Iseshu: collection of lyric poems of the early Heian period.

Issai-kyo (literally, "all the sutras"): the whole of the Buddhist canon.   ⌈dhist.

Issan Ichinei (1247–1317): famous calligrapher and Zen Bud-

Jakuchu (c. 1713–1800): painter of flowers and birds.

-ji: suffix usually meaning "(Buddhist) temple."

Jigoku Zoshi: Scroll of Hells (picture scroll).

Jikokuten: one of the Shi Tenno, guardian of the east.

jimbaori: coat worn over armor.

jingu: Shinto shrine.

jinja: Shinto shrine.

Jion: priest of the T'ang dynasty venerated by the Japanese Hosso sect.

Jittoku: one of two famous Zen practitioners (the other is Kanzan) usually represented as Chinese sages. Japanese name for Shih Te.

Jizo: very popular and frequently represented Buddhist deity, shown as a priest with a shaven head; generally regarded as the patron of children and of those in trouble.

-jo: suffix usually meaning "castle."

Jodo: Buddhist sect founded by Honen Shonin. It is also called the Pure Land sect and teaches that salvation lies in invoking the name of Amida Buddha.

Joga (fl. c. 1295): painter of Buddhist subjects.

Jokei: sculptor at end of 12th and beginning of 13th century.

Ju Dai Deshi: the Ten Disciples of Shaka Nyorai.

Juichimen Kannon: Eleven-Headed Kannon.

Juni Innen Engi: Scroll of the Twelve Fates (picture scroll).

Juni Shinsho: the Twelve Guardians of Yakushi Nyorai.

Juniten: the Twelve Guardian Deities; a group of twelve non-Buddhist heavenly beings who were incorporated into Buddhism as protective gods.

Juntoku: emperor; reigned 1210–21.

Ju O: the Ten Judges of Hell.

Jurojin: one of the Seven Gods of Good Luck.

Kabuki: the popular Japanese theater.

kaen-toki (literally, "flame ware"): type of Jomon pottery vessel with elaborate decoration.

Kagei: 18th-century painter of the Korin school.

kagen-kei: stand for a Buddhist temple gong.

Kaigetsudo: group of early-18th-century Japanese painters and printmakers.

Kaisen (1785–1862): painter, first of the Shijo school, then of the *nanga* school.

kakebotoke: hanging circular plaque with Buddhist figures in high relief.

kakemono: vertical scroll painting, made to hang on a wall.

Kakogenzai Inga-kyo: Sutra of Past and Present, Cause and Effect—a sutra relating events in the incarnations of the Buddha.

Kamakura-bori: type of carved lacquer made in Kamakura.

Kameyama: emperor; reigned 1259–74.

kan: hall, large building.

kana: Japanese syllabary.

Kannon: Japanese name for Kuan Yin.

Kano: name of a school of painting that started in the mid-15th

century, based on the Muromachi *suiboku* school plus a few
elements of the Tosa school. In the Edo period, it became the
official school of the shogunate. Masanobu founded the school,
and Motonobu put it on a firm basis. Hereditary members
carry the name Kano. Prominent members: Eitoku (1543–90);
Hogai (1828–88), one of the last; Masanobu (1434–1530),
founder; Motohide (early 16th cen.); Motonobu (1476–1559),
founder's son; Naonobu (1607–50), Tan'yu's younger brother;
Sanraku (1559–1635), noted for paintings on sliding doors and
screens; Sansetsu (1590–1651), Sanraku's pupil; Soyu (16th
cen.); Tan'yu (1602–74), one of the most distinguished Kanos;
Tsunenobu (1636–1713), son and pupil of Naonobu; Yasunobu
(1613–85), Tan'yu's younger brother.

Kansai: 18th-century painter of the *nanga* school.

Kansu: province in northwest China where much neolithic
painted pottery has been found.

Kantei: 15th-century painter of the Muromachi *suiboku* school.

Kanzan: one of two famous Zen practitioners (the other is Jittoku) usually represented as Chinese sages. Japanese name for
Han Shan.

Kao: 16th-century painter of the Muromachi *suiboku* school.

karabitsu: chest with four or six legs.

Kasuga no Miya *mandara: mandara* showing the Shinto Kasuga
Shrine as a Buddhist sanctuary.

kataginu: man's short, sleeveless coat.   ⌈invasion of Korea.

Kato Kiyomasa: one of Hideyoshi's commanders in the 1592

Kawai, Kanjiro (1890–1966): well-known contemporary potter.

Kegon Gojugosho Emaki: Zenzai Doji's Pilgrimage to the Fifty-five Saints
(picture scroll).

kei: flat, chevron-shaped bronze gong used in Buddhist temples.

Keibun (1779–1843): painter; brother of Goshun and member
of the Shijo school.

keko: flower basket used in the Buddhist flower-strewing ceremony.

keman: pendant ornament hung in a Buddhist sanctuary.

ken: prefecture.

kencho: prefectural office.

kenritsu: prefectural.

Kenshin (1130–92): writer.

Kenzan (1663–1743): well-known painter and potter of the Korin
school; younger brother of Korin.

kesa: Buddhist priest's robe.   ⌈ceremonial dress.

Kichijoten: goddess of fortune, depicted as a beautiful woman in

223

Kiko: Chinese priest of the Ming dynasty; visited Japan and stayed at Kamakura.

kin: musical instrument, the prototype of the *koto.*

kinen: memorial.

Kinkan Shutsugen: the Buddha reappearing from his golden coffin.

kinuta: mallet-shaped.

Kishimojin: goddess of children.

Kisshoten: alternate form of Kichijoten. ⌈scroll).

Kitano Tenjin Engi: Legends of the Kitano Tenjin Shrine (picture

Kiyochika (1847–1915): printmaker of the *ukiyo-e* school.

Kiyonobu (1664–1729): painter and printmaker of the *ukiyo-e* school; specialized in theatrical subjects.

ko: dagger; the distinctive weapon of the Yin and Chou dynasties
-ko: suffix usually meaning "lake." ⌊of China.

Kobo Daishi (774–835): founder of the Shingon (Esoteric) sect of Buddhism. His real name was Kukai, Kobo Daishi being his posthumous title. ⌈gardens.

Kobori Enshu (1570–1646): famous tea master and designer of

Kodo: lecture hall of a Buddhist temple.

koen: park.

Koetsu (1558–1637): painter in a very decorative style, potter of Raku ware, calligrapher, landscape gardener, maker of lacquer, and devotee of the tea ceremony.

kofun: tumulus or grave mound. The archaeological period to which it has given its name is known for its large grave mounds.

Kokei (1769–1836): painter of the Maruyama school, pupil of

Kokei Sochin (1532–97): monk of the Daitoku-ji. ⌊Okyo.

Kokinshu or *Kokinwakashu:* a collection of the best poems written after the compilation of the *Man'yoshu.* Put together by imperial order between 905 and 922, it is the most popular of all official anthologies and was the model for poetic composition for a thousand years.

Kokinwakashu: see *Kokinshu.*

kokogaku: archaeology. ⌈protector.

Kokuzo: a Bosatsu considered by Kobo Daishi as his personal

Komyo: emperor of the Northern Court; reigned 1337–48.

Kondo: main hall of a Buddhist temple.

Kongo Doji: deity of Esoteric Buddhism. He stands on lotus petals, amid flames, holding a *vajra* or a sword.

Kongokai: the Diamond Circle *mandara.*

Kongo Satta: a Bosatsu, shown holding a pestle and a bell, found in the pantheon of Esoteric Buddhism,

Kongo Yasha Myo-o: deity of Esoteric Buddhism; represented with six arms and standing on lotus petals amid flames. He devours evil-doers.

Korin (1658–1716): painter; also famous as a calligrapher and lacquerer. He founded the Korin school.

kosode: small-sleeved kimono.

kote: in armor, tight sleeves for the protection of the arms.

koto: a kind of zither with a long, narrow sounding board and strings of twisted silk.

Koyo (1717–80): painter of the *nanga* school.

ku: ancient Chinese bronze wine beaker with a slender body, a trumpet-shaped mouth, and a spreading foot.

-ku: suffix meaning "ward" (section of a city).   ⌈boat.

kuang: ancient Chinese bronze vessel resembling a covered gravy

Kuan Yin: the most popular Bodhisattva, generally represented as the god of mercy; in China and Japan, generally thought of as a female deity.   ⌈tea bowls.

Kuchu: potter, grandson of Koetsu, noted for Shigaraki and Raku

kuei: ancient Chinese bronze food vessel, circular in shape, with two handles and, sometimes, with a high square base.

Kujaku Myo-o: the Buddhist deity who exorcises poisons; depicted sitting on a peacock.   ⌈museum.

Kujiro: potter known only for his signature on a jar in the Arita

Kunisada (1786–1864): prolific printmaker of the *ukiyo-e* school.

Kuniyoshi (1797–1861): prolific printmaker of the *ukiyo-e* school.

-kyo or *-gyo:* suffix usually meaning "sutra" (Buddhist scripture).

kyodo: local.

Kyogen: comic interlude between performances of Noh plays.

Kyozo: sutra hall, or library, of a Buddhist temple.

Lang Shih-ning: Chinese name of Father Castiglione (1698–1768), the Italian Jesuit; painter of court pictures in a style that mixed Western naturalism with a pseudo-Chinese technique.

lei: ancient Chinese large bronze wine vessel, wide at the shoulder and narrowing towards the foot.   ⌈with hollow legs.

li: ancient Chinese bronze cauldron for food, similar to a *ting* but

Li An-chung: Chinese painter of the Sung dynasty; member of the Southern Sung Academy at Hangchow.

Liang K'ai: Chinese painter of the Sung dynasty who worked in the spirit of Ch'an Buddhism. His works are mostly in Japan.

Liao: name of the dynasty founded by the Khitans in northern China in the 10th century. It was destroyed in 1125 by the

Chinese and the Jurchen, a people from the Amur River region.

lien: ancient Chinese bronze cylindrical covered vessel.

Li Lung-mien (c. 1040–1106): well-known painter of the Sung ⌊dynasty.

Li Po (701–62): famous poet of the T'ang dynasty.

Li Ti: painter of the Sung dynasty; member of the Southern Sung Academy at Hangchow.

Lohan (in Japanese, Rakan): a Buddhist sage who has achieved enlightenment and is endowed with supernatural powers obtained through religious austerities; depicted, often as ascetics, singly or in groups of 16, 18, or 500.

Lo-lang: site of the capital of the Han-dynasty colony of the same name in Korea. Situated near P'yongyang, it was excavated by Japanese archaeologists before World War II and yielded much decorated lacquer.

Lung-men: site of the famous Buddhist cave temples, south of Lo-yang, Honan Province. The rock-cut sculpture dates from the 6th and 7th centuries.

machi: street or town.

mae: in front of.

magatama: archaic curved jewels of stone or glass.

Maitreya: the Buddha of the Future; sometimes depicted as a ⌈Bosatsu.

Ma Lin: painter of the Sung dynasty; son of Ma Yuan.

mandara: schematic diagram, generally in the form of a painting, of Buddhist deities, intended to explain the doctrines of Esoteric Buddhism.

mandorla: in Buddhist art, a large shield or screen placed behind a Buddhist figure. It is generally either almond-shaped or pointed at the top and straight at the bottom, with curving sides. ⌈riding a lion.

Manjusri: the Bodhisattva who represents wisdom; often depicted

Man'yoshu (literally, "Collection of Ten Thousand Leaves"): an anthology compiled in the middle of the 8th century and containing more than 4,500 poems; the first and possibly the greatest Japanese anthology.

Mao I: Sung-dynasty painter and member of the Southern Sung Academy at Hangchow; specialized in painting kittens and puppies. ⌈the *ukiyo-e* school.

Masanobu: see under Kano. Also the name of two painters of

Matabei (1578–1650): painter who worked in the Tosa manner; incorrectly regarded as the creator of the *ukiyo-e* school.

Maya, Queen: mother of the historical Buddha.

Ma Yuan (c. 1190–1224): famous painter of the Southern Sung
    Academy at Hangchow. His name is often linked with that of
    Hsia Kuei, and together their work gave rise to the Ma-Hsia
Michizane: see Sugawara Michizane.   ⌊school.
Mi Fei (1051–1107): great Chinese landscape painter, calligra-
    pher, and collector.
Minamoto Yorimasa: soldier and poet; for long, trusted and
    favored by Taira Kiyomori, but in 1180 plotted against the
    Taira; committed suicide in front of the Byodo-in at Uji when
    overtaken by the Taira forces.
Minamoto Yoritomo (d. 1199): leader of the Minamoto clan and
    founder of the military dictatorship of the Kamakura period.
Minamoto Yoshitsune: younger brother of Yoritomo, leader of
    the Minamoto forces in their victories over the Taira; commit-
    ted suicide in 1189 after his arrest was ordered by Yoritomo for
    supposed rebellious actions.
Mincho: see Chodensu.
mingei: folk art.   ⌈gin.
Minki Soshun (1262–1336): famous calligrapher of Chinese ori-
Miroku: Japanese name for Maitreya.
Mitsumoto: see under Tosa.
Mitsunobu: see under Tosa.
Mitsuoki: see under Tosa.
Mitsuyoshi: see under Tosa.
mizusashi: water pitcher for tea-ceremony use.   ⌈Kyoto school.
Mokubei (1767–1833): scholar, poet, painter, and potter of the
Monju Bosatsu: Japanese name for Manjusri.
monogatari: story or tale.
Morikage: 17th-century painter. Although he was trained in the
    Kano school, his work shows much independence.
Moronobu (c. 1625–c. 1694): painter, book illustrator, and
    printmaker who gave a great impetus to the *ukiyo-e* school of
Motohide: see under Kano.   ⌊prints.
Motonobu: see under Kano.
Muchaku: Supposed to be the elder brother of Seshin and re-
    garded, with him, as founder of the Hosso sect. An Indian
    teacher of Mahayana Buddhism.
Mu Ch'i: Chinese painter and Ch'an priest of the first half of the
    13th century. His monochrome ink paintings are mostly pre-
    served in Japan.
Munakata, Shiko (1903–): well-known contemporary printmaker.
Murasaki Shikibu Nikki Emaki: Kamakura-period picture scroll

227

based on the early-11th-century diary of Lady Murasaki, celebrated author of *Genji Monogatari*.

Muso Kokushi (1275–1351): leading Zen prelate of his day and head of the Rinzai sect; first served Emperor Godaigo; then, when this emperor went to Yoshino, transferred his loyalty and became adviser to Ashikaga Takauji. His name was Muso Soseki; Kokushi, or "National Master," his title.

Muso Soseki: see Muso Kokushi.

Myoe Shonin (1173–1232): priest and founder of the Kozan-ji, Kyoto, and contributor to the revival of Kegon Buddhism at the beginning of the Kamakura period. His name was Koben; Myoe Shonin was an honorary title.

Myo-o: "shining king." See Godai Myo-o.

naidaijin: inner minister, a high post under the Fujiwara regents.

Nakamura Kuranosuke: wealthy Kyoto banker and patron of Korin.

namban (literally, "southern barbarian"): a term applied to the first Europeans to appear in Japan (mid-16th century).

nanga: literary men's school of painting. It was originally influenced by 18th-century Chinese painting. Also called *bunjinga*.   ⌈*nanga* school of painting.

Nankai (1677–1751): painter and literary man; founder of the Naonobu: see under Kano.

Nayotake Monogatari: Tale of the Emperor Gosaga (picture scroll).

Negoro: a kind of lacquer in which a coating of black lacquer is painted over the priming and is then generally covered with a coat of vermilion lacquer.   ⌈the obi.

netsuke: toggle used in suspending an *inro* or tobacco pouch from

Nichiren (1222–82): priest; founder of the Nichiren sect of Bud-

Nihon: Japan.   ⌊dhism.

Nikko Bosatsu: one of the two attendants of Yakushi Nyorai.

Ninsei: potter active the second half of the 17th century; originator of gorgeously colored enamel decorations applied to pottery; worked in Kyoto.   ⌈Kongo Rikishi.

Nio (literally, "two kings"): temple-gate guardians; also called

Nippon: Japan.

Niten (1584–1645): painter, probably pupil of Yusho but developed independently of any school; also famous as a fencer. Also known as Miyamoto Musashi.

Nobunaga (Oda Nobunaga; 1534–82): first of the three military heroes of the 16th century (the others were Hideyoshi and Ie-

yasu) to dominate the contending clans and temple strongholds
and to make Japan a unified nation.

Noh: the classic Japanese drama.

Nonko: see Donyu.

Northern Wei (386–535): one of the Chinese Six Dynasties.

nyoi: staff held by Buddhist priests while preaching.

Nyoirin Kannon: one of the forms of Kannon, shown with two,
four, or six arms; worshiped in Esoteric Buddhism.   ⌐it.

Nyorai: a Buddha. The name of the individual Buddha precedes

Ogimachi: emperor; reigned 1557–86.

oi: priest's traveling case for sutras and Buddhist images.

Oju (1775–1815): painter, son of Okyo; member of the Maruyama school.

Okamoto Shuki (1767–1862): painter of the *nanga* school; worked
for the Okubo family in Odawara.

Okyo (Maruyama Okyo; 1733–95): well-known painter; founder
of the Maruyama school, which emphasized direct observation
of nature.

Otsu-e: folk paintings from the region of Otsu on Lake Biwa.

Ozui (1766–1829): painter; son of Okyo and follower of his style.

pi: ancient Chinese carved disc of uncertain usage.

Pu Tai (in Japanese, Hotei): a gay wandering monk, a favorite
subject in Ch'an painting. He symbolizes the carefree life of one
who, through the study of Ch'an, has overcome the troubles of
everyday life.

raigo: the descent of a Buddha to this world.

Rakan: Japanese name for Lohan.

Reigen: emperor; reigned 1663–87.

Reisai: 15th-century painter of the Muromachi *suiboku* school.

Rosetsu (1755–99): painter; follower of Okyo and member of the
Maruyama school.

Ryodohin: one of the Eight Taoist Immortals.

Ryokan (1758–1831): priest and calligrapher.

Ryutoki: goblin holding a lantern.

Saigyo (1118–90): priest and poet.

Saimei: empress; reigned 655–61.

sakè: wine made from rice.

Sakuramachi: emperor; reigned 1735–47.

Sakyamuni (in Japanese, Shaka Nyorai): the historical Buddha; also called Gautama.

Samantabhadra (in Japanese, Fugen Bosatsu): the Bodhisattva of the Highest Good or Universal Wisdom; usually depicted ⌊riding an elephant.

samurai: a feudal warrior.

Sanjo: emperor; reigned 1011–16.

Sanraku: see under Kano.

Sansetsu: see under Kano.

San Tsang: famous 7th-century Chinese monk who journeyed to India seeking Buddhist sutras; brought back to China many Buddhist relics, images, and books and was honored as a translator of Buddhist texts and a preacher of Buddhist doctrines. Also known as Tripitaka. ⌈the Kofun period on Honshu.

Satsumon: archaeological period on Hokkaido corresponding to

sekibo: prehistoric stone club.

Sekigahara: village between Gifu and Hikone, site of the great battle in 1600 in which Ieyasu gained a victory which led eventually to his becoming effective ruler of all Japan and first Tokugawa shogun.

Sekkei (1664–1732): painter; imitated the technique of Sesshu.

Sengai (1751–1837): painter and priest; worked in ink in a simple, rather eccentric style.

Senju Kannon: Thousand-Armed Kannon.

Sen no Rikyu (1520–91): famous connoisseur, tea master, arbiter of taste, expert in flower arrangement, and adherent of Zen.

Serizawa, Keisuke (1895–): distinguished contemporary designer of textiles in the folk manner and leader of the folk-art movement.

Seshin: said to be the younger brother of Muchaku (q.v.).

Sesshu (1420–1506): one of the greatest painters of the Muromachi *suiboku* school.

Sesson (1504–89): well-known painter of the Muromachi *suiboku* school; carried on Sesshu's style, but in an individual manner.

Shaka: see Shaka Nyorai.

Shaka Ju Dai Deshi: the Ten Great Disciples of Shaka Nyorai.

Shaka Nyorai: Japanese name for Sakyamuni.

shakujo: priest's staff.

shaman: medicine man or healer.

shi: city. ⌈kura.

Shigen Sogen (1282–1339): Zen priest at the Engaku-ji at Kama-

Shih Te (in Japanese, Jittoku): one of two (the other is Han Shan) Chinese comic sages and famous practitioners of Ch'an

Buddhism who lived in a Chinese monastery in the 7th century. They are regarded as incarnations of Bodhisattvas.

Shijo: school of painting, founded by Goshun; an offshoot of the Maruyama school founded by Okyo.

shikishi: decorated piece of paper on which a poem is written.

Shingon: the Esoteric sect of Buddhism introduced from China by Kobo Daishi.

Shinkai: 13th-century priest; painter of Buddhist subjects.

Shinran (1173–1262): priest, follower of Honen, founder of Jodo Shinsho (True Sect of Jodo).   ⌈of Japan.

Shinto (literally, "the way of the gods"): the national religion

shiritsu: municipal.

shiryo: historical material or records.

Shi Tenno (literally, "Four Heavenly Kings"): the four guardians of the Buddhist world.   ⌈era.

shogun: title of the military dictators of Japan prior to the Meiji

Shokado (1584–1639): priest, painter, calligrapher; independent

Sho Kannon: the ordinary form of Kannon.   ⌊of any school.

Shokei: painter of the Muromachi *suiboku* school; worked late 15th to early 16th century.

Shoki: the devil fighter; a figure from Chinese Taoism.

Shomu: emperor; reigned 724–49.

shonin: priest, saint.   ⌈school.

Shosen: early-16th-century painter of the Muromachi *suiboku*

Shotoku Taishi (572–622): prince regent for the empress Suiko; promoted the growth of Buddhism, developed relations with China, and laid down lines for political reforms.

-*shu:* suffix usually meaning "anthology" or "collection."

Shubun: painter and priest of the 15th century; pupil of Josetsu. Paintings attributed to him are close to the Ma-Hsia style.

Shungyu Ekotoba: Portraits of Famous Carriage Bulls (picture scroll).

Shunsho (1726–92): painter and printmaker of the *ukiyo-e* school; specialized in female figures.

Shutoku: painter of the Muromachi *suiboku* school; worked during second half of 15th century.

Sogyo Hachiman: the Shinto god Hachiman as a Buddhist monk.

Soma, Gyofu (1881–1950): poet, critic, translator of Tolstoy and Turgenev.   ⌈yama school; specialized in animal subjects.

Sosen (1747–1821): painter, first of Kano school, later of Maru-

Soshin: potter and painter of the early Edo period.

Sotan (1413–81): painter of great reputation; however, no certain works by him remain.

Sotatsu: brilliant painter of the 17th century; founder of the decorative school of painting which bears his name.

Soyu: see under Kano.

Spring and Autumn Annals: the first accurate chronological history written in China; a chronicle of the feudal state of Lu (where Confucius was born) from 722 to 481 B.C. It is the fifth of the Five Confucian Classics.

stupa: domed monument containing Buddhist relics.

Sue: hard-baked, non-porous grey pottery of the Kofun period.

Sugawara Michizane (845–903): man of letters, scholar of Chinese literature and adviser to the Kyoto court; intrigued against and banished to Kyushu, where he died; posthumously deified, and is worshiped as the god of learning and calligraphy.

suiboku (literally, "water and ink"): the leading Muromachi school of painting. The paintings are done in ink with light washes of color used only occasionally.

sumiaka: lacquer box with red corners.   ⌈near Osaka.

Sumiyoshi Myojin: deity of the Sumiyoshi-jinja, the Shinto shrine

Su Shih: Chinese court official, poet, painter, and antiquarian of the 11th century; also known as Su Tung-p'o.

Sutoku: emperor; reigned 1123–41.

sutra: Buddhist sacred literature; a book of the Buddhist canon.

Su Tung-p'o: see Su Shih.

Taiga (1722–76): well-known painter and calligrapher of the *nanga* school.   ⌈(Heike) clan; son of Kiyomori.

Taira Shigemori (1138–79): one of the leaders of the Taira

Taishakuten: Buddhist deity, Lord of the Thirty-three Heavens; one of the Juniten.

Takakura: emperor; reigned 1168–80.   ⌈school.

Takashina Takakane: 14th-century painter of the Yamato-e

Takuan (1573–1645): Zen priest and preacher.

Takuma: a family of painters (also a school) of the late Heian and Kamakura periods; specialized in Buddhist subjects.

Takuma Shoga: member of the Takuma family or group; worked in the late 12th century.

Tamechika (1823–64): painter, best-known member of the Fukko Yamato-e school, a 19th-century revival of the old Japanese traditional school.

Tamonten: one of the Shi Tenno, and also of the Juniten; guardian of the northern quarter of the Buddhist heaven. See Bisha-

Tan'yu: see under Kano.   ⌊monten.

t'ao t'ieh: decorative ornament resembling a mask, found on early Chinese bronzes; its significance is unknown.

tebako: Japanese cosmetic box, usually of lacquer.   ⌈Japan.

temmoku: the name by which Chinese *chien* ware is known in

Ten (literally, "heavenly or divine being"): The Ten were originally gods and goddesses of Brahmanism and Hinduism and were later assimilated into Buddhism.

Tendai: the Esoteric Buddhist sect introduced from China by Saicho (767–822), the Buddhist priest who studied in China from 804 to 805.

Tengu Zoshi: Stories of Conceited Priests (picture scroll).

tennin: Japanese name for *apsara.*

Tenryu Hachibushu: Eight Supernatural Guardians of the Buddhist Law and messengers of the Buddha.

Tentoki: goblin holding a lantern.   ⌈the 20th century.

Tessai (1836–1924): painter; carried the *nanga*-school style into

Thirty-six Poets: in Japanese classical literature, the best-known poets prior to the 11th century. They became a favorite subject for painters.   ⌈dynasties in Shansi Province.

T'ien-lung-shan: Buddhist cave temples of the Sui and T'ang

ting: ancient Chinese bronze cauldron for meats and cereals, with either a round body and three solid legs or a rectangular body

Tofu: 10th-century calligrapher.   ⌊and four legs.

Togan (1597–1618): painter; founder of the Unkoku school, an outgrowth of the Muromachi *suiboku* school.

toji: ceramics.

toki: pottery or porcelain.

tokonoma: alcove used to display a painting or an *objet d'art.*

Tomimoto, Kenkichi (1886–1963): potter; noted for his blue-and-white enameled wares decorated with delicate brush drawings.

torii: gate to a Shinto shrine.

Tosa: school of painting, founded in the early years of the Muromachi period; carried on the Japanese painting tradition, known as Yamato-e, of the Heian and Kamakura narrative scrolls. Promiment members: Mitsumoto (1530–69); Mitsunobu (c. 1430–c. 1521), chief court painter; Mitsuoki (1617–91); Mitsuyoshi (1539–1613), chief court painter.

Toshimi: one of the Sennin, or Taoist sages.

tou: ancient Chinese bronze food vessel with a hemispherical body resting on a high stem that spreads at the base.

Toyokuni (1769–1825): printmaker of the *ukiyo-e* school; specialized in female figures and portraits of actors.

tsuba: sword guard.

tsun: ancient Chinese beaker-shaped bronze wine vessel.

Tsunayoshi: fifth Tokugawa shogun, in office from 1680 to 1709; noted for his Confucian scholarship and artistic taste as well as for his cruelty.

Tsunenobu: see under Kano.

ts'ung: ancient Chinese ritual jade in the shape of a hollow tube with a square exterior.

tumulus: ancient burial mound.

Tun-huang: oasis in the far northwest corner of China on which the Central Asian trade and pilgrimage routes converged, and where many paintings, documents, and frescoes of the T'ang dynasty have been found.

Uda: emperor; reigned 887–97.

Uesugi Shigefusa: military lord of the Kamakura period; founder of the Uesugi family, members of which were advisers to the shoguns.

ukiyo-e (literally, "pictures of the floating world"): genre pictures and prints, particularly of the Edo period.

Unkei (d. 1223): sculptor; established a new style of Buddhist sculpture marked by powerful naturalism.

Unkei: priest and painter of the Muromachi *suiboku* school; worked in the 15th and 16th centuries.

Utamaro (1754–1806): printmaker and painter of the *ukiyo-e* school, well known for his elegant female figures.

vajra (in Japanese, *kongo* or *kongosho*): metal bar held by Buddhist priests during sacred rites.

waka: Japanese poetry.

Wakan Roeishu: Heian anthology of poems written in imitation of Chinese poetry, collected by Fujiwara Kinto (966–1041).

Wang Wei (699–759): famous Chinese poet and painter.

waniguchi: gong in front of a Shinto shrine.

Watanabe Shiko (1683–1755): painter; began as a member of the Kano school, then became a follower of Korin.

wei ch'i: Chinese game resembling checkers.

Yakushi Nyorai: Buddha of Healing.

Yamada Doan: see Doan.

Yamai no Soshi: Scroll of Diseases and Deformities (picture scroll).

Yamato-e: the national school of painting; developed in the Heian period; used purely Japanese subject matter derived from Japanese poetry and romances.

Yasunobu: see under Kano.

yen: ancient Chinese bronze steamer, cast in two pieces. The upper part resembles the body of a *ting,* the lower a *li.*

Yin T'o-lo: painter of the Sung dynasty, member of the Southern Sung Academy at Hangchow; better known in Japan than in Yoritomo: see Minamoto Yoritomo.   ⌐ China.

Yoshimasa (1435–90): Ashikaga shogun from 1449 to 1473; noted for his weak administration and his lavish buildings.

Yoshimochi (1386–1428): Ashikaga shogun from 1408 to 1423 and from 1425 to 1428.

Yoshimune: eighth Tokugawa shogun, in office from 1716 to 1745; considered to have been, after Ieyasu, the greatest of the Tokugawa shoguns.

Yoshitsune: see Minamoto Yoshitsune.

yu: ancient Chinese bronze wine jar with a cover and a swinging handle.

Yuima Koji: a disciple of Shaka. He had a famous discussion of the Buddha's teachings with Monju.

Yukimitsu: painter; worked from 1360 to 1371; chief court artist of his time. The use of the name Tosa probably began with him.

Yusetsu (1598–1677): painter, son of Yusho.

Yusho (1533–1615): painter; studied Kano technique; founded the Kaiho school.   ⌐ (picture scroll).

Yuzu Nembutsu Engi: Stories of the Origin of Yuzu Nembutsu Buddhism

Zao Gongen: a manifestation (*gongen* means "manifestation") of either Shaka or Miroku, revered as a mountain god in a combination of Buddhism and nature worship.

Zen: Japanese name for Ch'an.   ⌐ scroll).

Zen Kunen Kassen Emaki: Stories of the Zen Kunen Civil War (picture

Zochoten: one of the Shi Tenno; guardian of the south.

Zoku-Jomon: archaeological period on Hokkaido corresponding to the Yayoi period on Honshu.

Indexes

BY JAPANESE NAMES

NOTE: *Most of the names of the museums begin with the same word in both English and Japanese, and hence can be readily found in the alphabetized listing of the main text. Included below are only those few cases where the first word of the Japanese name is different from that of the English.*

BY PREFECTURES

BY TYPES OF COLLECTIONS

NOTE: *Boldface references indicate the more important collections—those of more than passing interest.*

The "weathermark" identifies this book as having
been designed and produced at John Weatherhill,
Inc., 50 Ryudo-cho, Azabu, Minato-ku, Tokyo | Book design
and typography by Meredith Weatherby | Composed and printed
by Kenkyusha, Tokyo | Photographic plates engraved by Misaki
Platemakers, Tokyo | Binding by Makoto Binderies, Tokyo |
The text is set in Monotype Baskerville, with display in Bulmer